D1550812

MICHAEL CHEKHOV'S

TO THE DIRECTOR

AND PLAYWRIGHT

COMPILED AND WRITTEN
BY Charles Leonard

238364

GREENWOOD PRESS, PUBLISHERS
WESTPORT, CONNECTICUT

Library of Congress Cataloging in Publication Data
Chekhov, Michael, 1891-1955.
    Michael Chekhov's To the director and playwright.

    Reprint of the ed. published by Harper & Row,
New York.
    Includes English adaptation of N. Gogol's
Revisor, with rehearsal notes.
    1. Theater--Production and direction.
2. Playwriting. I. Leonard, Charles, 1900-
II. Gogol, Nikolai Vasil'evich, 1809-1852.
Revisor. III. Title. IV. Title: To the
director and playwright.
[PN2053.C4 1977]   792'.023   77-8158
ISBN 0-8371-9615-9

Originally published in 1963 by Harper & Row, Publishers,
New York

Reprinted with the permission of Charles Leonard

Reprinted in 1977 by Greenwood Press,
a division of Congressional Information Service, Inc.
51 Riverside Avenue, Westport, Connecticut 06880

Library of Congress catalog card number 77-8158
ISBN 0-8371-9615-9

Printed in the United States of America

10 9 8 7 6 5 4 3 2

Contents

To the memory of my beloved Betty (1911–1961),
but for whom the teachings
of Michael Chekhov might never have been
recorded in these and previous pages

C. L.

Illustrations

[vii

MICHAEL CHEKHOV's To the Director and Playwright

Prelude to an Exploration

A few months before Michael Chekhov died (September 30, 1955), in one of our discussions pertaining to this book, he remarked:

"If you think the average grownup is embarrassed when a child asks, 'Where do babies come from?' just think how difficult it must be for the theatre professional to explain where so many directors and playwrights come from, and how."

Like most perpetual priers into the theatre arts, both of us had cause to conjecture about the manner in which modern playwrights, and particularly directors, proliferate in all countries where entertainment has grown apace and developed into ranking commercial industries.

Every year sees a new crop of literary and directorial entries into the stage, film, radio and television fields; names not only unheard of by audiences of all these mediums but little known even to the established professionals. What of their training, what of their actual experience, what of their qualifying achievements in the past? The majority of their backgrounds, it seems at first glance, would not bear close scrutiny, and some of the murky origins might even be downright embarrassing.

But where, in truth, *do* they come from? By what means *does* one become a playwright or director when there are so few schools of higher education specializing in or offering diplomas specifically for these most difficult and most creative of the theatre arts? In the schools of experience mostly? Perhaps. But is that really enough, and do most of these practitioners have sufficient experience if not scholastic preparation to do full justice to their chosen professions?

In his autobiography, a popular playwright-director states that he does not believe playwriting can be taught any more than acting can be taught. He may be right in one respect: far too many of the untaught seem to have found their way into and polluted the stage, screen and television. But he is not entirely correct in discounting the vast number of highly successful playwrights and stars who were, at the very least, embryonic products of the various college and university drama departments, inadequate as some of these courses may be, and the countless stars and directors who did undergo some kind of processing in the commercial and unregulated schools of the theatre, limited though many of their facilities are.

It is my firm conviction that every successful playwright or director must have had some kind of tutoring or training for his profession, must somehow or somewhere have spent sufficient time or study at learning at least the basics of his craft. I do not believe that any person without previous knowledge or experience can say, "I am going to write (or direct) a play," and turn out a hit right off. Even the first-shot geniuses are no exceptions. Each must first have been taught, must in some manner have learned the rudiments of his business and how to use the tools peculiar to it—even if he is self-taught, as that popular playwright-director confesses he was. For in the same paragraph in which he avers that it is impossible to teach playwriting and acting, he acknowledges that he simply read the plays themselves, dozens of them, studying and analyzing them like a scientist in a laboratory. And he admits that many of these investigations left their imprint on him, possibly without his knowing it, and he began to see and distinguish between the good and the bad in character-creating and plotting, to recognize the phony from the forthright, and that the secrets of the craft were thus gradually revealed to him.

There are thousands of persons who can assure him that play-writing students in the college and university drama departments do it no differently, though perhaps not so exhaustively, and that the curriculum he so fortunately stumbled on for himself—play-going, play reading, play study and analysis—is part and parcel of every good drama course. Perhaps, and regrettably, not all of these courses are as thorough as the one our playwright-director mapped out for himself, but the more dedicated and talented of the students manage to find ways of supplementing them on their own in their climb toward professionalism.

Even in his great skill as a stage director, that autobiographer does not deny some early process of self-education. Catapulted by dire necessity into directing a little-theatre group when he admittedly knew nothing about direction, he was compelled to bluff and blunder his way through while he learned the ropes. Ultimately, he confides, he learned considerably more from his amateurs than they did from him, it being impossible to direct any group without gleaning some knowledge from the experience. He was compelled, for example, to become aware of how a play is constructed, he relates, and after much fumbling he had to divine the author's meaning and intent and devise methods for obtaining the desired results. In short, by actually doing he learned that there is much more to directing a play than merely moving actors around the stage so that they do not trip over themselves and others.

In extension of my feelings that ample training for the theatre, in whatever manner obtained, is indispensable and should be made inescapable, permit me to point out that a large number of foreign countries regard the theatre as so vital to their native art and culture that many of them have long boasted government-sponsored playhouses and academies or other such state-endowed institutions for matriculation in the theatre arts *exclusively*. It is regrettable that in the United States such a complete course of specialized undergraduate study, comparable in depth and scope to other specific arts and sciences, and flying its own colors instead of masquerading under Eng. 7 or Lit. 8, is still unobtainable and often deemed unnecessary in the majority of our colleges and universities. This despite the fact that the academic theatre has been a vital force in adult education since the Athenian schools of the fifth century B.C.!

It may be that most colleges and universities still do not regard the theatre as an art of and unto itself. Only for the sake of argument, I shall grant that point. I shall even grant that the professional American theatre (entertainment) is today more commerce than art. Yet many a seat of higher learning offers degrees in Business Administration. How, then, can they justifiably show such disregard and disrespect for training which can sustain, keep supreme and even qualitatively improve such multi-billion-dollar American industries as television, motion pictures and radio, if not the stage? Why not a degree in Bachelor of *Theatre Arts?*

Whatever the cause for ignoring the full commercial, artistic and cultural potentials of the American academic theatre, the result is that comprehensive and truly *professional* training for the theatre in this country, as complete and as thorough as it is for the other professions, is not yet what it should be; such curriculums are, in the main, haphazard and still lumped with other academic degrees. The professional, nonacademic alternatives are a few private, commercial and not yet entirely adequate schools, studios, workshops and little-theatre groups, most of which cater largely to acting aspirants and scarcely any to the primary crafts of the playwright and director. It is quite obvious that training for the entertainment professions would be better and more profitably served if the accredited institutions of learning assumed the major responsibility. Some day, many theatre devotees hopefully predict, failing the establishment of a national theatre and School, the theatre arts will be accorded their deserving stature of a full, unencumbered, independent and important major in most of our colleges and universities. A few of the more progressive campuses are already pushing toward that goal. Hence, one of the objectives of this book is to supply a few of the missing ingredients for curricular inclusion until and when theatre *departments* become *Schools.*

Some years ago, when producing a play starring Mary Boland, I cast for the "accent part" of a maidservant a diminutive Hungarian actress named Iren Agay. I had never seen or heard of her before, but she was most highly recommended by the veteran playwright and director. On opening night of the tryout engagement, she made me regret my ignorance. For at the end of her third-act scene, this seeming "unknown" brought salvos of applause from the audience. She had stopped the play cold, stolen the show away from a seasoned trouper and incomparable comedienne like Mary Boland! I rushed backstage and bombarded her with questions about her training and background. No, she had never played an English-speaking part before; in this country she had made only recital appearances before Hungarian-community audiences in a few cities; but in Budapest she had been for some years one of the leading actresses of the state theatre, from whose acting school she had graduated. Then she threw me the eye-opener: "Do you know, at the state theatre we were not permitted to speak a single word on the stage until we had studied at least *four years?*"

God bless your memory, Iren, and my undying thanks for awakening the interest that launched my probes into the scholastic side of the theatre. For it subsequently attracted me to a genuine theatre worshiper named Betty Raskin (she became my wife), who, as the manager and close family friend of Michael Chekhov, in turn led me to him and into a long association which resulted in an honor that befalls few master-student relationships: he asked me to help him with the writing of his first book, *To the Actor* (Harper & Brothers, 1953).

A couple of years after the publication and success of that systematic "how-to" volume for actors, we began formulating and assembling material for this book, a similarly analytical and practical approach, but aimed more at exploring the techniques of the playwright and director. But his chronic illness, coupled with the growing demands for his teaching services from many of Hollywood's stars, directors and acting groups, permitted us to work only spasmodically, and then only for brief periods each time. His eventual death, though not unexpected, also left me bereft of all desire to pursue the project alone, regardless of how articulate I already was on the chapters he had charted for it and despite the promptings of many of his former students who were aware of our new undertaking. The inspiration which his genius sparked in all who came in contact with him seemed inexplicably to have vanished in me and defied recapture.

On the fifth anniversary of his death, I accompanied his eight-year-old goddaughter, Julietta (who also happens to be my own daughter), on her annual visit to "Papa Mischa's" grave. I am not spiritually aware enough to be able to explain why I left the cemetery with the feeling that the time had come at last to resume work on the book, but I did, and with the help of his widow, Xenia, I began reassembling all of the abandoned pages, chapter outlines, memoranda and lecture notes.

In this connection I must acknowledge with unlimited gratitude a mountainous windfall from Messrs. John Dehner and John Abbott and Mrs. Fanya Miroff, who headed the Drama Society of Hollywood, a group of seventy-five theatre students before whom Michael Chekhov lectured twice weekly for about three and a half years—not only on acting but on the creative philosophies of the theatre in general. Providentially, they had the dedication, wisdom and foresight to record twelve of his most valuable lectures and present the tapes to Mrs. Chekhov, who urged their inclusion in this book as an added memorial to his life's work. Their contents, edited and supplemented where necessary, have been incorporated into many of the ensuing chapters. Still ringing in the ears of the students who heard it is his memorable discourse on the five greatest Russian directors, whom he had known intimately during his sixteen-year association with the Moscow Art Theatre.

Further valuable assistance came from a series of rehearsal-by-rehearsal notes kept for Mr. Chekhov in 1946 by a group of highly professional actors while he was directing them in their production of Gogol's *The Inspector General*. Several years before that, many members of this acting company (The Actors Lab) had seen Chekhov's staging and portrayal of the title role of *Revisor,* as it was called in Russian, performed by former players of the Moscow Art Theatre who had been assembled in Europe and brought to Broadway by Sol Hurok. Thus, when Chekhov was asked to come to Hollywood for film roles, this group persuaded him to restage *The Inspector General* for and with them. The notes they kept on each rehearsal and presented to him are in themselves actual, step-by-step instructions for directors, most of them applicable not only to that particular play but to almost any play.

Finally, it must be stressed that because the functions of the playwright and director are frequently so closely allied, they inevitably become so closely alloyed that the points of confluence are barely distinguishable. Hence, the reader will discover that many chapters and segments intended for the director overlap those of the playwright and can be just as useful to him, and vice versa. Besides, it was Chekhov's opinion that a good director should be as conversant with the playwright's mental and artistic processes as the playwright must be with the technical and creative interpretations of the director. Their roles must be capable of interchange at any moment if they are to co-create and make optimum contributions to each other's art. And since the actor is so vitally and inextricably bound up with the work of both, many of the techniques dealt with can be equally serviceable to him; not only for the present, by giving him a better understanding of the playwright-director goals, but for the future, should he ever have occasion to venture into their areas of activity. Additionally, there are many new dissertations on the art of acting which originated since the publication of *To the Actor,* and these can have the double utility of benefiting the actor as a sort of postgraduate course as well as affording the director and playwright new insights into the performer's art.

CHARLES LEONARD

October, 1962

1. The "Method" Madness

No method, no technique, should deprive the playwright or director of his individual creative freedom; no rules should be so restrictive that they chain him as an experimenter and innovator. If he becomes so dogmatic that he fears to deviate from a single postulation in this book, it indicates that he is cutting himself off from investigations of his own and that the technique is not properly understood; or, if understood, then improperly applied.

The freedom of an artist's intuition always has been and always will be basic to his craft, and the task of this or any forthright technique is, fundamentally, to stimulate and cultivate the artist's inherent talent and pave the way for its utmost and untrammeled expression.

True, every valid technique, every effective method, has a tendency to refine itself eventually into scientific gospel. This should not be the fate of theories on the theatre arts, which should have greater latitude. But if it is, then let us think of theatre sciences as gay and permissive sciences which, having laid the groundwork for our inspiration, will not hold us so fast that we cannot go forward to something better.

Here we must digress long enough to debate with those columnists, commentators and interviewers who, whether out of carelessness or indolence, have denigrated theatre techniques by lumping everything under "method acting," as though it were a contemptuous implication.

The dictionary definition of "method" has not altered since the word made its way into the English language from the Latin *methodus* and the Greek *methodos*. It still means: 1. An orderly procedure or process; hence a set form of procedure, as in investigation or instruction. 2. Orderly arrangement, elucidation, development or classification; more generally, orderliness and regularity or habitual practice of them in action.

From that it should be clear even to the most uninformed that "method" does not connote in any way the chaotic, disordered acting which some of the theatre's pseudos have perpetrated and thus encouraged; nor is it the odius label which the scoffers and sneerers so conveniently, often unthinkingly, grasp at as a means of maligning the sincere craftsmen and experimenters in the theatre arts.

Everybody, whether conscious of it or not, has and uses some kind of method, style, manner or means in the pursuit of his work or professional practice—and that includes columnists, commentators and interviewers. All of us follow certain occupational rules and employ certain dictated devices, whether they stem from tradition, necessity, experience or expediency. But suppose our opinion-makers adventured with something new or different in an effort to improve and enliven their labors—would anyone be justified in ridiculing them with such appellations as "method columnist," "method commentator" and "method interviewer"?

Obviously, the "method" label has been too indiscriminately slapped onto all innovators in the theatre because of the posturings and failings of an anarchic few who, rather than evolving new and valid concepts or improving on the old ones, have gone "way out" into orbit like so many misguided missiles by disregarding all good form and taste of the past. But it is cruelly unjust to condemn a whole profession and its genuine ideals because of a handful of ostentatious rebels without a cause, who, in an effort to launch themselves with pretentious and tasteless styles, have not even succeeded in getting off their "pad." The same may be said for some of those "new wave" playwrights whose works are awash with enigmatic themes, wobbly construction and uncharacterized people.

So let us hear no more about "method" actors and let us not tar the theatre as a whole with that term's derisive insinuations. Every good actor, director or playwright, like every good artist or craftsman in whatever field, has and must have a method or technique, a set of precepts, rules, basic laws or principles without which he cannot function to the maximum of his ability, talent or efficiency. Some are old methods, some are techniques compounded of two or more methods, and some are pioneering supplements; but all must be soundly based to have any validity or enjoy any permanence; none can be so outrageously "new" that it departs entirely from, disregards and violates, the basic principles and high standards which have preserved and advanced its progenitive art or science. The formless, sloppy, beatnik style which has become an opprobrium of the theatre is, thank heaven, a meretricious and vacuous vogue. A short life to it!

The purpose of this book is not to espouse one method over the other. The ensuing chapters will deal with and clarify some of the *best* methods of the past; but primarily they will present and analyze those refinements and improvements which, after many years of investigation and experimentation, have been welded into a set of the most workable and exemplary *techniques* to date. In the belief that by so doing we will not have further disgraced or degraded the theatre, but *will* have taken some of the pejorative sting out of "method," we offer these findings in the hope that they will lead to "technique directors" and "technique playwrights"—in name and in fact.

2. What a Play Ought to Be

Over the entrance arch of a château-like edifice which houses the writers' cubicles at one of the major film studios in Hollywood, this inspirational legend is engraved:

A PLAY OUGHT TO BE AN IMAGE OF HUMAN NATURE
FOR THE DELIGHT AND INSTRUCTION OF MANKIND

In the film and television worlds east and west, the source of this quotation seems to have been obscured either by time, lack of interest or disagreement with its philosophy, or perhaps all three. Resident and transient writers whose attention has been drawn to it from time to time have been especially vague as to its origin. The late Herman Mankiewicz, a talented screen writer of his day and sometime wag, is reputed to have defended the ignorance of his fellow workers by saying that "The plaque has been placed too high and is figuratively as well as literally far above the heads of writers who have shown cause to hang theirs in shame." Perhaps it would be more charitable to say that, judging from many a script creation that emanated from the cells of that building, the precept of that quotation has been largely ignored, at that studio and in many another film and television fiction factory.

It may therefore come as a surprise to many of the high-priced

and most of the fast-buck writers that the legend is not some re-
cent, highfalutin admonition by a studio head or story-department
mentor; neither is it the aphorism of some modern-day prophet
who wanted to impress them with his erudition or immortalize
his personal philosophy. It is almost three hundred years old!
Written by John Dryden in 1668 in his *Of Dramatic Poesy,* the
full quotation is:

"A play ought to be a just and lively image of human nature,
representing its passions and humours, and the changes of fortune to which it is subject, for the delight and instruction of
mankind."

No wonder most of those writers did not recognize it!

There may have been room only for the condensation over that
building's arch, but I think that anyone who ever writes a line of
dialogue should commit it to memory in its entirety—and live by
it. Particularly the "new wave" playwrights. For while there are
numerous maxims applicable to the art of playwriting, it would
be difficult to find so apt a guide for both master and apprentice.
And if both used it as a yardstick for every character and situation
they put on paper, it is safe to theorize that young playwrights
would not have to struggle so hard for success and the seasoned
ones would be far more secure in theirs—not to mention the vast
reduction in financial losses to producers and the tremendous in-
crease in theatre attendance.

Now that we know what a play ought to be, I would like to express my views on what a talented playwright (and director) ought
to be:

1. He should have the ability to open himself to something
   higher than most people are capable of envisioning.
2. He should have the capacity to see and feel things, psychologically as well as physically, which are normally hidden to others.
3. He should develop the ability to express what is thus revealed
   to him.

4. He should have an individual *way* of interpreting what he sees and feels.

5. He should be able to find his own original *form* to express his thoughts, and state them so that the largest number of persons and peoples will understand.

6. He should be an emblem of one's higher self, a guiding light and clarion voice to humanity's blind, inarticulate search for the meaning and mission of life.

7. Primarily, he should be a creator and an innovator in word and deed—and with them.

3. Love in Our Theatre: Art or Profession?

PROLOGUE: The subject matter of this chapter, which Michael Chekhov first delivered early in 1955 as one of his memorable lectures to the Drama Society of Hollywood, requires an explanation as to its origin: it was born in anger—Chekhov's. Whether his choler was leveled at me or at the playwriting theories I once held and worked by is of no moment. What matters is that the disputatious mood it engendered inspired him to formalize his thoughts on love for and in the theatre as an objective principle and guide for the professional and layman alike.

It happened at his home in Beverly Hills one afternoon when we were outlining the chapter on character structure (Chapter 8) from the playwright's point of view, particularly on how to motivate a character. It was then that I made the now fortunate mistake of telling him the story of a *reductio ad absurdum* which I had learned in my youth and had compulsively followed ever since.

I told him how, when still in my teens, I had tried to break into show business by getting a job as a bellhop at The Friars, a theatrical club in New York. I worked the night shift, and in the coatroom was a kid with similar ambitions named James Cagney. Jimmy had already cracked the ice; he was a member of the Lenox Hill Players, an amateur group at the old Lenox Hill Settlement under the direction of Burton and Florence James, who later taught drama at the Cornish School in Seattle, then at the University of

Washington, and subsequently created the Repertory Theatre of Seattle. Through Jimmy's efforts I joined the Lenox Hill troupe and, like him, was soon deep in the study of the theatre through books, rehearsals, occasional performances and many passes to Broadway shows, which we cadged from the various producer and director members of the club—and even its playwrights.

Incidentally, George M. Cohan was then the Abbot of The Friars and we saw him quite often, a fact which may help to account for Jimmy's remarkable portrayal of him some twenty-five years later in *Yankee Doodle Dandy,* a performance so authentic that it won the Motion Picture Academy's "Best Actor" award for 1942.

Anyway, a highly successful playwright at the time was a cynical and seemingly lonely but democratic Friar named Eugene Walter, still remembered by old-timers for his *The Easiest Way.* His next play, *The Challenge,* also proved to be a Broadway smash hit and was then bringing him more money than he cared about. He was spending it lavishly at the Friars bar one night long after all other convivial members had departed, and when that oasis shut down, he reluctantly weaved his way toward us for his hat and coat.

We paid little attention to him because both of us were draped over the coatroom counter, engrossed in Jimmy's reading aloud from a text book on the early Greek dramatists. But Mr. Walter's derisive snort made us look up and snap to attention. Apparently, he had been standing behind us long enough to hear what was absorbing our interest, for before Jimmy could go fetch the man's apparel, Mr. Walter delivered himself of what to me became an unforgettable (now regrettable) theory, which I sustained through many years of theatre activity:

"You're wasting your time, kids. You can take all those thirty-odd Greek plots and chuck 'em down the sewer. There are only two human impulses, two human desires that underlie and motivate all plots and characters—*Sex* and *Property.* No play can be successful without them. Nothing in life can exist without them."

I can still remember how shocked I was at this brutal pronouncement from a current oracle, and how vainly I tried to refute him.

"What about a truly sacrificial emotion like mother love?" I argued.

"Just another sex manifestation," he elucidated dismissively. "Besides being a survival mechanism, which is the reproductive function of sex, the mother needs the child to empty her painfully engorged breasts and to contract her womb so that she can get ready to bear more children. Her continuing love for the child far into maturity is still that survival mechanism, her posterity insurance, plus the lingering and grateful memory of that once necessary physical contact."

The dialogue may not be verbatim after all these years; in fact, I recall it as being much franker, and it is easy to see how it could make such a lasting impression even on two idealistic pubescents. Mr. Walter said many more indelible things as he rebutted and demolished every exception I tried to think of in negation. In short, I was a bantam fighting a heavyweight in age, intellect and experience. He took my best haymakers and reduced each to the two simple denominators, his basics for true and successful playwriting —*Sex* and *Property*. And thus, they remained my beacons until that day when I tried to shine them as directional finders for Michael Chekhov.

Chekhov was outraged by the precept, and perhaps with me as well because I gave it credence and quoted it as gospel.

"It is ridiculous!" he fumed. "It is a low and terribly sad opinion of human beings that they are motivated only by their glands and their greed! What happens, for instance, when a person has all the sex he wants and all the money or possessions one can acquire? Must he stop living—does he? Is there nothing else which makes living worth while? No, it is not so. There are much higher objectives to life and much better reasons for a play, even a good commercial play. There is, for example, a pure love of life itself and all its natural and divine mysteries; there is an honest and selfless love of people; and there is a genuine love of the theatre as a cultural and creative force. Any of these gives the lie to the idea that sex and property are the only stimulants and indispensable ingredients of human existence—on the stage or off."

In the week that followed, Chekhov prepared the lecture which comprises this chapter. On hearing it, I gladly exchanged my role of catalyst for that of convert. Because it suddenly became clear to me what was wrong with the plays I had produced and those I had written—including even the one that was awarded some now forgotten writing honors by the Dramatists Alliance of Stanford University, and the one that Marie Louise Elkins was going to produce on Broadway and Gerald Savory direct, had a better attitude enabled me to rewrite it to their satisfaction. Had I held, instead, the view and respect for the fundamental ingredients of a play which Chekhov espouses in this chapter, I daresay that my years in the theatre might have been even more rewarding than I think they were.

C. L.

Deep within ourselves are buried tremendous creative powers and abilities. But they remain unused so long as we do not know about them, so long as we deny them. Although they are beautiful, powerful and wonderful, we are—and this is a disease of our time —we are ashamed of them. And thus, they often remain ignored and lie forever dormant because we do not open the doors to our hidden vaults and fearlessly bring them to the surface.

One of the treasures I would like to talk about quite shamelessly is the one we seem to be most ashamed of and frightened by. And yet it is the richest diadem that can crown our professional, practical and creative work, even our whole existence. In fact, the world could not exist without it any more than it could without oxygen, for example. But are we ashamed of and frightened by oxygen?

So, permit me to speak to you about—Love.

Have you ever watched two immature, frightened, inhibited people trying to express, to act love? They stare into each other's eyes for a while, begin to feel uncomfortable and start blinking. That makes them even more uncomfortable and they feel that they have to do something to conceal and overcome their embarrassment. So they tentatively touch hands, then start to giggle, then try to find escape in this giggling. Finally, they produce an almost idiotic smile on their faces and soon everything comes to a feral end.

It is a most pitiful spectacle, a mawkish pastiche which cannot even substitute for love. It is just one of the phantoms of our era that pass for love, copied from other phantoms like it, and is enough to dissuade any sensitive person from uttering or venerating the word. There are loves far more admirable.

Since a great many conflicting views are already rampant on the subject of love, it is not my purpose to add to the confusion but, rather, to ask you to examine another kind of love, one which is an ideal and an art and which inspires our creativity in the theatre. For, contrary to opinions engendered by some forms of entertainment and some show-business personalities, there *is* another kind of love in our theatre, and it is not the commodity or "profession" that the mercenary elements have made of love on the stage and screen.

In order to understand what real love in our theatre is and should be, let us first establish what love definitely is not.

It is not a commercial commodity in the carnal sense; it is not a peep show. Neither is it a sentimental something that we mistake for love. And it is certainly not the thing that is hawked and thrown at us so casually, so surfeitingly in cheap books, shoddy films and radio and television soap operas and violence vehicles, for the sole purpose of titillating us. That kind of love can have no other purpose.

But what is genuine love, love in our theatre, the love experienced by its creative persons—the playwright, director and actor?

Let us analyze that and see how it differs in theory and fact from the imitations that have been foisted upon us.

There are three kinds of love governing life, each very different from the other. The Greeks had to have three different words to classify them. We have only one, and that may make for some of our confusion and inarticulateness on the subject. Hence, a clarifying peek into what these three kinds of love are is necessary at this point.

One is the erotic love between the sexes and is the definition most commonly hurled at us, most easily understood and most readily accepted. Even its two poles or extremes are more or less familiar to us: its highest aspects we refer to as platonic love and romanticism; the baser, lowest end is just animal gratification. In between is a spectrum too wide to parse in these pages and not too pertinent to the kind of love we shall ultimately deal with. The only observation germane here is that the baser aspect of this erotic love is something which the theatre, being a visual and aural medium, cannot actually supply or even imitate, much as it often tries and pretends; the best such unworthy efforts can do is merely stimulate the carnal appetite for sex. That, to me, is not only cheating the theatregoer but cheating the theatre itself, which is capable of love's much nobler expressions.

This nobler love is definitely another kind of love. We might call it pure, human love. It is devoid of erotic elements; it is a love between one human being and another, regardless of sex. And this human love also has its higher and lower aspects. In its lower aspects it is usually linked with blood relationships, and here egotism plays an important part. It is the I-love-my-son, daughter, father, mother, cousin, brother—any and all who are "mine"—type of love. It is a form of I-love-*myself*-within-my-son, daughter—all the kinships. It is good and noble but it is not the highest or most selfless aspect of love. Somewhat higher, for instance, is our love of country. But even that is not yet its highest aspect.

Real and true love begins when we start loving every human being regardless of blood relationship or nationality, but only because it is another human being and we are able to love him without any specific reason, without the prefix of "me" or "mine." *That* is the highest aspect of human love. There is no need to know the human being personally. It might be somebody in China whom we never saw and perhaps never will see, but we love him only and simply because he exists.

By this I do not mean to suggest that we plunge headlong into the boundless, dangerous sphere of loving humanity in the abstract. Nobody loves "humanity" because nobody really experiences, feels or knows what humanity is. It is a generalization we cannot truly envision, much less portray. But if we say "I love human beings," we immediately get some firm, definite basis on which to build our ideas and emotions. Loving human beings, wherever they may be and whether we know them or not, is quite a different thing from playing with mass conceptions or generalities. Try to write, direct or act a scene demonstrating that you love humanity and you will invariably end up by showing that you have compassion for certain persons because they symbolize certain things and qualities with which you have an affinity.

And finally, there is the third kind of love, the highest of all its forms and expressions—Divine Love. This is a love so exalted that it is given to very few if any of us on earth to have any conception of it, much less experience it. It is the kind of love with which God or the Holy Trinity loves, and we shall not even attempt to profane it with meager descriptions and definitions. Besides, the purposes of this chapter will best be served if we confine ourselves to that frame of reference that we know as purely human love, and see what practical uses we can make of this treasure.

One unmistakable manifestation of that human love is the thing that devoted theatre people feel for the theatre per se. The question that inevitably arises in the minds of its creators is: What is it that we actually love so much in the theatre—and why?

The true professional loves everything in it, of course. Why? Primarily because he loves the wonderful world that is opened up to him through that magic of make-believe which is acting. "Acting" is the key word. The playwright at work is mentally acting all the characters of his play; the director vicariously sees himself acting all the roles in the play while he is rehearsing it; the actor enjoys the pleasure of transforming himself into every character he plays and expressing himself through their masks or personalities.

The world at large knows very little of the sacrifices most people in the theatre usually make in order to become an active part of its viable creations. They read and hear only about the glamorous exceptions who "made it" the easy way, however they managed it, because those are the phenomena most freely glorified. But what about the numerous, untold rejections suffered by the average playwright before he turns out his first hit, and the bitter disappointments undergone by the average director striving for his first big chance, and the privations and humiliations endured by the average actor while waiting for his first big role?

Yet no force on earth could possibly divert them from this desire, this overpowering love which impels them to express themselves on the stage. If it were only the lure of money or fame, most of them could do far better at other careers and achieve them in far less time. There are much less painful and much more lucrative ways of securing one's livelihood and insuring one's comfort and position in life. But these mean nothing to the person who chooses the theatre. It is the love of creating through "acting" that leads him on despite all hardships. That, too, is a vital form of human love. Without it the theatre would have become extinct long before the days of the first Greek playwrights. They understood this love, and their imperishable creations are their monuments to it.

Besides this act of creating for and through the theatre, another thing we love is the creation itself. As soon as a play is born, the author begins to love it as though it were so many living beings. They exist for him objectively. Even if they are not perfect, and in spite of their fictitious existence, they represent human creatures and he loves them dearly. He loves even his most hateful, most despicable characters. He understands them and the forces that make them what they are, and to feel for them in this sense requires not only a higher but almost a divine love. The same may be said for the director and actor when they bring the characters to life.

The same kind of love must be extended even to the audience. Playwrights, directors and actors may sometimes claim indifference to those "out front," may even say they hate them. It is only an illusion or perhaps a studied attitude. Did they honestly dislike the audience, they would not be so relentlessly driven to create for it. The unalterable truth is that they love it, need it and cannot live unless the audience reciprocates this love for their creations. Subconsciously they may resent the fact that the audience has the power of life and death over the characters; intensely loving the people they created, they fear and cannot bear to see them suffer or die. But that does not detract from their desire and efforts to please the audience and win its love (i.e., approval) in return.

Please note that at no time did I say that the playwright, director or actor *ought* to love his profession. I always said that he *does* love it. It is only a question of how much he is aware of this kind of love constantly working within him. And here we come to what I regard as a very interesting and even curious point in our professional psychology.

Among many others throughout the world, I subscribe to the spiritual philosophy which asserts that there are two currents working within us, two powers of influence constantly struggling for supremacy. One is positive, creative, helpful; the other is negative, hampering, destructive. Now, if we are not conscious and responsive to the creative powers, they inevitably become weaker and weaker; their influence upon us becomes negligible; they might even vanish entirely if we ignore or neglect them. Conversely, if we are not aware of the hampering and destructive powers working within us, they grow and develop alarmingly; their negative influence upon our creative work becomes stronger and stronger. However, if we know about and acknowledge the positive forces, it is they instead that grow and increasingly help us in our creative work. And by being constantly on guard against the negative powers, it is these that diminish and eventually die out. With this premise I hope to establish my belief that human inspiration is forever the object of a power struggle between the forces of good and evil, creation and destruction, and it is only our degree of awareness that determines which way the battle will go.

The positive forces I refer to are, of course, implicit in the theatre creator's higher sense of love. So let us consider the practical rather than the esoteric values of this kind of love to the theatre professional who is courageous enough to acknowledge it and its latent power for wooing inspiration. Let us see how we can develop this higher sense of love within ourselves.

First, as I have tried to establish, all creative feelings on the stage—meaning the feelings of and for the characters—are based upon this higher love. We might even say they are its progeny. And if we think of this love as a field which must be properly prepared and cultivated, then all the creative feelings we grow upon it will be strong and healthy.

Consider a more extreme or inverted example of this love in action—say a character on the stage who is filled with hatred. Did we not create even him, too, with love, he would only engender hatred within ourselves and the audience, as it often happens in many a play. Without this love, the hatred of the character would become so realistic, so ugly and repulsive, that we could not write or perform him in proper perspective. He would exude hate, he would be all hate, devoid of all other qualities that humanize him and make him interesting for us to portray and the audience to watch. And what would happen when the curtain went down? We and the audience would continue hating. Whom? Nobody in particular, not even the character who saturated us with this hatred. Nevertheless, the hatred would remain and infiltrate our workaday lives, become one with us and confuse us to the point where we could not distinguish our creative from our personal emotions. That way lies failure for us as artists and irrationality as social beings.

If I were to be asked what the most characteristic feature of our kind of love is, I would name its constant process of expansion. For it is not merely a state of mind; it is never static. Susceptible to the stimuli of attention and exercise, it spreads and permeates our inner artistic being, and our talent flourishes in proportion to its growth. The more we indulge and lavish it, the more it can give us in return. I have actually seen this at work in myself and in many of my colleagues.

Test this out for yourself by defining the essence of our profession or that of any other art. Its essence is to give—to give constantly. What is it that we in the theatre give? Instead of images on canvas or in the form of statuary or music, we give our body, voice, feelings, will, imagination—we give a form of pulsating art to life itself; we give it to our characters and we give it to our audiences. Nothing, absolutely nothing remains for us save the pleasure of having given pleasure. And yet it is only by this miraculous process that our love grows and our talent is fulfilled and replenished.

There are many ways of developing this very special sense of love right within the framework of our everyday life. The first step is to believe it and become more and more aware of its existence. Then, almost automatically, the opportunities to nourish it will present themselves in your daily routine. You will find, for example, that you can render help to people around you. It doesn't always have to be some grand gesture or a piece of superaltruism, and it doesn't have to be made deliberately and you don't have to go seeking it mechanically like a boy scout his daily good deed. It can be some trivial, spontaneous little thing like lighting somebody's cigarette or yielding the right of way in traffic. If it is sincere and unpremeditated, its significance will lie in the fact that by doing something for your fellow man you become cognizant of the positive qualities of considerateness and kindness. These are some of the foods that this love feeds on.

Another suggestion: There are many things around us which we feel are ugly, unsympathetic, unpleasant, and our impulse is to shun them, have nothing to do with them. That is an understandable, atavistic, animal reaction. But suppose the very next time you encounter something unpleasant you try to find in it at least a grain of something which is not ugly or repulsive. I don't mean this as plain blind optimism; it literally *is* possible to discover something good or pleasant in everything unpleasant. It might be so minuscule that it is almost microscopic, or it might even be something intangible, but finding it will be extremely worth while. This act of kindness, this perceptive, artistic form of love, will help you to understand why no character on stage can ever be all black. In order to like and enjoy even the most hateful of our character creations, we must see in them or endow them with something admirable.

Still another suggestion: Listen to conversations and discussions of people around you and pay particular attention to the way they utter such possessive words as "I," "mine," "to my way of thinking," "in my opinion," etc. Frequently, they put more emphasis on those than on the things they have to say. Your impulse is to be highly critical of their egotism. But if you stopped to view this failing in a charitable light, you would soon be asking yourself, "Don't I measure the thoughts and opinions of others through the prism of my own agreement or disagreement?" I don't mean to say that nobody should express opinions; without them no discussion or conversation would be possible. What I am suggesting is that we curb this small ego within our own selves. The best way to treat it is with a gentle and tolerable humor; laugh at it, but without your justifiable sarcasm or cynicism. Learn to laugh at and discourage your petty ego because it is one of the numerous foibles that work in opposition to selfless love. Our kind of love, the creative person's love, must be all-pervading and expand us; the small egos of our life only contract us. These two cannot coexist; sooner or later one or the other must be victorious in the eternal battle for our creative souls.

One final suggestion: Try to develop the habit of thinking about everybody, like yourself, as a bearer of two different selves—the higher and the lower. In time this will grow into something tangible and expressible. For instance, when we speak about our love of other persons in general terms, it implies that we accept each *in toto,* with his good, bad and indifferent qualities. But the moment we make that separation between the higher and lower selves in a person, it becomes inconceivable that we would choose the baser self in him any more than we would in ourselves. We instinctively prefer the better, higher self in everybody. Therefore, this habit of thinking and believing that there is a higher self in others will awaken a concrete sensation of the higher self within you as well. For it is from no other source but the higher self within us that our artistic, creative love derives. And love in the theatre is infinitely nobler as an art than as a "profession."

4. Materialism Versus Play Material

> The beautiful is the appearance
> of the idea in material form.
> The sublime is the idea predominating
> over its material form.
> The comic is the material form
> predominating over the idea.
>
> —Friedrich Theodor Vischer
> on Hegelian aesthetics

In the world of inspirational ideas, in the world of art, everything that is built on a materialistic outlook is limited, confined and restrictive. We in the theatre are already pushed against the wall by a surfeit of materialistic concepts and presentations. But the theatre can and must be developed without limitations of any kind, and that can be achieved only if we shy away from a strictly materialistic outlook on the things the theatre has to say to the world and his brother.

In harsher terms, it means that the theatre, primarily through the playwright, must break the shackles of flat naturalism and devote itself largely to the inner psychological truths.

A civilization that builds solely on the foundation of exerting its materialistic powers cannot hope to advance the cultural life of humanity. The human being does not become more cultured because technological improvements increasingly bring him more of the commodities and comforts of life. Cultural development requires the refinement of the human being's inner life, demands searching for and realizing the *ideals* of the individual, the family, society, nations and the whole human race. Without those ideals, "civilizations" of the past succeeded only in becoming the enemies of humanity, plagues which drove us back into darkness, symbols of cruelty, egoism and hostility which resulted in destructive rather than constructive aspirations. Each war is the end result of a lack of true culture, an absence of ideals and inner human values. The decline and fall of all such materialistically overdeveloped "civilizations" is in nearly all instances traceable to their preoccupation with more powerful methods for the annihilation of the human race. What a pity to spend one's passions on death rather than in furthering the arts and sciences for a better life. It is time we learned something from the fact that such civilizations crumbled while their arts survived.

The contemporary theatre, films, radio and television are influences too wonderful to be wasted merely as so many of life's materialistic comforts, to be used simply as minor entertainment and diversion. They have too vast, too vital a cultural potential. The fact that the greatest number of our contemporary playwrights, and most of the public and play critics, are habituated to the theatre as it is now constituted, and do not envision its transcendental aspects, possibilities and obligations, is scarcely conclusive proof that all is right with its (the theatre's) world. Human beings can become accustomed to anything through constant repetition, usage and habit, and eventually they can be subverted into a passive acceptance of everything mediocre and deleterious that's fobbed off as "entertainment."

My materialism-steeped readers should not be offended by this outburst. It is not my intention to demand of them that they change their world outlook at once or completely. I realize that in the realm of everyday life, in the sphere of our own "civilization," everyone is compelled to be sufficiently materialistic in order to contend with the practical side of existence. But in the theatre, as in all artistic domains, one cannot sincerely approach his problems without a spirit of idealism. While it is true that nobody, not even playwrights and directors, is exempt from paying rent and taxes and buying groceries, it is equally true that these things need not and should not be the only or even the dominant motivations and criteria of life. In the worlds of artistic endeavor, one must be somewhat of a materialist by necessity and more of a dedicated idealist (even one with a spiritual goal) from choice. One should always be "practical" and yet flexible enough to be able to attune one's mind to the artistic demands of whatever occasions or problems confront one. A richness and flexibility of mind is indispensable to the artist as well as the artistic appreciator.

Once, while directing *The Inspector General* in Hollywood, I asked an actor to enter a scene as though he were about to step into an atmosphere of awe and veneration, as if the character he was about to encounter were a symbol of God.

"I can't play it that way," he replied. "I don't believe in God."

"I am not asking you as an individual to believe in God," I reasoned with him. "I am asking the character you are playing to believe in Him. I am asking you as an actor-artist to give me that kind of portrayal regardless of your personal beliefs."

The talented artist in him finally prevailed and he gave a magnificent performance. Proving that no true artist can afford to be resolutely inflexible; he must be able to see all of life, and he must be able to view it from all perspectives.

The true artist, be he playwright, director or actor, must be aware that of all the world's viewpoints, the purely materialistic one is the most relentless and destructive. Given full reign, it will vitiate, corrupt and corrode all else. Time and again in history, as history itself has shown, it has proved to be the malignant cell which invades, overruns, overrides and eventually depletes all human aspiration and inspiration. It is especially pernicious in the bodies of art, anesthetizing the nerves, denuding the flesh and pulverizing the bones.

Materialism's baneful effects on the playwright are that they occlude his artistic mind, kill his deeper feelings, distort and destroy his imagination and render him uninventive. A playwright thus deprived of his originality and ingenuity would, obviously, be better off dead, for all concerned. The tragedy he will never write is that he continues to live and work like an automaton, and, in an effort to conform to the materialistic pattern—i.e., concentrate on making only money—he is forced to accumulate and draw upon all kinds of theatrical clichés, character and plot banalities, and become a kind of mechanical imitator of the ordinary, the tawdry and the inconsequential in people and subjects that pass for life. Unable to portray life's more profound truths, he concocts instead a copy of life's meaningless surfaces—sans depth, sans creative ideas and without showing the higher and more laudable inner impulses which are ever present and vibrating beneath human beings' outer manifestations.

It is therefore the function, the very responsibility, of the sincere playwright to avoid vapid and valueless themes and people and devote himself more to subjects and protagonists that can better advance our cultural development. (And by that I don't mean being "arty"; artiness for its own sake is just as inartistic.) The dedication is not a simple one when the clink of easy dollars keeps dinning in his ears; but do it he must if he is to be a playwright of substance, if he is to make any memorable contribution to his time and his civilization. Because that has been his God-given role from time immemorial, because sometimes he can be more effective than the pulpit. Yes, he can and he has been—but he must not, need not, preach.

He may do it with allegory, allusion or even attack; he may do it with satire or symbolism, with anger or ridicule, with any and every device his words can create. Sometimes the illustration or a parable is so apparent that he need only hold the mirror up to nature to reflect the images of humankind worthy of our admiration and emulation, and those that merit only our disgust and pity. For the playwright's weapon is the right word, his persuasion is the right gesture, his emblem is the inspirational idea which can, by exposure and example, assail or guide the manners and morals of humans today and point a more desirable direction for the future.

How can he do it? That is where his artistic techniques come into play—and the pun *is* intended. Because, without sound craftsmanship, his loftiest inspiration will come to naught. Some of the techniques available to him will be dealt with in the succeeding chapters. For the present, though, permit me a necessary restatement by way of summary:

It is an unfortunate fact that the venality of our materialistic age frequently diverts the artist from thinking of the Higher Being within us; and yet it is exactly from that source, acknowledged or not, that we draw our greatest inspiration. Therefore, in this book I declare open war on excessive materialism in our arts, especially the arts of the theatre, for materialism brings with it the inevitable superficialities which intrude so ruinously upon our creative work. The main task and obligation of an artist is to explore and reveal the depth of his subjects.

In this book, as in all my work, I shall try to keep before my mind's eye a kind of ideal actor who will be able to utilize the maximum of his spiritual abilities while creating his characters, an ideal director who will be able to extract the maximum in such spiritual values from the play and players, and, *ab ovo*, an ideal playwright who will be able to portray our world and its people with the profoundness and wisdom that can spring only from the truly godlike qualities within himself. For the playwright's creations, like *His* creations, should also strive to become exemplary human beings!

5. No Conflict, No Play

In each play of any consequence, you will find two powers interlocked in combat. Whatever form or guise the playwright has devised to represent these powers, they must carry on their fight or conflict throughout the entire play, else the play stops, just as the play stops when the conflict is resolved either way at the end. Conflict, therefore, is a quintessential of good playwriting, just as it is one of the inescapable conditions of life itself.

In fact, life and the elements in all their manifestations are a macrocosm of sempiternal conflicts, and human existence consists of the microcosmic conflicts within the larger plan. As water forever fights fire and heat forever fights cold, so every living thing does incessant battle with the endless hungers, ills, problems and difficulties that beset it and challenge its survival, comfort and happiness. Indeed, all of life, from the very moment of conception, is a constant defense and battle against the ever-threatening menace, Death; and each encounter with it, in whatever form or magnitude, constitutes a dramatic action.

For it is a curse of Nature that life's conflicts never cease, and human beings have good reason to identify with them. Let them triumph momentarily over one menace, and another of greater or lesser magnitude inevitably looms to threaten and be overcome. Even such seemingly commonplace functions as "making a living" —getting and holding on to a job, the animal counterpart of foraging for food—are fraught with life-and-death conflicts. Stop struggling for and winning the things you need and desire for physical, mental and emotional pleasure, and living soon comes to a painful halt. For pleasure (victory) means survival and pain (defeat) means death, and these unceasingly contest against each other, as we know so well. It may be tragic or ironic, depending on your personal philosophy, but it is nevertheless true that life declares no lasting truces, and our efforts to achieve that illusory permanent peace and serenity in human existence make for the greatest conflicts of all.

So conflict, being ineradicable in life, is indispensable to the portrayal of life; and whatever kind of emotional or ideological conflict the playwright chooses to project must be made easily discernible from the very outset. Failing that, his play will have no shape, no driving force, no life. The sooner the conflict becomes apparent and the clearer its nature, the better will be the play's structure.

For the moment the audience discovers the essence of the conflict, even if only in general terms, it comes into possession of the key to the play and with it unlocks the motives behind the ensuing events or action. Therefore, the sooner are the conflict and its nature established and clarified, the sooner is the audience's interest engaged and held, the sooner does the audience become involved in the emotions of the characters.

What must become apparent to the playwright from the moment he conceives the play is that one of the two struggling powers leads the action of the play while its opponent constitutes its counteraction. Also, in a well-defined conflict, every action meets with a reaction which not only clarifies the action that preceded it but leads to the next action. For action is the drive toward the objectives and the superobjectives, both of the whole play and of the individual characters. The obstacles put in the way of the objectives and the superobjectives are the counteraction, and the resulting clashes with these obstacles comprise the reactions. Action = drive; counteraction = obstacle; reaction = clash; conflict—drama.

Every well-constructed play's characters can be divided into and arrayed as two groups representing the armies of action and counteraction, and so can the events or scenes of a play.

In some instances, in addition to these two basic groupings, you may discover a third group of people who do not participate in the actual fight or conflict itself. But these characters must not be regarded as entirely innocent bystanders. There are no such things as neutrals in a play. They are, rather, the catalysts who cause the battle to go one way or the other, depending on whose sentiments they unwittingly if not unwillingly represent.

It is these "catalyst characters" who usually form and dominate the third grouping of a play's events and scenes, commonly called its subplot. And since true catalysts remain unaltered by the battles they precipitate and the changes they effect, it may be said of the subplot that it has a life of its own and is as independent of the main plot as the main plot is dependent on it.

It will be well for the playwright to bear this in mind when he is dealing with character structure and motivation.

6. Improvising by Playwrights and Directors

The art of improvising—what to do and say in a given scene at a given moment—is not confined to the actor alone. The playwright practices it, too, consciously or unconsciously.

For what is a playwright but an actor on paper?

In fact, there is not a single instant of the playwright's creations that is not preceded by improvisation, even though the largest percentage of it, or maybe all of it, is done mentally.

Hence, just as the actor must be his own playwright when he is improvising without a script, so the playwright must be his own actors when he is devising their dialogue.

And no matter how fresh the playwright's theme, or novel his plot, or unusual his action or scenic inventions, dialogue is still the greatest brush and canvas of his creative equipment. Therefore, this word of caution is necessary: just as faulty, unclear and overlong dialogue destroys tempo and a feeling of ease in an actor, so does it make unreal and inartistic the characters and scenes of a play.

The shorter, clearer and more meaningful an actor's improvisation, the better it is. The same may be said for a playwright's dialogue.

As for the director, he must expect that improvisations (if he allows his players this latitude in their search for just the right business and gestures) will differ with different casts.

It is natural that they should, since no set of playwrights will invent the same dialogue for the same scene and no set of actors will perform and speak the lines in the same way if given the freedom to do otherwise.

The director will find it almost instinctive in the actor to respond differently to different words. All human beings do, as the psychologists and semanticists will tell you, and actors are even more sensitive to words than the average human being.

You will notice that when a playwright changes dialogue during rehearsals, the players' improvisation of the new lines will almost automatically suggest different action, different bits of business. And sometimes the different qualities or degrees of talent in the actors themselves will even inspire different approaches to the situations.

It is good to give the actor this creative freedom, but it devolves upon the director to see to it that it does not become too tangential, that it does not veer off into something alien to the character the actor is portraying, or become untrue to the particular scene or the over-all theme of the play.

Thus, one of the primary functions of the director is to maintain the psychological truth of the scene at all times. And looking ahead to the next scene, as he must at all times, he should be careful to forestall any premature actions and dialogue that are not natural steps and links to that ensuing scene, that will unhappily jump the logical transitions. In the performance of comedy or drama especially, these linking steps are vitally important and there should be no gaps or unbridged moments in the psychological transitions from one scene to the next.

And just as the actor should never start without the Sensation necessary to the beginning of a particular scene, so a director should never start a scene without firmly establishing its Atmosphere and defining the Qualities he wants from the cast. If a scene is to be played for comedy, then what kind—straight, light, broad, farcical? Only then can the director rightfully maintain truthfulness to the scene throughout.

7. Techniques of the Great Russian Directors

To the majority of us in the theatre the world over, the name of Constantin Stanislavsky is magic. Even to the laity it is a prime symbol of the actor's art and sometimes the only name among the great Russian directors that is easily remembered or readily associated with the establishment of the theatre arts as a universal culture. And it is not undeservedly so, since his pioneering efforts in founding the Moscow Art Theatre in 1898 and formulating and inditing the first set of theoretical codes on acting were of inestimable value to the growth of the theatre in general.

For myself, I owe two great personal or family debts to the founders of the Moscow Art Theatre which I hope will never be erased from theatre annals: they made their first big success with my uncle Anton's play *The Sea Gull* (after the work had been a failure in its initial production at St. Petersburg the year before), thereby launching him as one of the great playwrights of the late nineteenth and early twentieth centuries; and thanks to Uncle Anton's influence a few famous plays later, the Moscow Art Theatre became my training school as an actor and director. Also, my subsequent work and experiments with the First Studio of the Moscow Art Theatre, and as head of the Second Moscow Art Theatre, would not have been possible had not Stanislavsky and Nemi-rovich-Danchenko created the mother theatre and, later, given me the latitude to explore theories of my own within this cradle of the theatre arts as we know them today.

But there were many other directors who in their own way made unique and outstanding, though much less publicized, contribu-tions—such as Stanislavsky's inseparable partner and cofounder of the Moscow Art Theatre, the overshadowed Nemirovich-Dan-chenko; and Vsevolod Meyerhold, Eugene Vachtangov and Alex-ander Tairov. I shall discuss only these five, because they were the forerunners and I was privileged to work with four of them in their capacities as actors and directors during my sixteen-year association with the Moscow Art Theatre, and because I knew them intimately and studied their methods closely.

As I look back on the happy years when I observed Stanislavsky at the peak of his creative activity, and try to pinpoint the most characteristic feature of his method from among the numerous facets of his talent and interesting personal qualities, one memory remains pre-eminent: he was obsessed with, virtually possessed by, what he called the "feeling of truth." He could accept many things with which to express his art, even those that were inimical to him or against his principles, if he believed they were true; that is, true to life. That's what he looked for in all things and people; that was his most organic quality, his criterion of appraisal and ap-proval, and he demanded it of all his playscripts, actors, directors, settings, *décor,* lighting and props.

The way in which he applied it to his productions was a kind of twofold principle: not only did everything on his stage have to be true to life, including the actors, but the actors had to be absolutely true to the psychology and *inner life* of the characters as well. I, for one, was bewildered by this theory because it raised such questions in my mind as: "What if the character's psychology and inner life are *not* true to life? Was Don Quixote true to life? How does an actor play a character who is one such person among millions, or one for whom there is no norm because he is so different, and still convey the feeling of being 'true to life'?" But in Stanislavsky's burning, undeviating imagination, everyone and everything was capable of imparting this feeling of truth. And so, when working in his productions, we had to make many compromises with our own theories in order to guess and give him what we thought he wanted. But I never stopped wondering what was so imaginative and creative about merely copying life around us in every detail, photographically as it were, and I regarded it as one of the beclouded facets of Stanislavsky's many-sided talent. Nevertheless, and aside from my personal indebtedness and despite a difference or two of theoretical opinion, his pioneering achievements on his own and in collaboration with his coworkers must be acknowledged as the first monumental contributions to the art of the theatre in the past and present centuries. Others are said to have surpassed and even bypassed him but he, together with Nemirovich-Danchenko, was the first to break the land that opened up the new fields which all of us later tilled in our own distinctive ways.

Quite a different kind of artist was Vsevolod Meyerhold. Both as an actor and director he was absolutely polar to Stanislavsky's techniques. He, too, possessed tremendous imagination, but he applied it in exactly opposite ways. He *re*imagined everything, he reconstructed everything, he destroyed reality. He stretched his imagination to unheard-of lengths in order to avoid imitating life. Even his strong feeling of truth was exerted in a different sense: every play he directed, all his actors, had to be true to things only as *his* despotic imagination conceived them. He was just as certain of his own imagined feeling of truth as Stanislavsky was of his photographic sense of truth. If something was actually true to life, it didn't interest Meyerhold. His criterion was: Is it true to *my* imagination of it?

And the thing most characteristic of his imagination was his amazing ability to look beneath and beyond life's realities, to probe much deeper and farther than those true-to-life replicas which Stanislavsky loved so much. With his overdeveloped gift of imagination he saw things that, he believed, were hidden from everybody in the world but himself. Not only did he see these obscured things when he let his imagination run riot, but he saw them in his own peculiar and sometimes bizarre way—and what he saw he tried to incarnate through his actors and incorporate in his productions. Whereas Stanislavsky underplayed his imagination by confining it only to life's images, Meyerhold overplayed his with his more-than-life excesses. And yet, despite their contrasting techniques, they admired each other's results and loved each other as artists. This interested and puzzled me greatly, because I could not reconcile Stanislavsky's naturalistic approach with Meyerhold's almost diabolical conceptions. That's what they were, diabolical, as I shall explain in a moment.

Anyway, in the early days, Stanislavsky invited Meyerhold to join the Moscow Art Theatre family as an actor. To everyone's surprise, they managed to work well together for three years. As an actor in Stanislavsky's productions, Meyerhold seemed to submit to the founder's doctrines. Perhaps he was interested in learning how Stanislavsky made them work so well; or perhaps he was as overpowering an actor in concealing his opposition to them as he was a directorial personality later on. As extremely difficult as it must have been for him to go against his own artistic inclinations, he never showed it. But when he finally attained his own theatre in Moscow, and the freedom that went with it, he was his own autonomous self again— and a firebrand!

What was it that Meyerhold actually saw in life, in people? His imagination always led him to what we now call archetypes. For Meyerhold there was no such thing as one person or one character. To him it was the predominant type that was all-important; not alone the simple type or the stereotype, but the one that categorized vast numbers of persons or multiple groups of the species. His was some contorted archetype that combined and symbolized the strange qualities of large masses of human beings, and somehow it became a more easily recognizable archetype. It was, as I said, a truly devilish creation of his fantasy.

Why devilish? Because he saw everything from its evil side. He saw all our sins and shortcomings in huge dimensions, and when producing his plays he worked like a malevolent psychoanalyst. He dug the cruelest things out of human beings and events, their darkest deeds and most frightening qualities, made archetypes of them and put them on the stage for all of us to recognize some of our baser natures within them. All of his presentations were tremendously attractive, just as sin and wickedness can be magnetic to the average spectator. I must confess that it was enormously interesting to me—as a student of the theatre more than as a sinner, of course! Like Stanislavsky, I too loved him as an artist, for his startling ability to probe for and reveal those hidden facets of life which we could never have glimpsed had not his fiendish imagination ventured beyond the reaches of our own. Perhaps a couple of minor examples as I remember them will better illustrate his technique.

When Meyerhold directed Nikolai Gogol's *Revisor* in his own theatre in 1926, his wild imagination led him not only through the characters of the play but into the entire world of Gogol's own imaginings. He penetrated the very sphere of Gogol's whole character arena. But Gogol, as is well known to students of the theatre, was himself a very strange character; he also dramatized persons in archetypes, and all his concepts, artistic as they were, also were somehow twisted or exaggerated. Well, Meyerhold decided to exaggerate what Gogol had already exaggerated! It brought an astounding reaction from his audiences and colleagues: they either accepted it wholeheartedly and adored him or they denounced and hated him with a relentless fury. It was the same with all his productions.

One of the most violently debated characterizations in this Meyerhold production of *The Inspector General* concerned the main role of Khlestakov. As Gogol wrote him, he is an attractive young man, gay and lightheaded, almost a fool. He comes to the small town, plays a big shot and everybody mistakes him for the real Inspector General and kowtows to him. In the course of his silly prank, he even makes love to the Mayor's wife and becomes engaged to his daughter. But what did Meyerhold do with the character? He dressed him in black like a monk and gave him dark glasses that hid his thin and insipid face. Further, as Gogol limned the character, Khlestakov moves very fast and speaks rapidly, has nothing in his head and less in his heart; he is just a butterfly. But Meyerhold twisted the whole thing and mischievously went even beyond Gogol in exaggerating him. He gave him lackadaisical movements and, with his dark glasses and hanging hair already obscuring those necessary facial expressions, made him speak ever so slowly. Then, when he came to the famous main speech of the play, wherein Khlestakov begins to lie more and more and almost goes mad as his lies ensnarl him—in the middle of that speech, and for no apparent reason, Meyerhold had him slowly raise his leg skyward and hold it there like a sore thumb for several long moments! It was idiosyncratically Meyerhold and absolutely contrary to the character Gogol had intended, but it made a powerful impression. Even so, no playwright then or now would have tolerated it. Fortunately for Meyerhold and his startling directorial eccentricities, Gogol was long dead.

Another startling Meyerhold innovation made his *The Inspector General* equally memorable. Believe it or not, he injected a *brand-new* character into the play, one that Gogol probably had never dreamed of and certainly had never indicated either on or off stage. But that did not stop Meyerhold. Suddenly, this military-looking individual, an officer of some high but imprecise rank, entered the activity. This nonexistent character, wearing a uniform of the palest blue, which was also nonexistent in Russia, spoke not a single line but walked and walked among the other characters, looking very contracted and sad, almost weeping, having nothing to do as well as nothing to say. The other characters ignored him as if he didn't exist. He was just there, with his ultrapessimistic and almost cranky expression, just walking aimlessly back and forth and all around. And just as aimlessly, right while the dialogue and action were going on, he sat down at the piano and played things as sad as himself! It was as though this character had been left over from some other play, or had wandered in from a musical comedy at a theatre down the street, and everybody was too busy with his own part to socialize with him so he paid no attention to them.

Fantastic? Yes, but it also had a powerful impact. Again Meyerhold had created a tremendous impression on his audience. For as unreal and irrelevant as this character seemed to be, he nevertheless possessed a certain psychoanalytical something which somehow made you identify with him, made you feel what he symbolized, made you say, "Somewhere in the hidden corridors and labyrinths of my soul, there is something of this light-blue, lost, sad, aimless thing which nobody sees or recognizes, which is obscured even to myself. But there *is* something like it in me."

So again had Meyerhold been devilishly penetrating, punishing, but revealing. It was not some evil genius of his own which deliberately made him figure out these soul-torturing devices. It was simply his nature, as I said, to see things which nobody else saw, and his performances convinced you that they actually did exist, in yourself and others. And he always managed to dig them out, without fear of audience acceptance, opinions or reactions. That was *his* feeling of truth, and he was possessed by it and secure in it just as much as Stanislavsky was in his diametrically opposite view of the truth. Extreme as their techniques were, both made you see and feel the verisimilitudes of their creations.

Now, between these two fascinating artists, just in the middle, as it were, was Eugene Vachtangov, whose way of creating was influenced by both of them at the same time. One must marvel at the manner in which he was able to take these two techniques, which seemed to pull us in different directions, and reconcile them and combine them and put them to work harmoniously. He took Stanislavsky's reality and Meyerhold's fantasy and welded them with his own theatricality, his own eclectic sense of artistic showmanship, so that his own stage creations became as distinctive a trade-mark as theirs.

Instinctively, intuitively, Stanislavsky tried to persuade his audiences that they were not in a theatre, that his performances were real life, that after the curtain went up, they were one with the characters on the stage. With Meyerhold's superpsychology, you were taken by the scruff of the neck and thrown out of this world and into another of his own imagining. Vachtangov, on the other hand, did everything possible to remind the spectator: "Look, it is the *theatre*. It is not Stanislavsky's reality or Meyerhold's other-world images. It is just juicy theatre." With Vachtangov, you remained in your theatre seat; nothing was too naturalistic or too illusional; everything was theatrical. And he developed this theatricality to such a degree that you began to love the theatre in a new way—the theatre as such. There were always the elements of amusement and imagination in everything he did, but at the same time, his theatricality managed to include the powerful feelings of truth as Stanislavsky and Meyerhold used and justified them.

And so you might say that these three directors, these three points of view and approaches to the theatre, actually encompassed the entire scale of directorial and even playwriting possibility and impossibility. I see them as milestones, at or between which we can stop as we choose. And if we do not forget the workable extremes of Stanislavsky and Meyerhold and the median efforts of Vachtangov, we can be inspired by the feeling that everything in the theatre is not only permissible but possible. We have only to make our creations come alive, artistically and convincingly, no matter by what means we achieve this.

There were two other directors contemporaneous with those formative years of the twentieth-century theatre whose functions and contributions, while not as genetic as those of the foregoing three, should also be examined if we are to know precisely how the Moscow Art Theatre family tree grew and where it branched.

The theatre as we know it today, its artistic philosophies and various technical methods, was actually created by two persons: Constantin Stanislavsky and Vladimir Nemirovich-Danchenko. They were both equally responsible for founding the Moscow Art Theatre. But by some strange destiny, Stanislavsky's name is always mentioned in connection with it and Nemirovich-Danchenko's only rarely if at all. Perhaps it was because Stanislavsky was a physical giant of a man while the bearded and slightly paunchy Nemirovich was not very much taller than Toulouse-Lautrec. I always thought it grossly unfair that both nature and history has conspired to deal so inadequately with him. But measured by what they each gave to the world, Nemirovich-Danchenko was as much of a giant as Stanislavsky. Both cut their ties with a comfortable past and both worked equally hard and sacrificed in equal proportion in order to realize their dream theatre. Once they came together, they collaborated for the rest of their lives and influenced each other greatly. Nemirovich was also a playwright, which Stanislavsky was not; his *The Price of Life* had shared a playwriting prize with my uncle Anton's *The Sea Gull*. In fact, it was Nemirovich who later overcame the resistance of the other members of the Moscow Art Theatre and persuaded them to include *The Sea Gull* in their first season's productions and, as I mentioned in the beginning, it proved their first big financial hit. Hence, a seagull became the theatre's emblem.

Nemirovich-Danchenko was a trained mathematician. By avocation he was a psychologist and continued one even after he entered the realm of the theatre. Thus, in everything he did, his genius lay in going directly to the crux of the matter and immediately finding the main idea, the guiding theme. Then the separate elements materialized before his brilliant mind and formed themselves into a sort of scaffolding or skeleton, which he slowly and painstakingly fleshed out in every minute human psychological detail. His performances were like a symphony conducted by Toscanini, and like that maestro, he heard and corrected all the little mistakes unnoticed by the average ear, saw and remedied all the little blemishes not apparent to the average eye.

His little-known influence on Stanislavsky during their close collaboration was this sense of oneness, wholeness, completeness. Stanislavsky grasped at it and developed it into his now famous theories of the superobjectives—of the play and the characters— and the smaller objectives. These were Stanislavsky's interpretation of Nemirovich-Danchenko's ability to see the main line always and unmistakably. In turn, Nemirovich-Danchenko learned and applied Stanislavsky's "human" approach to the theatre and charac-

ters. From the brilliant mathematician-playwright-psychologist
came the skeleton of the play, from the great humanist came the
real-life moods and atmospheres to flesh it out. Together they created not only the Moscow Art Theatre as an organization but the
style and face of the theatre-and-school which has made such a lasting impression on the world and has yet to be rivaled.

Much as they complemented and inspired each other artistically
and creatively, they were a most oddly matched pair outwardly.
Stanislavsky was a very elegant man; his every movement was a piece
of art, every word and term he used conjured up a picture, and his
attire was always impeccable. He was a joy to watch and listen to.
Nemirovich was a gentleman in a different sense. He always wore a
top hat, which nobody else did; his clothes were clean and not
unfashionable, and his manner dignified. But he was terribly awkward. He used to step on his own foot and walk into chairs and get
angry with himself because his dignity was diminished. Stanislavsky being so tall and graceful and Nemirovich so short and clumsy,
it was painful for both of them to be so physically incompatible, so
Mutt and Jeff, as they used to say in this country. And when the
two were together, it was just as comical as that cartoon to see
Nemirovich always trying to step up on something in the hope of
looking a little taller and Stanislavsky always slumping or sitting
down to make himself a little smaller. But inwardly, to my way of
thinking, they were on a par—men of equally gigantic stature in the
theatre.

It was from this combination of talents, as well as Meyerhold's,
that Vachtangov borrowed and compounded a theatre philosophy of his own. That was Vachtangov's special genius. He was a
vessel into which all the positive things could be poured and he
quite naturally gulped and ingested them. I do not mean to imply
that he baldly imitated them. In a minor sense he did, but whatever
he accumulated and refined emerged as a fresh amalgam of his
own. What he borrowed from Meyerhold, for instance, was transformed into something pleasant, not offensive. Vachtangov gave
nobody umbrage or cause to hate him; he was a gay and happy

Meyerhold with a tremendous sense of humor. Where Meyerhold's creations were permeated with pessimism, evil and sardonic commentary, Vachtangov's were suffused with gaiety, happiness and lightness of spirit. Even Meyerhold himself admired this ability in Vachtangov and, since they all influenced each other artistically, made several unsuccessful stabs at borrowing some of this lightness and optimism. But somehow they always came out ponderously Meyerholdian.

Also luminous during this golden era of the Moscow Art Theatre, though not connected with it, was Alexander Tairov. His characteristic technique, his label, was that he deliberately made everything on his stage overly beautiful. He was in love with beauty. On the surface, his productions seemed to contain no ideas and have no depth. His settings were always elaborate and colorful, his costumes pretty, the actors' movements like dancing and their speech almost like singing. Everything seemed lightheaded, lighthearted and very superficial. But they were none of these. Behind all his flossy and glossy creations there was an arresting quality that defies definition. It was extreme beauty, to be sure, but it also had strong, undeniable undercurrents of earnestness and sincerity. It was more than beauty for the eye alone. He expressed himself and the meaningful things of his plays through the *soul* of beauty. Vachtangov was most impressed by this kind of beauty, drew upon it and transmuted it into a quality of his own.

In this visual respect, Tairov was the exact opposite of Meyerhold, who increasingly denuded his stage as the years went by, eventually winding up with the red bricks of the rear wall showing —just a repelling, dirty, dusty, starkly lit stage with a piece of scenery here and there. But when Vachtangov adapted the setless or bare-stage idea, it was without Meyerhold's dust, dirt and ugliness; he made everything pleasant to look at and inviting by an ingenious use of drapes, scrims and colorful lighting. He was gifted enough to beautify Meyerhold with Tairov, as it were, which was no small accomplishment.

If Vachtangov had accomplished nothing else, he still would have won his place among those early "greats" by proving that the seeming irreconcilables of the theatre can be reconciled—that the diverse techniques of Stanislavsky, Nemirovich, Meyerhold and Tairov could be brought together, amalgamated and metamorphosed into a new and wonderful product without doing violence to any of them. For each of Vachtangov's productions was a harmonious blend of the very beautiful, very deep, very light, very mathematically clever and humanly true. He believed, as do I and think we all should, that for the imaginative craftsman of the theatre, there were no artistic boundaries that could not be crossed without some benefit to the adventurer. Hence, it is ridiculous for the artist within us to say, for example, "I love only Stanislavsky. I reject Meyerhold," or vice versa, or deprecate the merits of any of the theatre's other creators. Why be narrow-minded, why cut ourselves off from any of these rich heritages when, like Vachtangov, we have the freedom to make the most of the best in all techniques? There are no prohibitions against it. All it takes is a little wisdom, imagination and courageous experimentation.

II

Now I would like you to join me in delving into the egos, the assertive temperaments of these creators, which formed the bases of their respective techniques. But by way of elucidation I must immodestly reminisce about one of my own theoretical contributions around that period.

During one of our summer vacations in the late 1920's, Stanislavsky, Meyerhold and I sojourned in Berlin. By that time certain of my own ideas were fairly well developed, so Stanislavsky invited me to discuss them and our differing approaches to the theatre. We spent more than five hours at it in one of those Kurfurstendamm cafés and I don't remember all the details of our exhausting conversation, but I shall try to give you that essence of it which is germane to what I am discussing with you.

Stanislavsky's viewpoint was that when an actor gets a part he has to imagine that the character he will play is, figuratively speaking, seated within himself—absolutely and completely occupying the actor's inner self—and the actor has to imagine what his character will do in given circumstances. He called this mental process of the actor the "Magic If." It was supposed to tell the actor how to play the character which the playwright invented for him—how to behave, speak, react and fulfill the business under the conditions the playwright had set forth. In sum, the character dwelt within the actor, and the actor's voice and body expressed in a true-to-life manner what the character was supposed to think and feel and do according to the playwright's intentions, and yet in such a way that it was also true to the psychology or inner life of the actor himself.

To me, this made for confusion in the actor's mind and could lead to conflicts with the playwright's conception of the character. But that was Stanislavsky's point of view. Mine was a different one.

I told him that to my understanding, the actor should be able to imagine every thing and every place, but not with the character sitting within himself. My technique then, as now, was to imagine the character as being *outside* of me and to ask myself what I would do, and how, if I were in his circumstances. Then I could stand off and watch myself, not here any more as Michael Chekhov the actor but there as the character—actually seeing the character in the process of acting out all the things the playwright had prescribed for him. With this more objective means of inquiry, it is like asking the character himself to show you how to do it.

Another and perhaps deeper reason for my disagreement was that, if the character is seated within me, according to Stanislavsky's notion, I can never separate myself from him nor he from me; the character will have no free will; it will always be the actor manipulating the character as if he were a puppet instead of the sentient being we must try to make of him. But according to my theory, the character should have a free will, life and personality of his own and have the liberty to exercise them, and by so doing, demonstrate to the actor what to simulate and how. But when the character lies buried within the actor, the actor can get no proper perspective on him, and so the character can exist only as the actor permits or dictates. In other words, a character thus imprisoned cannot guide and instruct the actor; he must adapt himself to the limits of the actor's personality and way of doing things, when the reverse should be the case.

The actor must divorce his own personality and mannerism from those of the character and give himself over completely to the will, feelings, habits and appearance of the character. When the playwright imagined the character and wrote how he lived certain incidents, it was not the actor whom he visualized nor the actor's way of life. Neither was the character seated within the playwright, doing things the playwright would do and in the playwright's way. It was the playwright who initially gave the character an independent life and personality; therefore, it is the function of the actor to collaborate and cocreate with the playwright, not by confining the character but by imagining him and seeing him and performing him objectively.

Seeing and hearing the character thus in my mind's eye and ear, as the playwright saw and heard him, studying him in every detail as he lives out his brief life on the stage, I am better able to absorb the qualities which will transform me into the character; I am better able to alter my body, my voice and my emotions to conform with those of the character instead of forcing his to conform to mine. By so doing, I become the character's instrument for conveying his life to the audience, as the playwright saw it. I do not make the character just another instrument for conveying my own personality.

I told Stanislavsky that I differed with him because he placed the emphasis on "the actor's ego," and by his "Magic If" method, compelled the actor to reimagine everything unnecessarily and ineffectually. If, for example, I were a character whose child is ill and I racked my brain and tried to imagine my ailing child lying there, I tell you honestly that nothing would happen to me. It would only be the child I was seeing from my place within the actor. I would only be sorry in a psychological, dispassionate way for this nonexistent child who is not mine, the actor's. Besides, it is not the child I must observe and portray.

But if in my imagination I watch the *father* whose child is ill, if I see myself acting *him,* there in the room or at the bedside, and I study *his* emotions, movements and facial expressions, then it is much easier for me to emulate what *he* does and to feel what *he* feels. I am looking objectively, as if I were an unseen spectator (later the audience), upon this as my future performance. I am the observer, student and critic at the same time. In the latter capacity, my judgment tells me whether I am performing it artistically and convincingly enough as an actor and correctly enough in fidelity to the playwright's conception. The difference is that with Stanislavsky's method, the character's child becomes the actor's focal point, since the actor must see only the things seen by the character residing within him. With mine, the *character* becomes the focal point, which after all is the actor's true objective, and through the character the actor is able to feel so much more of what the father feels for the child than he could possibly be capable of on his own, by doing it *for* the father, as it were.

That was the gist of what we discussed—the supremacy of the character's ego (mine) against the actor's ego (Stanislavsky's)—and I must confess that neither of us convinced the other. But I was honored that he gave so much time to exploring my formulations and subsequently proved that he respected my viewpoint by permitting me to put my ideas into practice. Now I can resume our present discussion of Stanislavsky's special characteristics and of those who surrounded him at that time.

Let us examine Stanislavsky's unalterable view of the creative actor's ego. When directing us, or watching us as actors under other directors, his ever-questioning concerns were: "Is he really using the 'Magic If'? Is he really believing those nonexistent things of the character? Is he imagining them as if they were reality?" And when he criticized us, he always appealed to his "feeling of truth" to determine whether the character was solidly seated within us, and whether we were being true to the character's behavior in the various situations, and whether what both of us (the character and the actor) were doing was true to life and reality. When he said, "I don't trust you. I don't believe you," it meant that you were not doing all these things, not fully utilizing that actor's ego which he deemed of paramount importance.

He tortured us with his complex theory on other occasions, too. During one of the times when we were lunching at his home, he was already eating heartily and I was about to lift my fork when he said, "Now, Michael, I want you to eat like Malvolio and I'll see if you really grasp this feeling of truth."

I tried but was too full of confusion and fear. Never having actually seen Malvolio eat, I could not truly duplicate it with the exactitude of Malvolio's reality that Stanislavsky expected of me; I could only give him my impression of how a Stanislavsky type of actor tenanted by Malvolio would do it. But Stanislavsky criticized me with the authority of an eyewitness who had not only gone back through the centuries to observe the table manners of the time but, while there, had peered into Shakespeare's imagination in order to ascertain Malvolio's eating habits.

"I don't believe you. Malvolio would never eat this way," he said.

"Well," I hedged, "it all depends on whether he was eating out at an inn or as a dinner guest in somebody's home, or in the privacy of his own home; and if at his own home, whether he was alone or with guests."

"And where was he when you were acting him just now?"

"He was eating out," I improvised, "and his host was a wonderful man but a tyrant who wouldn't let him enjoy his meal."

He laughed. "In that case, I'll consider it convincing enough to make me keep quiet and let you eat."

So you see, his whole preoccupation was with the actor's ego. But in our theatre at that time, there was no distinction between what we today call our Higher, Creative Ego and the everyday ego that is concentrated only on self. Then it meant only the actor's personal ego, the attitude of the actor as applied to and by himself, and that was the basis of the "Magic If" with which Stanislavsky's actors were expected to search for, find and evaluate the "feeling of truth." It stemmed, no doubt, from his own personal psychology as an actor. But the directors around him, consciously or not, concentrated on other egos which guided and characterized their respective techniques, and these likewise originated with their own personal attitudes or psychologies.

Nemirovich-Danchenko, doubtless because he was a successful playwright himself, inwardly searched for the author's ego in approaching his own productions or when viewing those of others. It can make for tremendous differences when the playwright sits within you, to use Stanislavsky's image; one kind of differences to the director and another kind to the Stanislavsky type of actor. Frequently, they tend to negate each other, or at least it seemed that way until Vachtangov came along and disproved it. Nevertheless, Nemirovich always tried to direct with a burning fidelity to the playwright and required of his actors that they express with true feelings what the playwright's ego was aiming at through the play. That he was highly successful with this technique was proved by his numerous triumphs. And so you might say that these two collaborators represented two different kinds of theatre within the Moscow Art Theatre.

Then Meyerhold appeared. He was younger than the founders and represented a new kind of ego—the hard, autocratic director's ego. No viewpoint existed for him save his own. "I see it this way and I want you to do it my way." And since he had a tremendous, almost superhuman imagination, always dark and infernal, he mercilessly and ruthlessly imposed upon his actors his own creative ego. He was forever dissatisfied with his actors; none could completely incarnate and incorporate what he saw. I often wondered whether he himself, great an actor as he was, too, could have brought to life his strange and wild images to his own satisfaction.

Thus you might say that there were three theatres pre-eminently working and creating within the Moscow environs, though in different ways—via the actor's ego of Stanislavsky, the playwright's ego of Nemirovich-Danchenko and the director's ego of Meyerhold. You could take your choice but you couldn't without prejudice take sides because each in its own way achieved remarkable results.

The successes which Alexander Tairov achieved with his beautiful, colorful, rhythmic, seemingly superficial but really profound productions added a fourth ego and yet another kind of theatre to the Moscow milieu. In case you haven't guessed whose ego he represented, it was the spectator's. For to him the focal point of a performance, the criterion, was whether the spectator would accept it and be immensely impressed. He saw everything through the eyes, soul and desires of the spectator first and foremost and made all existing viewpoints conform to his own, which was that the spectator passionately loved beauty.

And so we come full circle again to that wonderful artistic sponge who was Eugene Vachtangov. His ego, his influence upon our theatre, was that he had no particular ego of his own, so to speak, and could open himself to all the blessings of all the others. To me it was extremely revealing to watch his brilliant mind at play, like a juggler, with the four egos I have described. He took them all into consideration, combined them, and in all his productions they were perfectly, ideally balanced. None of the other directors could achieve such a consummate blend of his own with the others' special talents.

Vachtangov and I were approximately the same age and good friends, so I asked him point-blank one day, "Tell me, Eugene, what is the secret of your success? How is it that whatever you direct is an unmistakable hit?"

His answer was, "First of all, I never rehearse without imagining that the theatre is already full. The imaginary audience is always there, from the very first rehearsal to the last."

This appeal to the future audience was Tairov's technique, to be sure, but Vachtangov could carry it farther and more fluently endow it with all the others' atributes, collectively or in turn. In a flash he could also switch to the director's ego of Meyerhold, to the playwright's ego of Nemirovich-Danchenko or to the actor's ego of Stanislavsky. He had everything going for him, as the saying is, plus his own artistic agility to make each technique even more dazzling. It was like a game with him, and he loved it passionately.

What especially endeared him to me was that he never cloaked his talent with an air of mystery or an aura of inimitable genius. In fact, he often made light of it between ourselves, such as by giving impersonations of himself wearing and applying the four egos. Once he did it while we were in the midst of a game of pocket billiards, at which I was depressingly bad. Whether to cheer me up or improve my game, he showed me how he could approach it as if he were directing a play. Now he pocketed the ball like Stanislavsky, now like Nemirovich, now like Meyerhold, now like Tairov —and each time he vividly materialized the proper image behind the cue. And do you know, he not only played better than they did in this demonstration, but he even outdid himself!

Which is by way of saying that his enormous sense of humor and mimicry were still other ingredients that served him creatively in the Moscow Art Theatre. None of the others had much humor, Meyerhold least of all. But Vachtangov was as free as a bird. He could create performances of the most profound and tragic content, but always with a grain of humor. There was always a little laugh or two in his sad plays, always a little tear or two in his comedies—mixtures which would have been incomprehensible to the others did not these light-and-dark, serious-and-humorous touches meet with such overwhelming audience approval, as they since have in many a play throughout the world. Even when he expressed unfathomable philosophical concepts there was a twinkle in his eye.

Thus to me, of all the directors whom I consider the greatest contributors to our theatre during that richly formative period, Vachtangov, next to Stanislavsky, will always stand out as the universal theatrical personality.

8. Character Structure and Motivation

Before discussing the problem of character structure and the dialogue and plot motivations with which it is linked, it is necessary to make this statement:

All true artists, especially the talented creators for the stage, bear within themselves a deeply rooted and often unconscious desire for transformation.

Speaking in our theatrical vernacular, this is the urge to achieve that most elusive quintessential of good playwriting and good play acting—characterization—and the subject will be greatly simplified if examined on the basis of that premise.

As there are absolutely no identical people in life, not even so-called identical twins, so are there no identical characters on the stage. We must distinguish between different *types* of people (or their counterparts on the stage) and the particular, individual *characters* within these types. These are never the same, never identical or equal in every respect. They are always different from one another in some or many ways.

Whether it is a tough guy that the playwright conceives, or an absent-minded professor or a bitchy woman or an irresistible young girl with long eyelashes and slightly parted lips—these are only some of the *types* of his cast, but they are not yet nor automatically the fully developed *characters* which the director, actors and audience expect them to be. For each particular tough guy or bitchy woman or any other person is by nature a different *variation* within these types, and must be even more so on the stage. They are *individuals,* and each must be written, interpreted and played differently. That is the indispensable, the primary function of characterization.

In other words, the *type* which the actor plays is given to us by nature, but each individual *character* must come from the playwright. That is what he creates, or should—each character anew each time, and each time endowing it with different characteristic features. Even the slightest characterization, even a hint of it, is part of the process of transformation.

What would happen if playwrights failed to distinguish between the *type* and the *individual* of their characters? They would always portray only the type but not the character itself. They would always describe and delineate the nature of the type but not the characteristic variations within it. All their absent-minded professors or seductive girls would be clichés, dull copies of all others that preceded them in other plays. It would be analogous to an artist who painted all clowns alike, when we know that it is only the different grotesqueries of makeup that distinguish each and make him unique. Thus, a clown is only a type; his different makeup converts him into a distinct personality and a unique character. And it is a most desirable condition of good playwriting that each character should have equally distinct and unique trade-marks in keeping with his role.

But how does the playwright arrive at these different characteristics in his types, by what process of deduction, elimination or selection does he settle on the prognostic set of characteristics for each, which will make each of his types different from all others of its kind?

One of the simplest ways of dissecting the type and discovering its characteristic differences is, contrary to popular notions and practices, not for the playwright to contrast it with other such types but to compare it to himself, the playwright! Ask yourself three questions:

1. What is the difference between my way of thinking and the character's way of thinking? Or how does his mind contrast with mine?

You might discover, for example, that the character thinks much faster than you do, or perhaps much slower. Or perhaps his manner of thinking is more ardent or intense. Or perhaps you will find that you shape and convey your thoughts with greater clarity and precision and that by contrast your character is a very vague thinker. The more differences you can discern between your mind and that of the character, the more distinctly will you begin to understand what your character (the type) is and devise the symbolic features (characteristics) which can best assert and identify his uniqueness.

2. What are the differences between the feelings and emotions of the character and myself?

In this case you might discover, for other examples, that you are rather passionate, easily inflammable, or that you are inclined to love people and forgive them their weaknesses and stupidities, and so on; whereas, in contrast with you, your character might appear to be calm or even cold, never losing his temper, or he might be inclined to accuse and criticize people around him.

3. What is the nature of my will and inclinations as against those of the character?

Investigated in the same way, your will might be strong, unbending, and your inclinations more commendable than the average (as a playwright's should be!), while the will of your character might be weak and his inclinations feeble or substandard. Or, obversely, being honestly introspective, you might be shocked to discover that you forget and lose your aims, purposes or objectives long before you are able to achieve them, whereas the character pursues them with great insistence or persistence. But whatever strengths or weaknesses you discover in yourself are of no consequence save that they help you uncover the *contrasts,* those vital differences, in the character you are dealing with and are trying to form into a unique and distinctive entity.

So accumulate and write down all the differences you are able to establish between yourself and your character in these three spheres —mind, feelings and will impulses. Consider these differences as the character's most outstanding, most "characteristic" features.

And now, with these differences in mind, go over the character's entire part or his function in the play, experimentally speaking some of the tentative lines you plan for his key scenes, or perhaps only whispering them. Then imagine or even actually test out some of the accompanying business. You will notice that gradually the respective characteristic features (differences) of the part will emerge, clarify themselves and become integral elements of the character's personality. But please do not force the result. Do not "brain-suck" too hard, as some of my TV-playwright friends call it. Just do it easily. Approached honestly and patiently, the results will come by themselves.

Further, in going this way through the character's entire part, don't try to keep in mind all the differences at once. If you have, say, ten characters to deal with and at least a handful of differences for each, it will take superhuman mental juggling to remember what belongs to whom. Eventually, as you get to know your characters better, it will become second nature to identify each and his set of distinguishing marks, like a parent does. So in this exercise of testing some of the lines and business, take the differences of each character one by one.

I hardly need to mention that by using these gentle and subtle means of exploration in order to give form and substance to the character, you still remain within the framework of the type you intend to represent on the stage. That is another reason why it is not absolutely necessary to commit each character's entire dossier to memory. Just a general idea of what is in each will be enough to start with. More important at this point is getting properly launched on the various transformations. Once you have identified and established the differences for each, they will automatically, almost subconsciously, click into place when necessary as you deal with each character in turn.

The foregoing technique might be terned a form of character structure and motivation "in depth," as the current phrase is for exhaustive and penetrating study. But if it is too technical for the average or young playwright, especially those unfamiliar with the principles elucidated in my first book, *To the Actor,* then permit me to suggest another way of finding and developing the characterization, which some of my playwright friends have also found quite productive:

Begin with making observations of people around you. If it is true that every individual, every person, is different from every other, and that we can describe to ourselves in so many words exactly where the differences lie, then it is possible to try a more visual approach by defining the differences *without using any words* —purely artistically, as it were, using only our creative imagination rather than tentative dialogue and business.

How can it be done? Very easily and perhaps with great humor and self-amusement, too. (By the way, the more humor, lightness and ease that goes into such explorations, the better. If the playwright's efforts are not labored, the character won't be.) But there is a secret to this kind of observation, so let us investigate that secret for a moment.

Every living person, according to his general character, his main psychological qualities and peculiarities, is, if I may express myself with such an image, *centralized* within himself. Our imaginations can easily find where this *Center,* as I call it, sits within this or that person. Let us take a few examples at random:

You observe, for instance, a person who is selfish and conceited and you ask yourself, "Where is the Center of his entire being located?" Your creative imagination, or purely your whim, might lead you to the discovery that his conceit and snobbishness built a warm and cozy nest for themselves in one of his slightly raised eyebrows. Or in his protruding jaw. Or in that barely noticeable, frozen, wry smile permanently lingering on his lips. Or perhaps in the lower part of his spine, which makes him feel superior, especially if he strains slightly at that spot. Any of these spots or places might be regarded as a Center if your imagination defines it as the center of his being.

Another example: You observe a woman who is highly inquisitive and knows it, and you see that her Center sits right on the tip of her nose, or in one of her eyes, or in one of her ears. You might also find the Center in the back of her neck, which gives her a tendency to walk with her head thrust forward so that she will not miss anything going on around her.

Some more examples: There is a noble, quiet man before you, without any specific characterization. Has he got a Center? Yes, he has. Everybody has some characteristic Center. But where might that man's be? Let us say right within his chest; the way it is positioned on his body, the way he stands or moves with it might bespeak his dignity.

But the imaginary Center might also be located somewhere outside or away from the body of the character, as in the type of person whose main characteristic is cowardice. In this case, your imagination might show you the Center as located externally, as if hanging in the air somewhere low, such as beneath his posterior. Or take a warm, truly loving person who is always possessed with the desire to do something good for somebody else. Her Center, too, would be away from her and could easily be imagined as residing within other people, within those she loves. The same might be said for a character who is full of hatred; his Center would undoubtedly repose in those he wishes to destroy. Or imagine a strong, willful, active and even aggressive man. Most likely, such an individual could not keep his Center within himself if he tried; it wants to jump out of his body; it wants to cling like a phantom to all kinds of events and all sorts of business going on around him.

Another thing to remember about the Center is that it is like a character itself, since it reflects the most symbolical feature of the character it personifies. As such, the Center, wherever it may be located, must have certain definite qualities. It can be large or small, dark or light, dull or shiny, warm or cold, crisp and dry or soft and gentle; it might be aggressive and boisterous or calm and tranquil. Your creative imagination is free to endow it with any qualities which seem compatible with the character you have in view. Thus, the Center of our nosy woman, for instance, might appear before your mind's eye in the form of a needle, a cold and hard needle, whereas the Center of our truly loving person can be imagined as a big, warm, shining sun. But while working on the form or quality of each Center, do not restrict or limit your imagination by making each choice final and unalterable. Try investing each Center with different qualities until you have found the one or more which suit it best and activate it the most.

Furthermore, every Center can be either static or mobile. If, for instance, the Center of our snobbish and conceited person is easier to imagine as a static one, then by contrast the Centers of our nosy woman and hateful or aggressive man would undoubtedly be better visualized as constantly moving, shifting and restless.

Properly utilized, the device of the Center serves at once to define not only the general types you wish to represent on the stage but each particular character within his type's frame of reference.

Test this out in still another way. Instead of observing people around you, observe the characters from different plays. Where and what are *their* Centers?

A little practice will soon give you sufficient skill to use this Center as a dexterous prop in character structure and motivation, hence in your plot progression. Never ask anybody whether this or that idea of the Center is the correct one. Rely only on your own selective judgment. Your imagination, your intuition, your creative talent invariably will tell you whether it is good or bad, genuine or phony.

If, let us say, a Center you found satisfies or amuses you, then you may be sure it is correct. Besides, I may see the Center of a certain character in my own way, another person may see it his way. That is each person's prerogative, but the careful craftsman within you, who in his imagination is always projecting the character before an audience to test their receptivity, is the one who must be guided and satisfied. Further, there are no mathematical rules or infallibly logical approaches to inspiration. To create your inspiration in the way that makes you happiest with it, because it will make others happy with the result, is frequently the essence of originality. Hence, I caution you again not to struggle with this Center device. Take it as simply as it can be made to work; play with it and enjoy it as a child does a ball.

There is a third and equally enjoyable technique of transformation or search for characterizations. Like the imaginary Center, it is also a game, a form of make-believe which we shall call the Imaginary Body, and may be used in a similar manner either as an aid or as a substitute.

When studying your proposed character, even from the very first glimmering of the type, your intuition gives you certain ideas, perhaps very vague ones at the outset but still some notions of what the character of the type might be. Therefore, it is a simple thing to imagine what kind of *body* your character might have. Soon, or perhaps instantly, you will see that the imagined body of your imagined character is different from yours. Observe this body for a while and then pretend that you are stepping right into it and that both of you are occupying the same space. It is you inside the character, not, as with Stanislavsky, the character seated within you. Now, what will be the psychological result of such a merger? Again let us resort to some examples.

Let us say that your intuition prompted you to envision the body of the character as slightly taller than your own. What, then, would be your sensations as you remain within this Imaginary Body? Feeling that this being is slightly taller than you are in reality is bound to alter your psychology. Instinctively you will have the urge to move and speak like a taller person. It will happen by itself and you will not have to force yourself to do things differently. Just being *within* this taller Imaginary Body more or less compels different speech and movements peculiar to itself and its comfort.

Or imagine that this Imaginary Body is shorter or heavier, or plump or stooping, and so on, and each time try to comply with its impulses. What happens to your psychology and even to your own body each time? You may safely anticipate that the Imaginary Body technique, properly applied, will exert a tremendous influence on your psychology and actual physical body, thereby leading to a better understanding and shaping of your character.

In this game of dealing with the Imaginary Body, it will be additionally helpful if you can remember that it is composed of three elements. One is the character, another is the Imaginary Body and the third is your own body. The Imaginary Body stands, as it were, right between the character and yourself, acting as a sort of catalyst to your imagination by influencing your own body and psychology as you transform into the character.

You could, of course, dispense with this Imaginary Body method and force yourself to imagine the characters without it. But I assure you that the result would not be nearly as pleasant, artistic or satisfying; the hard struggle and the resultant stereotypes would be painfully evident. It makes for great differences whether you cudgel your brain and claw into the thin air for the things that can transform your types into valid characters, or whether you let them develop by themselves with a few slight assists from your imagination. The Center and the Imaginary Body not only can simplify this work for you but, additionally, guide the characters into fresh and engaging situations and dialogue that ultimately will advance the play as a whole.

If you doubt this, give yourself the benefit of a series of experiments with different Imaginary Bodies. Only then will you be able to see how useful this aid can be and how practically it can serve you. It is not always necessary to imagine the whole body of your character; sometimes imagining only a part of it will open the door to his traits and mannerisms.

Let us say, for example, that you imagine the neck of your character as longer and thinner than your own. What would be the result? You might feel that you are, for one sensation, constantly on the alert. And this is already an assumption of your character's psychology. You have at once begun a transformation of your own psychology by using only the image of the neck.

Or imagine that the arms of your character are longer than yours and the legs shorter. It is quite possible that you suddenly will feel very awkward. Or, say, the imaginary nose of your character turns upward, and immediately you might get the sensation of a certain lightheaded, superficial attitude toward life; or perhaps that retroussé nose might bring a mischievous quality into your psychology.

You can use the Center and the Imaginary Body separately or simultaneously. There are no inflexible rules about it. It depends entirely on your free will and artistic decision.

Simple as these aids are once you have acquired a facility with them, there is still a fourth means of transformation or characterization, which is perhaps the simplest of all. That requires that you make a tentative mental list of the business which your character is going to fulfill from his first function in the play to his last. If possible, the list should be in proper sequence and contain as much of the major and minor business as you anticipate for him—even all his entrances and exits, his sitting down and getting up, or just turning his head to the right or left, or just throwing a glance at another character, or sitting quietly and listening to what the other characters are saying to him or someone else, and so on.

When your list of business is ready, start to fulfill it step by step. Having a vague idea in mind of the type who is not yet your character is enough of a skeleton with which to start working out his business. But now your whole interest must be concentrated on *how* he fulfills it. The *how* is tremendously important.

There are two sides to this *how* of your character and the given circumstances for each particular bit of business. Let us say that the type you begin with is sitting quietly on the stage, reading a book, and then he hears the doorbell. In your imagination, you (as the formative character) will get up, go to the door and open it. Your friend (his) enters and you greet him heartily. You fulfill this business several times until you discover *how* your character will ultimately do it best, with the proper characterization that will eventually creep into this bit of business. That is one way.

Another is *how* this bit of characterization will and must be carried out in the given circumstances. I mean, quietly sitting and reading the book and then—*excited* and *happy* that your friend came to see you? Or are you *unhappy* or *embarrassed* or *afraid*— or what—should the visitor turn out to be a bill collector or an enemy? Similar business may be required several times by the final script, but naturally this getting up and opening the door will be fulfilled under different circumstances. So although the character remains the same, the circumstances and his mood of the moment certainly will be different in each particular case.

What do you achieve by repeating this same bit of business several times, experimentally? First of all, you will discover exactly *how* your character should fulfill this or that business, his most characteristic way of doing it, and you will become more familiar with the true characterizations (differences) of the role. That will be your main achievement.

Another achievement will be your ability to preserve the same characterizations in different circumstances and thus maintain them throughout the entire play. At no time will they be "out of character" in whatever they do and say. Moreover, by searching for the characterizations in this way, by elaborating them, you inevitably become more familiar with each character as a whole. For in the process, you will make new discoveries in each character, you will be digging deeper and deeper into him and finally get to his very core, the very heart and essence of the full-blown character as opposed to the mere type you started with.

Although you are concerned mainly with the business in this fourth method of transformation or characterization-finding, your probings should not be reduced solely to a kind of mental panto-mime. To avoid this danger, you will have to combine the tenta-tive business with appropriate lines—not necessarily the verbatim dialogue as it will finally emerge in the finished script but enough of a suggestion of what would be most apt and most suitable for the character to say in each particular situation through which you are putting him. You are not at all obliged to speak the lines aloud as though from the stage. Whispering or thinking them will be enough, else the emphasis on the way they sound or the manner of delivery may obscure the pantomimic differences you are searching for in the character.

While suggesting that the playwright thus give each of his characters this kind of "acting test," I must at the same time caution that the characterizations or transformations must not be so strong, so obvious or overdone that the basic types from which they derive will no longer be recognizable. No, the absent-minded professor must not be drowned completely in multifarious characterizations; the tough guy must still retain vestiges of the type from which he springs, and the irresistible young girl should not be denuded of the beautiful attributes within her type by, paradoxically, covering her with every characterization you can imagine for her. So no need to go destructively overboard with your transformations. Choose only the best elements for each.

Another important thing to remember is that characterization has two sides to it—one purely psychological and the other physical. If, for instance, I were probing for the characterizations of my absent-minded professor, it would be helpful to me to make that separation first. Absent-mindedness in this case would be the purely psychological side of it. But since an audience cannot read an actor's mind except through his actions, I must also find a way to express it bodily. I might find some gestures or movements for him, a position of his head or a certain way he has of looking strangely and abstractedly, so that his psychological absent-mindedness would find its physical or outer way of being expressed and shown to the audience.

You might consider these as general rules in the search for and development of all kinds of characterizations, however simple, subtle or passive their generic types might be.

II

The introduction of psychological factors at this point in our discussion of character structure and motivation is intentional, for without them it would be impossible to put all the preceding approaches into action.

As talented playwrights have long been aware, there are two psychological processes that interest them most. One is to express themselves via the stage, the other is to absorb and accumulate all kinds of life experiences and all sorts of knowledge. The better the playwright, the larger his capacity for both. For undoubtedly you have noticed that the richer your experiences and knowledge are, the more colorful your stage creations become, since one writes best of the people and things he knows best.

These two processes may be likened to and considered as vital as breathing. When you are expressing yourself, you exhale; and while absorbing your experiences, you inhale. The more you inhale of life, the more you can exhale.

But since all playwrights live and breathe in the field of art, their inhaling and exhaling must be of a very special kind. For the playwright never expresses himself directly but always indirectly, never through himself but always through others, never through the words he would use but always through those of others. In order to express himself on the stage, the playwright, like the actor, needs a mask. The true playwright is one who is able to create and wear all the masks which the actors ultimately will wear, the masks of his characters.

Here, then, we have established that like all artistic creations, the playwright's must first undergo mental processing and psychological refining in the crucible of his knowledge and experience. For the people he creates are born only of that knowledge and experience, and the masks he devises for them symbolize them as his characters. But how do these masks serve him and the actors?

In order to make them wearable on the stage with sincerity, truth and artistic dignity, he has to find and clothe his people (types) with the individual attributes that will transform them into the masks (characters) through which he will speak. He has to become the masks themselves for the duration of his creativity. For only these so-called masks can give him true opportunities to express himself anew each time and in each case and with utmost ingenuity and originality. Else, to write each part straight, only in his own words and his own image, would be like creating a series of self-portraits, appearing before the audience only in the playwright's own physical personality or psychological garb; and the characters he set out to portray would still be only naked types, reflecting only a playwright type regardless of the sex, height, weight or apparel with which he invested them. Such a dilatory playwright is only a more or less skillful loudspeaker for his own ego but not a playwright in the truest sense; his dialogue conveys only his own thoughts but not the deepest feelings, emotions and will impulses of his characters; his creative imagination, intuition and talent remain unused; he does not contribute anything to the theatre or the playwright's craft. That kind of writing is better suited to the treatise form. It will not excite or satisfy an audience. It is doubtful if it would entertain the playwright himself were he a little less lazy or shallow and a lot more discriminating.

What, then, *is* the nature of the kind of playwright who wants to and must express himself in full through the medium of the mask of this or that character? Certainly he is not a person who is concerned only with his own happiness and sorrow and doesn't mind the suffering of others, or who glides over the surfaces of life, or who naïvely paints only self-portraits. Presumably there must be a great deal more inherent in his own character, another and deeper self, let us say, which, when properly invoked, brings his most creative powers to the fore.

In fact, there is another, better self within all of us, but unfortunately it is mostly hidden beyond the threshold of our consciousness. Yet it wants to express, to reveal itself. It would take hours, perhaps days, to discuss fully the true nature of this other self. For the sake of my argument, please grant me that it does exist and let us content ourselves with picking out just one feature from among the great variety of creative qualities possessed by this wise, loving, compassionate and powerful other self, this higher being within us.

The feature we will concentrate on is the attitude which this higher self takes toward life, people, events and all happenings around us. This attitude is very much different from the one we see in ourselves when we merely skim across life, as most persons are inclined to do. Normally we might always be inclined to accuse, blame and criticize the behavior of others, often with great cynicism. These are faults which the playwright frequently and unconsciously carries over in his attitude toward his characters. But in those hidden, occluded depths of our truer selves, we are more likely to understand and forgive them. We might feel, instead, compassionate and rather sorry for the mistakes and shortcomings of others.

Nonetheless, this other, more generous attitude toward life and people around us is, I reiterate and ask you to believe me, hidden until we make a sincere effort to call upon it, until we open ourselves to its wonderful influences. When working upon the characters, try giving this other self the benefit of the doubt by appealing to it for assistance; try discovering what its generous attitude would be toward the characters you are about to delineate. For this higher self is the voice of the true artist within us, the bearer of our talent, the creator of our genuinely aesthetic endeavors. Listen to it, learn to uncap its volcanic power to express itself without bias or prejudice. Neglect or imprison it and you cut yourself off from your most inspired collaborator.

I am aware that this may sound rather "mystical" to a lot of playwrights, especially the beginners and those who have not gone too deeply into why they want to write plays and the historical function of the playwright. I ask only that you suspend judgment until you have tried it—until, while working on a new play, you have asked yourself the invocatory question: What is my true, human attitude toward the type of person and the particular individual character which I am going to portray on the stage?

First of all, you will have a firmer starting point for delineating the role. Inevitably you will feel that the way you draw that character is your very own individual approach to it, that you didn't borrow it from anybody else, didn't copy anyone, that you are expressing yourself through the mask of the character into which you transformed yourself, and that the character's words and movements are as original as you can make them.

Innumerable nuances, too, will emerge from this approach, this appeal to the sensitivity of your higher self, and at the same time all sorts of clichés and banalities will fall away and disappear. You will experience a new freedom of expression, gain new confidence in the independence of your creativity and find the true playwright within you at last.

In conclusion, permit me to suggest a couple of rather amusing exercises which may help to give you a better insight into a person, i.e., the character you are probing:

Using the same means of transformation, look at the face of a person you don't know at all or know very little. Then, in your imagination, try to borrow and put on the various components of his face as though they were so many items of makeup, so that you will feel: "Now I have his eyebrows on my own face, the same nose, the same kind of lips, ears, the shape of his face, the form of the head and forehead, the shape and expression of his eyes," and so on. The more you can imagine your face as resembling that of the person you have under scrutiny, the more will you feel the psychology that this person awakens within you, the more will you be able to experience what this person experiences. For by thus penetrating his psychology, you open the door to a truer knowledge of his inner life.

The variation and continuation of this exercise is to observe the person's entire body, and in your imagination try to imitate his characteristic movements and gestures. The predictable results will be the same.

The practical extension and application of these exercises is to do them without observing anybody in real life, but while you are mentally assembling the types who will eventually people your play as its characters.

Another variation: Look at some picture of a man or woman dressed in a period costume. Now imagine that you are dressed the same way. Study the person's position and then, through the period costume you are wearing in your imagination and through the possible movements which you imagine will be in harmony with such a costume, also try to imagine the person's characteristics. No matter if your imagination runs riot. What matters is that you actually *feel* you are transforming yourself into somebody else and acquiring some knowledge of this imaginary person and his individual inner life.

Still another variation: Choose a very good cartoon or caricature. Study it in the same way and try to move, even speak if you wish, as this cartoon figure would move and speak if your creative imagination suddenly animated it.

And now to the last and unquestionably the most interesting and creative variation of these exercises: Do not use any real person or picture or cartoon as a model, but try it on the types of your new play who are giving you the most trouble, who simply refuse to be realized convincingly and entertainingly, or who give you nothing in return by way of motivation and plot progression. Put them through all the paces if necessary. They must be made to become valid, interesting and entertaining characters, for without such characters there can be no valid, interesting or entertaining play.

9. Director-Actor Baptism

One of the actor's chronic difficulties nowadays is that he depends too much on his directors, with the result that the director often has to spend more time being a crutch than a cocreator. Many an actor never seems to have enough time or true inclination to work on his part alone. This may stem from the fact that he does not genuinely love his parts, as every actor should, or from his defeatist attitude that no matter what his conception of the role and how to interpret it, he will ultimately have to do it the director's way anyhow.

Whatever the reason for this "holding back" on the part of the actor, and whether it exists among his cast or not, the director is frequently put upon to find short cuts to character approach, so that his cast will not flounder aimlessly and waste too much rehearsal time while settling themselves into their parts.

In truth, there are no short cuts to character development by the actor, certainly no infallible ones. But if the director happens to be stuck with a box-office name, a so-called star who has not bothered to learn the subtle arts of his craft or is not conscientious enough to dig and delve into the depths of the character for himself, what else can the director do for the preservation of the play but help him in the fastest way possible? Here, then, are some quick pointers for stimulating the cast and accelerating the development of the characters.

When an actor encounters difficulty in acclimatizing himself in his role, ask him to take those sections of his part which give him the most trouble and single out the key emotions, feelings or sensations of each. Then let him name the sections accordingly—baptize them, as it were. These sections should not be too small; the larger the better.

Let us say that the key or strongest emotion of one section is *Fear,* the strongest sensation of another is *Doubt,* and the strongest feeling of a third is *Courage,* or whatever. When the actor has found these difficult sections and named them according to their predominant emotions, let him start reading the lines of each section in keeping with its respective sensation or feeling.

Some directors use this also as a preliminary technique when starting rehearsals on each new play, when the cast is seated around the table for the first readings. Each member of the cast is encouraged to break up his part into these big sections and label each with the word that best describes its major emotional content.

When the sections and names are established for each part, the cast can start reading in a low voice or even a whisper, adjusting the mood of each section to its lines. Avoid the use of loud or full voices during these preliminary readings because they tend to arouse uncertainties, inhibitions and bad acting habits if resorted to prematurely. It is best to withhold full vocal expression until the cast has settled on the sections and is quite comfortable in the parts.

The next preliminary step is to suggest that each member of the cast go over all the business of the part in the same way, not necessarily during rehearsals but at home; that is, in his imagination start moving in the different tempos which he thinks will be compatible with each of the baptized sections of his part. (See chapter 13, Tempos and Other Directorial Aids.) When exercised at home, the cast can actually move about in these various tempos while testing them and searching for the right ones; it will make correcting and polishing so much easier for both director and actor at rehearsals, when the members of the cast are finally using them while on their feet.

10. Director-Actor Responsibilities

To the average or mechanical actor, a play consists only of his part, the cues and a lot of gaps in between his lines. Some of these gaps he expects the director to fill in with bits of his character's business. The rest of the play is not his concern but that of the other members of the cast and the director.

That kind of attitude in an actor is bad enough; the greater sin is when he *shows* it on the stage.

The more ideal actor is one who inwardly plays (and even rehearses) *all* the parts, who feelingly follows all the scenes and remains *active* during the entire performance, regardless of whether he is onstage or waiting in the wings for his next cue. Each time he makes an entrance to pick up his role, he must convey the feeling that he is continuing not only his portion of the performance but the play as a whole.

In order to execute his part constructively, an actor should be encouraged and guided in bridging the so-called gaps with a chain of his own business, large or small, and whether indicated in the script or not; and that chain must remain unbroken for the entire length of the performance, whether he is on or off, so long as his role continues active.

No intelligent actor, of course, will invent or sustain business that obtrudes upon the speeches of others in the cast and detracts from or mars their performances. But if he is onstage, in the midst of other characters while waiting for his cue or next piece of business, he cannot remain inanimate or impassive to what the others in the play are saying and doing. A look, a gesture, a facial expression, however slight, is expected of him as proof that he is still *alive* and responding humanly to the others' speeches and situations, that he is still part of the play and not somebody misplaced from the audience.

An awareness of this and other possible lapses on the part of the actor should be one of the prerequisites of a good director's intuitions. Long ago, I prepared for myself a sort of Baedeker for director-actor discussions when an actor encounters difficulties in building his characterization and maintaining an interest in the other characters. I pass on its seven points both as a guide to the director and a stimulus to the actor who requires "instant inspiration":

1. Let the actor appeal to his own creative intuition for the first indication of his role and its relationships to the other roles. On behalf of his character, let him ask, "Who am I?" Holding the image in mind, let him next emulate what the playwright must have done—ask *how* the character would fulfill specific bits of business in the play; then, in more detail, *how* he would carry out every movement of the action, and *how* he would speak the lines in the various situations. The criterion of whether the actor's answers are correct, as the director must judge, is how *truthful* they are to the character and the life surrounding him.

2. Should an actor have difficulty in evolving his characterization, let him experiment with an imaginary Center (see *To the Actor,* Chapter 1) until his creative intuition confirms the correctness of this approach. But to be certain that he is not deluding anyone, let him demonstrate exactly where the Center he has chosen is located. Is it in or out of his body, is it movable, is it flexible, and how is he adapting it to his characterization?

3. Failing that, the director may suggest that the actor have a try

at using the Imaginary Body technique (see *To the Actor,* Chapter 6) in whole or in part, depending on his need and intuition.

4. For actors less versed in these aids to characterization, the director might make more progress by suggesting that the actor again emulate the creative processes of the playwright and ask himself, "What are the differences between me and the character, our thoughts, feelings and will impulses?" The comparisons and the contrasts deriving from them will help to establish the role's characteristics more clearly in his mind and to interpret them with greater confidence.

5. Carry the actor a step further by suggesting that he ask his creative imagination to tell him the main inner or psychological qualities of his character. Then, what is its spine or scaffolding, what are its qualities?

6. Make sure that the actor has a fairly good notion of what his *individual atmosphere* is, as opposed to that of the scenes in which he participates.

7. Now ask him to imagine that he is actually incorporating all these images into the characterization, and double-check by requesting that he concretize the characterization (all the discovered differences and images) into one psychological gesture, that one all-embracing movement or position which he deems most symbolical of the character.

Note: The use of the above directorial aids is optional and not necessarily sequential. The director might have better success with one than the other, or with more than one in different combinations, depending on the degree of professionalism or nonprofessionalism of his cast.

11. Toward Better Ensembles

Implicit in every good playwriting and directorial method is the effort to discover all kinds of principles which can develop our own talents at the same time that we are developing the play and its individual roles. That is the most positive side of our work.

As far as his own progress is concerned, a director may count as lost the play, even the most financially successful play, from which he has derived no new knowledge or failed to add improvements to the old. The director who does not aim for the new, the novel and different in his work is, like some of his actors, a hamstrung creature; he is inhibited by fears of experimenting with the producer's money or the playwright's conceptions. And yet it is only by experiments, by attempts at innovation, that he can bring his ingenuity fully into play and add new artistic and material dimensions to what the producer and author have entrusted to him.

It is these inhibitions that I wish to deal with here. Everyone has lots of them and, though seemingly deep-rooted and successfully hidden, they nevertheless manifest themselves through the shortcomings in our professional work. The director is as prone to them as the actor, and it is my proved experience that if he can overcome the inhibitions of his cast, he will triumph over his own.

One of the better methods for ridding ourselves of whatever

professional inhibitions beset us is the application of the *ensemble feeling* in rehearsals, for a lack of it evidences one of the greatest of all stage inhibitions. Only through the cooperative, collaborative and cocreative ensemble feeling between director and cast, and among the cast themselves, can we understand and acknowledge our connections with one another and the imperative need of open-heartedness toward our coworkers. Let the participants in a play project fail to meet one another halfway (director with playwright and producer, director with cast and cast with director, cast members with other cast members) and all will be working in isolation, all efforts to establish contact will be hampered. And the results will show themselves in a myriad of subtle, inexplicable imperfections.

Establishing almost perfect contact with, by and among those whom the fates have thrown together to create a moment in theatre history is therefore one of the director's prime functions. If anything can help him achieve this desirable condition, it is the uncomplicated ensemble feeling he imparts to and instills in those around him.

He can start as simply as establishing contact between the cast and the setting(s), familiarizing the players with their environment. A vivid description of it will suffice, since sets and props are seldom ready or available before dress rehearsal. For if the setting happens to be strange or foreign to the cast, not the familiar milieu in which they normally move in their private lives, then they are apt to be unaware of or unresponsive to the surroundings in which they will eventually have to perform. That is one of the strongest inhibitions in most players in that it impinges on their freedom of movement and makes for unaccounted awkwardness. If they do not feel or look "at home" on the stage, it is often because they have not anticipated or been made to establish contact with everything that will be part of the setting in which they will live their new stage lives.

Long before they are "on their feet," perhaps as early as the first readings of the play, let the cast start imagining the set, let each become aware of everything that will belong to it before they start moving about within its boundaries—all the tables, chairs, the walls, their color, their shape, the height of the room, its doors and windows, the floor and its rugs or carpeting, the steps or stairs if any—and try to absorb them, just absorb them as a general impression. It is not necessary to remember them in detail or whether they will use them as props or involve them in their business. At this point, it is only desirable that they make contact with them, mainly because it is such an ingenuous way of stimulating the ensemble feeling and setting it in motion. In addition, the salutary side effect is that the process of becoming better acquainted with all these things will make them more comfortable in actually using them if they have to. They will better relate themselves to their surroundings for having first imagined them. Try it and you will see how much better and faster the cast is acclimatized when the doors and windows are eventually marked out and the furniture positioned.

The director can also obtain excellent results by applying the ensemble feeling in the use of properties. We all know how a sudden lapse or lack of facility with properties, especially hand props, often disconcerts a player and makes him look and feel awkward. He may use such familiar things as his spectacles, his cigarette lighter or a pencil a hundred times a day in real life, but the moment he is called upon to use them on stage, either palsy or mechanical failure sets in. So you can easily imagine what may take possession of him if he has to use hand or other props with which he is *not* familiar! Or, if his role requires him to sit at a desk which is as strange to him as the things and papers on it, he is apt to handle them as though they were time bombs and their detonations horrifyingly imminent.

There is no need for the cast to undergo these torments if they start using at once the hand props called for, even while still grouped around the table in those early rehearsal-readings. All a player has to do is *imagine* that he is holding the object or prop and go through the motions of using it, just as tentatively as he is softly speaking his lines, but in keeping with the atmosphere and tempo of the section being rehearsed.

If he is sitting at his desk, for instance, encourage him to try touching every thing on it, to move it slightly, to take up pencils or papers or whatever again and again until that comfortable "my things" feeling creeps into his movements. Not only will it give him that desired freedom and ease but it will lead to many subtle and charming bits of incidental business. Sometimes just toying with and studying the hand props, learning their weight, shape and structure intimately, will delicately awaken the actor's instinct and make the performance more pleasant for him and more enjoyable to the audience.

Costumes or clothes other than normal apparel can also be enemies of the actor, but they need not be if he is "fitted" into them early by means of this same ensemble feeling. Usually, costumes are not worn until the dress rehearsal. Then and for a long time afterward, the costumed player may look and feel as though he were inhabiting a kind of coffin. Frequently, too, he goes through the needless nonsense of finding and fighting all the strange buttons and buttonholes of his outfit and invariably losing both the buttons and the battles. So why not "fit" the actor into his new clothes from the very first readings by his imagining that he is already wearing them, in the same way that he is already imagining and pretending to use the hand props?

Now we come to perhaps the most difficult but the most essential step in the use of the ensemble feeling—helping each member of the cast to apply the principle to all other members of the cast, opening themselves to one another as persons and as the characters they play, making mental and emotional contact in an unrestricted and unlimited give-and-take exchange.

At first blush, this may seem like an impossible, almost utopian undertaking; not because the cast is composed of actors but because actors are people, only more intensely so, and most people do not by nature accept all other people unconditionally or on command. Even if they were capable of admitting all others into their hearts and minds, they would admit some more freely than others. It is these idiosyncratic preferences which frequently make complete rapport impossible among the cast as human beings or as play characters—and which the ensemble feeling must combat and overcome as its major objective.

It is far better for the play and the individual performances if each player, as a human being and an artist, is equally sympathetic to all and disturbed by none. While feeling otherwise may be an instinctive and subconscious human reaction, it is nevertheless a tremendous inhibition and scarcely conducive to fast and optimum results. Hence, whether he does it by suggestion, brief lecture, stern measures or fiat, it will be a happier director who can triumph over such negative attitudes in his company as: "Why should I be more warm and human to somebody I'm meeting for the first time, or open myself to So-and-So, with whom I've worked in previous shows?" Or, "I like her (or him), but I'm more interested in somebody else at the moment."

The feeling of ensemble cannot tolerate such separatism or distinctions; it is a thing which requires the frankest and friendliest artistic relations from all while on stage. After the rehearsal or performance is over, each member of the cast may revert to his private life, preferences and prejudices if, unchanged by the ensemble's warmth, he wishes to retreat into his cold, insular pattern. If somebody incurs his dislike or indifference, he need not go have coffee with him as a friend simply because he happens to be a member of the cast. But, while on the stage, while rehearsing or performing, it is artistically compulsory to find the inner power to be friendly, open and receptive toward everyone, regardless of personal attitude.

By the very nature of the social instincts which lead him to his profession, no actor is such a hopeless clod that he is incapable of exerting a little compassion toward another human being with whom he must share a common effort toward a mutual benefit. But should he be unable to like the other person or bring himself to be liked in return, then let him begin a reformation by at least trying to enjoy the other's acting. This virtue may be easier to accept, since others have deemed the man or woman good enough to be signed for the role. That may be one way of lessening the isolation. In fact, the happy, perfectly functioning company is one in which everybody admires, to a greater or lesser degree, the artistry of the others.

But suppose he cannot like even the acting of the person he dislikes? Then let him try to find some moments of the other's performance, at least something in the other's role or his portrayal of it, which he does like. True, this would be only a small beginning; but once the effort is activated, it is conceivable that he will gradually find more and more things to like, where before there was room for nothing but criticism. And criticism can be more destructive to the ensemble than indifference.

Another obstacle to the proper functioning of the ensemble is a lack of atmosphere, which often is also due to the cast's unawareness or indifference. Mind you, I said "lack," not absence, because atmospheres are ever present and all pervading. There is a correct atmosphere for every play as a whole and for each of its scenes or segments. It remains only for the director to establish and make the cast conscious of the atmospheres they are working in. (This technique is elaborated on in the final section of this book, which deals with the direction of *The Inspector General*.)

For the moment, however, let us define the atmosphere as an aura or floating mood which is superimposed over a scene and influences the persons in it. Just as the sections of a role, when given a name, can clarify it and make the player respond accordingly, so can atmospheres, when properly identified and brought into play. But whereas identifying the sections assists only the individual player, atmospheres extend to the entire cast. And whereas sections only galvanize action with intangible words, atmospheres can also induce responses with palpable things.

Thus, in describing the set and its shape, the distribution of its furniture, the walls and their colors, etc., the director has already taken his first step in establishing the over-all atmosphere of the play, or of one of its acts if the play has more than one set; he has already generated a better ensemble feeling. And if at this point he tells the cast exactly what the over-all atmosphere of the play is, and if later he imposes the atmospheres of the various scenes as he tackles each in turn, his ensemble results will be enormously facilitated. For atmospheres are microcosms of mass psychology in action and can exert a tremendous and lasting power over the cast and, ultimately, the audience.

12. Toward Better Rehearsals

As practiced throughout the world today, the stage rehearsal is perhaps the greatest area in which the theatre has remained at a standstill. Certainly that has been true from my personal knowledge and observation during more than half a century.

The torches and braziers that illuminated the earliest acting platforms in time gave way to candles, the candles to oil lamps, oil lamps to gaslight and gaslight to incandescent bulbs. Scenery underwent transmutations from none to too much, then to bare-wallism and impressionism. Acting styles changed from the heroic to the realistic and even the beatnik. Entertainment forms altered and yielded to films, radio and television. But the poor stage rehearsal, for some inexplicable reason, save perhaps a lack of enterprise and experimentation, has remained undisturbed and unimproved not only within my own time but throughout centuries of theatre activity. It is still hidebound by the tradition that it must start with the beginning of the play and go through it to the end!

No one has ever been able to tell me why or convince me that it should continue that way, but I have discovered many good reasons why it should *not*.

Ever since my student days at the Moscow Art Theatre, I have maintained that such a procedure makes for wooden acting and mechanical performances. It is like learning the multiplication table by rote: the recital will be accurate enough but not very inspiring or stimulating to the auditor. That kind of result has no place in the theatre.

If the director is thoroughly familiar with the play, and if the players know their parts, there is neither need nor reason to adhere slavishly to the beginning-to-end rehearsal system. One of the major factors militating against this inflexible succession of lines and business is that it tends to codify and formalize everything into a monotonous pattern, and in the course of following it we are bound to neglect important moments in the play and apt to stress quite unimportant things. For in a sequential rehearsal, there always exists some psychological compulsion to get to the next line and the next piece of business in a hurry. That physical and mental process becomes the objective of the performance, and not the contents of the scenes themselves. Thus, it is always the *next* things that become important, unimportant as they may be, and the dialogue and action that should be emphasized are often left unstressed.

In this headlong rush, little or no time is given to analyzing the part or the entire play from the point of view of its significant or less significant moments. Screenplays, too, suffer from this handicap, even though their scenes are frequently shot out of sequence because of time schedules and other exigencies; for each scene thus shot becomes the whole play of the moment, and the same tendency prevails of always focusing on the *next* dialogue and action, which is quickly superseded by the *next,* and so on until the whole scene has been dispatched and nothing has been treated importantly.

But let us see what can happen when a director upsets this orderly but antiquated rehearsal procedure. Let us say that the director starts the day's rehearsals with the second act instead of the beginning of the play, or with only a scene from the second act, or with just so many pages from anywhere in the script that he chooses to experiment with. At once a new beginning has been created and instantly the cast is out of the rut of repetition and on the alert.

Now, in addition to this new beginning, suppose the director takes the end of the second act, or the end of the scene he may have selected from it, and tries to find the polarity between its beginning and end. Forget for the moment its middle part or the rest of its action. Select only the short segment and few lines of the beginning and its polar segment and lines at the end. This polarity might best be exemplified in the opposite atmospheres of the beginning and end, or in contrasted characters, or in divergent meanings, thoughts or moods. Any of these will do if their polarities are also present at the end—and they invariably are in a properly constructed play, for no action and dialogue are purposeful unless they change something in their progression.

Having temporarily sidetracked, as it were, the middle section between the two polarities, we now get a clearer view of where we are going and what we have to do to get there. And by thus rehearsing only the polar segment at the beginning and its opposite mate at the end, we are certain to get a special sense of the composition of the entire scene which we couldn't have gotten otherwise, a sense of the well-balanced harmony that pervades it. Taken and rehearsed separately in this way several times, each important scene or situation is better exposed for polishing and highlighting so that it will stand out by itself as a piece of art.

When the director is satisfied with the result, his next step will automatically lead to ascertaining the truly important thing or things. He need only ask himself (or he may ask it of the cast) as a test of this new-found clarity:

"Between these two polarities, what will or should be the most important and significant moment of the act (or scene)?"

Whether it is a moment of the plot itself, a piece of business, a certain speech or the dialogue in general, or anything else, it must be an important link as well as have an important function of its own accord.

Then, having determined what it is, start rehearsing this important moment of the middle part separately, as was done with each of the polarities. Not only will rehearsals become more alive and enjoyable, but soon it will become apparent to everyone in the company that three identifiable gems now stud the beginning, middle and end of this part of the show. And it is no idle syllogism that if this can be done to one section of the play, it can be effectively applied to numerous others that require it, so that the whole performance will emerge as a lustrous jewel that sparkles at every turn and every moment of its display.

Now, by what miracle has the director accomplished all this? By none save changing a dull, monotonous rehearsal method into one that can inspire the players, make them think more deeply about what they are doing and clarify for themselves the idea and philosophy of the play, so that in turn they can better convey and clarify the play and its characters to the audience.

"Won't this new rehearsal technique take longer?" I can almost hear you ask. No. Because in actuality it is also a tremendous time-saver in that the cast, by thus becoming intimately familiar with each and every important part of the play, will do much less floundering than is par for the average rehearsal.

13. Tempos and Other Directorial Aids

Our theatre today suffers much from the evil of uniformity, much more so in the work of its directors and actors than in that of its playwrights. Many a simple means of expression that can give greater variety and relief to the stage performance has been overlooked or neglected. Figuratively speaking, most of our performances today rather resemble straight lines drawn on a sheet of paper. There are no curves, no ups and downs, no climactic moments to make them interesting. They are just dull, colorless straight lines which make for excessive uniformity and often monotony in the majority of our productions.

But before discussing some ways of remedying the situation, I would like to caution that any suggestions I offer should be tested with great care and discrimination. Also, their application should by no means be obvious to the audience, but should be handled with such tact and taste that they will not affect the content of the play to the extent that they will offend the playwright. Merely a hint of these techniques will often be sufficient to cure the ills here under diagnosis.

Suppose we begin with the problem of tempo. If you recall our discussions on the subject in *To the Actor*, or can refer to them, you already know that there are two kinds of tempo: Inner Tempo and Outer Tempo. The Outer Tempo, whether it be fast or slow, concerns speech, movement and business—all that we can see or hear. But the Inner Tempo is something different: it is the speed with which all that is *not* visual or aural—our feelings, emotions, desires and will impulses of every kind, our thoughts and images— can appear and disappear, change and follow one another with greater or lesser rapidity.

In this connection, we must never lose sight of the fact that each character has his own general tempo, which is a combination of his Inner and Outer Tempos, and so does every play as well as every individual scene of every play.

These two different tempos—the Inner, which is purely psycho- logical, and the Outer, which is visible and audible—are absolutely independent of each other. They can also occur simultaneously, with both being either slow or fast, or one of them slow and the other fast. A character on the stage is always much more interest- ing to watch when these two tempos run concurrently within him, the slow contrasted with the quick. In *To the Actor,* you will find several examples and exercises concerning these different tempos.

Every character without exception affords us many opportuni- ties to play with these tempos and weave them into expressive and interesting patterns. If the playwright has not anticipated or indi- cated such tempo patterns, then the director must use his ingenuity in finding them and his inventiveness in creating them for every character and every scene.

When dealing with the fast- or slow-moving inner life of the character, it is not essential to think or feel or wish for something definite and tangible to depict. It is only necessary to have the *sensation* that what is happening, what the actors are doing, is either slow or fast, and to what degree. Merely having the sensa- tion, just being aware of it, is often enough for the actors to reflect it in their performances and convey it to the audience.

It is well to remember that while using the Outer Tempo, the actors should not unduly accelerate their speech, movements or gestures or prematurely hasten toward the result. To manifest Outer Tempos with untoward or artificially generated motions or lines always creates the impression that the actor is helpless or not sure of himself in the scene, that he is doing it without thinking or feeling it and wants to get it over with as quickly as possible. It is therefore incumbent upon the director to set the tempo not only for each scene but for each character in it.

A good exercise for developing a better sense of tempos might be this:

Choose some characters from different plays or watch people around you and try to define the general tempos in which they live—Inner as well as Outer—and you will always find great differences between them. Lady Macbeth, King Lear, Hamlet, Ophelia or Cordelia—every one of them has an individual or general tempo, which is a pattern made up of a combination of their Inner and Outer Tempos. Compare these general tempos, then try to find within them what changes they might undergo in different scenes or situations. Take Malvolio as an example: his Inner and Outer Tempos would definitely be different before his famous letter scene and after it.

Thus, understanding and using tempos in their various contrasts and combinations will do wonders in eliminating that monotonous evenness which dulls interest and sparkle in many a character and many a scene.

Another way of making a scene more vibrant would be to concentrate on all kinds of contrasts and polarities within the situation and among its participants. From this point of view, try to consider their tempos as we have just discussed them. You can always make fascinating patterns by distributing them throughout each characterization and each scene. This can be done in many ways. You can direct the beginning of a scene in one tempo and the end of it in another, regardless of whether it is played for comedy or drama. Add the tempo patterns of the characters to this new effect and you will truly have a kaleidoscope that will be irresistible to watch.

By that I mean that between the beginning and end of the scene you might wish to create smaller contrasts and polarities and make wonderful transformations from one to the other, either changing the tempos abruptly or making slow and beautiful transitions so that you have the over-all effect of a smoothly blending series of crescendos, diminuendos, legatos and so on. The same effects may be gained through such transformations and transitions when applied to the feelings, emotions, movements, gestures and business of your characters.

You can achieve still other lively effects with the tempos by using them alternately in the Radiating and Receiving techniques described in *To the Actor,* or with various Qualities of the performance.

Excellent directorial results may be gotten, too, with the devices of what we call Outer and Inner Action, which are not to be confused with their namesakes in the Tempos. Outer Action may be described as those moments or longer sections of the play when the actor expresses everything fully, almost completely, with the character's voice, movements and gestures. Inner Action is everything in which the actor veils, mutes or underplays the character; it is the opposite of Outer Action only to that extent. The very extreme of Outer Action would be a complete stage pause, when nothing is expressed outwardly and everything is conveyed by radiation, atmosphere or any other kind of inner suspense. In other words, a pause or the utter extreme of Outer Action may consist of any or all the *intangible* means of expression, but can contain no outer expression at all. Properly executed, the stage pause can sometimes be much more effective than either Outer or Inner Action; hence, we shall deal with it briefly but separately in the chapter after this.

Having achieved a necessary degree of skill and experience in creating these contrasts, try them while rehearsing those of your cast who seem to suffer a letdown at certain moments, especially in the vis-à-vis or two-scenes. Find what you think are the contrasts between their acting styles or interpretations. If one speaks slowly, for instance, the other should speak faster. If one uses broad molding movements, the other might counterbalance it with radiating only. If one of the team is inclined to use mostly outer acting, muted responses from the other might supply the necessary shadings.

A third means of avoiding monotony or letdowns is to determine the different *attitudes* which the characters have toward those with whom they play their scenes. And not alone toward the other characters, but the attitudes of each toward all the important situations of the play and during them. This is even more useful to the playwright. For ascertaining these differences will lead quite naturally to the discovery of the different qualities, feelings or sensations with which each character can convey his reactions most convincingly and yet with sufficient contrast to highlight the whole portrait. In one case an attitude may be fearful; in another, loving; in a third, intimate. And so on.

A subtle development may result from this approach, which is worth mentioning. After having experienced and expressed this or that attitude toward the other characters and situations, each character becomes slightly altered in the process. That is as it should be, for no play ever leaves its characters unchanged, even temporarily, by what happens to them as the plot progresses. Therefore, at each moment of change, each character has to a greater or lesser degree a certain plus or minus quotient within himself. The same thing happens in real life. We may not always be aware of it, but after encountering some persons or events, we ourselves become different or respond differently. So if during such a metamorphosis the character reacts fearfully toward somebody or something on the stage, this fear invariably must leave its traces on the character for the rest of the role. And while the possibilities for these interesting character changes are not always present in a play, failing the playwright's efforts to provide the proper "events," we know that they must go on regardless if the characters are to be absorbing as well as thoroughly human. It therefore devolves upon the director's imagination and ingenuity to ferret out the moments when these transitions can at least be indicated if not strongly asserted. A classical and perhaps prime illustration of character alteration is that of King Lear. You can follow his transitions step by step as though they were charted on a graph. After each meeting with different persons in different events, he undergoes a radical change, each time virtually before your eyes, and yet the core of the character never fails to retain its essence. By this reckoning, neither playwright nor director need fear that too many such changes or transitions will destroy what is basically the character; they will only make him more interesting.

A fourth approach to stimulating the characters and highlighting the situations is to clearly define and understand what idea or leading thought each character represents. Sometimes, however, this is not too easy, for the reason that the author may have keyed certain situations to the business of the play rather than to the dialogue. That is to say, the deeper meanings of a play are frequently and often deliberately hidden behind such business or behind certain emotions, feelings or desires, or behind the objectives and superobjectives of the play or of the character. Why? Simply because the playwright's intuition tells him when these components can be more eloquent than dialogue in expressing some of the deeper meanings of his play.

Nevertheless, the director must uncover these leading thoughts and meanings and subject them to his scrutiny. And if they are not evident in the dialogue, he can usually find the answers by asking himself: Which moments of the business are so vital that without them the scenes and characters will mean nothing? The answers should be found in the same way for the various emotions, objectives and so on, for it is only when these data are put together and taken together that the deeper meanings of the characters will become more apparent.

It often happens that after such a computation, much of the dialogue takes on added significance and bears reinvestigation in a more detailed way. Toward that pursuit, the director might try to underline in pencil what are now more clearly the most important lines, and even single words if they are indicative of the main ideas or guiding thoughts. When this is satisfactorily accomplished, he will see that the entire text of the play figuratively falls into two parts. The smaller half will consist only of the important lines and significant words, those without which the characters and situations would lose their meaning. The larger half will consist of lines and words which serve only as reiteration, clarification or embroidery, as it were, of the main lines and words.

In this search for the main ideas or guiding thoughts of a play, the director therefore has four avenues of investigation to traverse: the feelings or emotions of its characters, its business, its objectives or superobjectives, and the lines. The underscoring procedure just described can be used in all these four directions. The director should not be alarmed if he changes his mind several times about what is important or significant and what is less so. In all probability, he will. At first it may seem to him that this or that emotional scene is most important, but after feeling his way a little further, his judgment may tell him that something else, some different place along this avenue or that should be underlined. He should continue being selective until he is satisfied that all his markers along the road definitely point up something *indispensable.*

Of course, the director must bear in mind that these avenues often cross and recross many times. So, having marked the most impressive places for his objectives, for example, he may find that one or more of these places can have a dual or multiple function; that is, they can serve just as well as the most important moments for feelings, emotions or dialogue.

But the fewer the number of underlined places, the better. Then the really important and significant things will become more apparent. Everything should not blend into one big exclamation point, else nothing will stand out.

Once he has found these important points in a play, the director must next think of the ways, the *hows* of conveying them to the audience as significant moments. And since he can do so only through the characters, he must tell himself from the very beginning: "I do not have to push, I do not have to stress these things by means of increasing the volume of my actors' voices or by any other of the obvious and primitive means." Because there are finer methods available to him.

He might, for example, insert very short pauses before and after one significant moment (see next chapter). Or he might change qualities before another important moment, then introduce a different quality during it, and then again add a new quality after it is over. Or he may find places where lines can be "thrown away," say the lines before and after a significant moment or perhaps only during it. Incidentally, throwing away lines sometimes not only tends to stress them but also heightens the situation, its business and its feelings. In short, any contrast which the director can find for the beginning of each significant moment, during it or after it will serve to make it more expressive and will spare you the necessity of pushing and proving it to the audience, as though you were saying, "Look, here is an expressive moment in this play. Please pay more attention to it." The four ways we have just dealt with will make the important moments create and sustain their own interest.

14. The Stage Pause That Refreshes

Not enough use is made by directors of that invaluable device known as the Stage Pause. This is not to say that it should be invoked indiscriminately for its own sake or that a performance should be punctured with pauses for no valid reason. "Punctuated" would be a preferable word in this case, since that is the primary purpose and function of the stage pause in its correct usage. For each correct pause has in it the power to stimulate the spectator's attention and compel him to be more alert than he already is.

There are two kinds of pauses and each results in a different audience alertness. But first it is important to establish that a completely vacuous pause, a blank gap, an empty space in time, simply cannot and does not exist on the stage. A pause must be germane to the scene and appropriate to the moment or it is pointless and ruinous to both.

Obviously, each pause either precedes an action or follows it. It can be used to precede an action only if the ensuing action quite naturally develops out of it; and if used *after* an action, it is only because that action must logically disappear into a pause.

A preceding pause prepares the audience to receive the forthcoming action, forecasts its content and sometimes even preconditions the effect which that action will have on the audience.

A following pause serves to summarize and deepen the impression which the audience received from the action just completed.

Not infrequently, both kinds of pauses merge into one: the action just past results in a pause which punctuates it for emphasis and, unbroken, turns inwardly into a pause from which a brand-new action originates.

Such combined pauses usually have the strongest effect, since they relentlessly hold the audience's attention. But unfortunately, too few of the modern plays take them into consideration, so do not give the director an opportunity to use them to the fullest advantage. The most effective stage pauses in plays of the last decade were not those designed by the playwright, but those which the director had to develop and insert out of necessity.

Perhaps the director and playwright of the future, aware of this lack, can help each other to overcome it by closer cooperation during those preproduction discussions or during rehearsals.

Note: This is not intended to goad playwrights and directors into the indiscriminate use of stage pauses. When employed, stage pauses must be as necessary to the syntax of a scene as punctuation is to the proper structure of a sentence.

15. Many-Leveled Performances

In the second half of the chapter on character structure and motivation (chapter 8), I spoke about the so-called mask which the playwright must wear in order to express himself, or rather, in order to express the attitude of his higher, creative self toward the characters he is going to bring to life via the stage. But this mask has numerous other aspects and problems which I postponed discussing until the propitious moment of this, the penultimate chapter. Before we can do so, however, some preliminary explanations may be necessary, especially for those who are not familiar with the techniques described in *To the Actor*.

To facilitate this communication, all of us should know what the atmospheres of a play are. No play is without its general or *objective* atmosphere. This kind of atmosphere usually surrounds all kinds of buildings, places, events and so on. If, for example, you enter a library or a church or a hospital or a cemetery or a curiosity shop, immediately you will feel the existence of its particular atmosphere. It belongs to nobody; it is just an objective, general atmosphere which envelops this or that place or building or home or street, and even whole cities, were it possible to encompass them on the stage. Different landscapes, too, have different atmospheres. So have all kinds of events, such as a carnival, a ball, a bullfight or a street accident. Different seasons and times of year also have their own atmospheres: Christmas, Easter, New Year's have especially strong general or objective atmospheres.

You can t see these atmospheres but you undoubtedly sense that they hang and float in the air around you, and from your own personal experience you must know that they influence people who enter the orbit of this or that atmosphere. On the stage, atmospheres envelop the entire play; to what degree depends on how sensitive the director and players are to them and how, in turn, they make them contagious to the audience.

But there is another kind of atmosphere which we shall call the individual, personal or particular atmosphere of this or that character. It is a *subjective* atmosphere and can be pleasant or unpleasant, sympathetic or unsympathetic, tragic or happy; dull, aggressive, dangerous, mischievous, pessimistic, optimistic, loving, hateful —as many kinds of individual atmospheres as there are personal descriptions.

This particular atmosphere of the character belongs only to the character. The character carries it with him wherever he goes and whatever he does; he walks, as it were, within this subjective atmosphere as in a cloud, as in an aura that surrounds him, regardless of what the general or objective atmosphere may be. The objective atmosphere remains fixed with its scene or event; the subjective atmosphere moves everywhere with its character. Another and to us a more important difference between the objective and subjective atmospheres is that the objective atmosphere influences the character from the *outside,* from the air surrounding the whole place, while the subjective atmosphere comes from within the character himself.

A further distinction between the two atmospheres is that the individual or subjective atmosphere itself can be of two kinds: either it is an atmosphere which remains constant with the character throughout the entire play, or it is with him only during certain sections of the play and is replaced by another when and if the character changes for better or worse in the crucible of the plot. But the objective atmosphere changes only with the change of scene; it can momentarily be changed by a certain dramatic occurrence within a scene, but only temporarily.

A small example of the latter possibility might be a scene of a beautiful and inviting lake. Suddenly, an accident, and a child is drowned! The atmosphere of beauty and invitation gives way to influences of fear, hatred and sorrow on those affected. When the unfortunate people have left the scene and unwary newcomers arrive, the original atmosphere would be restored. Or take a festive bullfight in which a famous and beloved matador is gored to death! Festivity surrenders to tragedy, at least until the next favorite bullfighter appears and changes the atmosphere back to anticipation and excitement, which are now heightened perhaps by the influence of revenge.

But atmospheres, whether objective or subjective, whether they are caused to change or not, always exist and are there to be made sensate by the playwright and director.

In the case of the subjective atmosphere, the character carries it around with himself and radiates it for as long as it is needed. To prove its existence, just watch people around you in daily life more intently than you normally do. In time, you will develop an almost radiological ability to observe and define the individual atmosphere that surrounds each person. Of course, in some instances, the subjective atmosphere may be more strongly expressed than in others, but by close study you will always manage to find at least some traces or hints of the individual atmosphere in even the strangest and most recalcitrant persons.

Therefore, imbuing his players with a keen sense of these objective and subjective atmospheres is indispensable to the director from the very first moment of the very first rehearsal. They are one of our strongest intangible means of expression and can be made powerfully provocative to the audience as well.

Next to remember is that two objective or outside atmospheres cannot exist within the same place at the same time; they will battle each other until one of them becomes victorious. As witness the scene of the lake where the child was drowned: were the unfortunate characters still there with the dead child when the unwary newcomers arrived, the atmospheres of beauty and tragedy would vie with each other and the dominant one of the moment—tragedy, no doubt—would triumph.

But the individual atmosphere of the character and the objective atmosphere of the scene *can* and do exist perfectly, even if inharmoniously, no matter how diverse their auras may be. For when the objective and subjective atmospheres contrast and clash, they create a most wonderful effect while in collision, and the sparks they generate bring extra illumination to the suspense of the play.

Unfortunately, many of our modern playwrights do not create their characters so completely that an audience can sense immediately and clearly just what kind of atmosphere surrounds them. That being the deplorable situation, the director, for the sake of the many levels which a perfect performance should have, must establish and even invent if necessary the atmosphere for every character to be portrayed. And here a word of warning to both playwright and director is necessary:

Do not confuse the individual moods, feelings or emotions of the character with its subjective atmosphere! A character can maintain the same individual atmosphere for a long time, perhaps for the entire play if that is most suitable for him, but his mood, his feelings, may require change several times. Take the character of Sir Andrew Aguecheek in *Twelfth Night:* he might carry the atmosphere of stupidity, emptiness and lightheadedness throughout the entire play, if that is your interpretation of him, but think of how many changes of mood he undergoes during his various scenes in the play. Or take an example from everyday life: somebody comes to you in a bad *mood,* but that is not yet a reason to hate him or feel unsympathetic toward him. But should he carry a bad *atmosphere* with him, you might feel that you dislike or even despise him.

To better understand the difference between the subjective atmosphere and the mood of a character, try this little experiment: Choose a character from a play or novel, or invent your own character. Surround yourself with the atmosphere of this particular character. Try to radiate it and fill the space around you with its aura. Then try to walk, move, whatever you wish, but relying only upon this definite individual atmosphere. It would be even better if you did not know the character too well but had only some general idea about it. Let us suppose that you are not too familiar with the details of the life of Joan of Arc, but from a general knowledge about her there can be no doubt that she must have had a very strong individual atmosphere surrounding her. It is of no consequence whether the atmosphere you create around yourself while thinking of Joan of Arc is the correct or true one. What matters is that that which you will call the atmosphere of Joan of Arc is there. So while trying to move or speak in her atmosphere, pay no attention to any possible mood in which she might be at this or that moment during which you imagine her. Concentrate only on her personal atmosphere. Carry it with you in this exercise and you will see how easily you can divorce these two things—the mood or feelings and the subjective atmosphere. Because the subjective atmosphere lasts as long as the character; its moods and feelings fluctuate. This is not to say that the subjective atmosphere cannot influence the character's own feelings, emotions and moods; it can and often does, but these two elements should not be considered as identical things.

Another thing I must mention is that many characters, both in old and modern plays, are written so that they have to conceal many things from one another. These hidden things can comprise the characters' objectives, their true feelings or true desires and even their entire natures. And they may use many different disguises for such concealment: pretended feelings, pretended attitudes toward the other characters or pretended reactions to what is happening around them. Cases in point are Goneril and Regan in *King Lear*. Their dialogue speaks to Lear about their love for him while inwardly they hate him. Or Iago in *Othello,* a classic example of a character who hides everything—his objectives, thoughts, true nature and true attitude toward Othello and Desdemona. In order to discover such secrets if their existence is suspected within an individual atmosphere, we have only to ask two questions of the character: What are you hiding from other characters? By what means do you do it? Finding out what and how will help immeasurably in wearing the character's atmospheric cloak.

II

Now, I think, we have a better foundation for our discussion on the "mask" which the playwright, momentarily his own actors, has to wear while creating his character. But what exactly is this mask? We know that it is the mask of the character with all his characteristic features, and that it can serve all who are involved in bringing him to life, that it is a means of revealing and expressing him to the utmost on the stage. Those are its functions. But what is its morphology, its idiomatic form and structure?

Each and every mask consists of several elements, too many to deal with as succinctly as we must here, so we shall confine ourselves only to the most important, those most applicable to our tasks of better playwriting and play directing:

One element is the dialogue. This is usually the most appreciated by most directors and actors. It is as enticing as the frosting on a party cake, but it is not always a token of the substantial ingredients the playwright should have put inside the cake itself. Anyway, because this surface element may sound smart or wise or funny, directors and actors tend to rely too much on it, often neglecting or forgetting the other, deeper elements.

Another element is the feelings and emotions of the character. They permeate and give life to the lines, and true meaning to the character.

A third element is the objectives of the character. Objectives also are permeated with the feelings of the character. The character uses his lines to achieve his objectives.

Still another element is the various means or disguises which the character uses to hide his true feelings and/or objectives from the other characters.

Yet another element is the individual, subjective atmosphere of the character which, naturally, permeates all the other elements.

For the sixth element I shall include what in previous discussions we called the voice of our other, higher self; that is, our attitude as artists toward the characters or the types of people we have to create and present on the stage.

And so we have the six different elements which comprise a many-leveled performance. All of them are closely interwoven with one another, all of them influencing every other element of the mask, all of them operating simultaneously—the objective atmosphere of the play or scene serving them additionally as a general background or habitat.

If you should wonder which of these elements is the most important, the answer would be: None. One of them might be more important at one moment and another more important the next. They are like living and shifting cells, transparent or translucent, moving with and within each other as the occasion may require, and thus creating a very intricate and rich psychology for the characters and the scenes whose forms and structures they compose.

Playwrights and directors who find these formulations too complicated to grasp or apply should be reminded that they are not alien to the actual creative processes which both craftsmen undergo when they are in their most inspired moods, whether they realize it or not. These elements are merely the result of an analysis of such creative processes, an attempt to bring them into focus, to replant them in the author's and director's consciousnesses. For, being unconscious of them, you cannot perfect them; consciously you can.

It is not necessary to remember them all at once; in fact, it would be impossible to do so unless you had a photographic mind. Neither is it advisable to try using them all at once; they are not tricks one can easily coordinate and incorporate like a juggler. But it *is* advisable to test one element here, experiment with another element there, combine two of them somewhere else, later three, then more —and to do so *consciously,* until a facility with them makes their application a kind of second nature. I know a father of five active young children who can listen to good music, keep time to it with his rocking chair, smoke a pipe, do double-crostics, answer his wife's questions and remember to sip his beer now and then. The analogy may not be a good one except to illustrate that with practice, one can acquire the skill to do a combination of things simultaneously and habitually.

So start by taking the objective alone, for instance, and concentrating on it for a while. Then take the individual atmospheres of the characters separately. Then go over all the devices which your characters may resort to in order to conceal things from other characters. Put them to work for you one at a time and leave it to your innate talent to merge them at the proper time and place. Without your having to force them, they will blend into a psychological oneness, into a true semblance of life. The more you try to rid yourself of the modern tendency toward oversimplifying your characters and making them flat and primitive, the more will you be aware of this defect in most performances, the more will you notice that our unifying elements can bring breadth, depth and scope to your own creations, the more will you realize the power these levels have to make actors and audiences more conscious of them, too.

When I decry the tendency to oversimplify characters, I do not imply, and you are not to infer, that I am opposed to simple, natural acting which resembles life itself. I am only denigrating the trend to make it so simple that it becomes primitive, artificial and even ludicrous. It is not acting any more, nor is it life. Human life is never, never as primitive as I have often seen it performed on our stages. Human life is a many-leveled, psychological process, and efforts to achieve "naturalness" by means of oversimplified characters or acting only make puppeteers of playwrights and directors, mere string-pullers trying to "make like life" but never quite succeeding. To think that by acting "naturally," mostly on the surface, without too much introspection, we are being true to life is the great delusion of today. That kind of "simplicity" only takes us farther away from life's truths. Life is a multileveled, often complex affair with many elements constantly operating, interweaving and interlocking all at one time. And for the sake of a better theatre, we must never forget it.

If you will permit an illustration from my personal experiences as a young actor, I would like to relate how I discovered this multi-leveled psychology for myself. It was during a period in the life and work of the Moscow Art Theatre when its audiences were not mixed, not socially heterogeneous. Every night, a certain class (people from a special profession) was invited. Audiences were composed of only teachers or only workers, or all doctors or all soldiers, peasants or farmers. Even all directors and actors sometimes.

At that time, I played in my own production of *Hamlet,* and to my great amazement, I realized that every night I played the role differently. Not because I deliberately wanted to play it differently. It was no experiment; it just happened by itself, every night. I sensed, as it were, the special demands and desires of the audience each night. I was not being intentionally subservient to them, either. I simply felt that my Hamlet of tonight became different from last night's and the night before last night's only because I seemed to be sensitive to what each audience expected of me *in its own terms.*

Mind you, my original interpretation of Hamlet always remained unchanged, but still it was somehow definitely different each time, and these differences lay in just *how* I performed it. Without realizing it, many nuances, many fresh and unaccounted-for things crept in and changed my performance of the character several times without disturbing the basic interpretation. I was fascinated, once I became conscious of this, as I watched myself from different angles and saw these interpolations click into place as though they had a life and time of their own and came forth volitionally. One night I was Hamlet and a medical doctor at the same time; the next I was Hamlet and a farmer, or a writer, but always remaining Hamlet on the upper level. This experience taught me that there must and can be deeper, stronger links between the characters and the audience, and only by appeals to multileveled performances can we forge them.

16. A Play Is Born

As every playwright well knows, a play, though it is an image of life, is not yet born when he puts the final word "Curtain" to the last act. That is only part of a play's biological process. The rest depends upon the love and skill of the world into which he hopes it will be brought. For though conceived and gestated, the still enwombed infant must await delivery until an X-ray view (the script) persuades some godparent (producer) that it is worth footing the hospital bill. Even then, actual parturition cannot take place until the obstetrician (director) and his staff (players, set designer, et al.) are able to bring it into living reality.

Frequently, the gestation period is longer than an elephant's, or finding a willing godparent proves impossible, producers and their unpredictable preferences being what they are. And sometimes the fetus is miscarried or the delivery is stillborn, or the child born with the best of professional care is for some inexplicable reason short-lived. For the theatre, being life's counterpart, is beset by the same mischances.

Our concern here, however, is not with life's failures and mishaps but with the obstetrics of the successful deliveries. To that end, there is not a better materia medica for the playwright, director and actors than a daily, step-by-step account of how a play should be directed and rehearsed.

For our text we shall take Nikolai Gogol's *Revisor (The Inspector General)*, because I am fortunate in having the rehearsal notes on my work for the Hollywood stage production of the classic.*

In this elaborately annotated section, we shall assume that the director has already started his rehearsals in one or more of the ways suggested in the chapters on better ensembles (chapter 11) and better rehearsals (chapter 12), so there is no need to dwell on these preliminaries. It is only necessary to explain that because the Hollywood cast was highly professional, most of them former Broadway actors of stature, and had long worked together as a group on the West Coast, I chose to start my rehearsals with the atmospheres and a description of the characters.

A final word: Even if the reader is already acquainted with *The Inspector General,* I urge that he first read this new version of the play and familiarize himself with it before embarking on a study of the directorial notes and suggestions. Following the descriptions of the scenes and characters, the play's pages will be found on the left-hand side of the book, the directorial data on the right-hand pages.

* The simplified, modern-theatre adaptation used in this book was especially prepared and contributed by Charles Appleton. It is protected by copyright. Performances or public readings of any kind are subject to royalty payments. Permission to perform or reprint must first be obtained from the author or his representatives.

Michael Chekhov in the title role of Strindberg's *Erik the Fourteenth,*
produced by Chekhov's First Studio of the Moscow Art Theatre, 1922.

As Khlestakov in the Moscow Art Theatre production of *Revisor*, 1922.

Michael Chekhov as Khlestakov in the Moscow Art Players' repertory production of *Revisor*, Shubert Theatre, New York City, April, 1935.

Vera Gretch as Anna, Michael Chekhov as Khlestakov and Maria Krijanovskaya as Marya in the Moscow Art Players' repertory production of *Revisor*, Shubert Theatre, New York City, April, 1935.

Pavel Pavlov as the Mayor and Michael Chekhov as Khlestakov in the
Moscow Art Players' repertory production of *Revisor*, Shubert Theatre,
New York City, April, 1935.

Michael Chekhov as Hamlet in his Second Moscow Art Theatre production, 1924.

Michael Chekhov as Skid in the Max Reinhardt production of *Artisten*,
Vienna, 1928.

As Polisch in *A Fool Through Love,* a German film directed by Olga Chekhova in Berlin, 1929.

In the starring role of the embezzler in *Phantom of Happiness,* a German film of 1929–30, directed by Reinhold Schunzel.

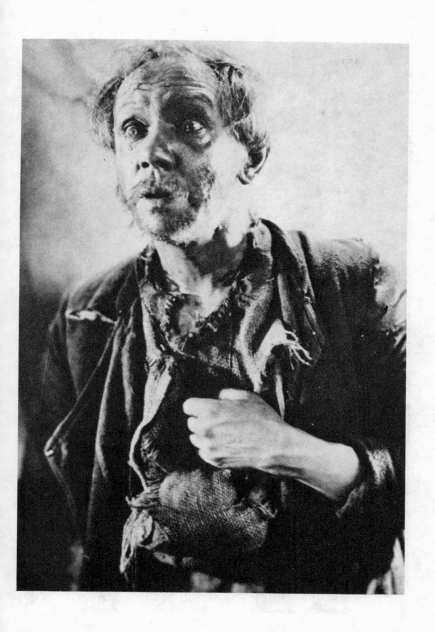

In the role of the beggar in *Troika*, a German film produced in Berlin in 1930.

Michael Chekhov with Sergei Rachmaninoff, Paris, 1931.

Michael Chekhov with Feodor Chaliapin at Riga, Latvia, 1932.

Michael Chekhov in the title role of *Ivan the Terrible*, by Alexei Tolstoy, produced at the Government Dramatic Theatre at Riga, Latvia, in 1933.

In the role of Opiskin in Dostoievski's *Village Stepanchikovo,* Russian Drama Theatre, Riga, Latvia, 1933.

Michael Chekhov as The Buyer in Anton Chekhov's sketch, "I Forgot,"
from *An Evening of Anton Chekhov*, Majestic Theatre, N.Y., 1935

The Student in Anton Chekhov's sketch "Rendezvous," from
ning of Anton Chekhov, Majestic Theatre, N.Y., 1935.

As The Drowned Man from *An Evening of Anton Chekhov,* Majestic Theatre, N.Y., 1935.

"Father of the Bridegroom" from *An Evening of Anton Chekhov,* Majestic Theatre, N.Y., 1935.

The Sexton in Anton Chekhov's sketch "The Witch" from *An Evening of Anton Chekhov,* Majestic Theatre, N.Y., 1935.

Michael Chekhov as snapped by a student at the Chekhov Theatre School in Ridgefield, Conn., 1940.

The village patriarch in Metro-Goldwyn-Mayer's *Song of Russia,* his first Hollywood film, 1943.

Michael Chekhov co-starring with Ida Lupino in the Warner Bros. production of *In Our Time,* his second Hollywood film, 1944.

Gregory Peck, Ingrid Bergman and Michael Chekhov as the psychoanalyst in *Spellbound,* Hollywood, 1945.

With Judith Anderson and unidentified actor in the Ben Hecht film,
Specter of the Rose, Hollywood, 1945.

Michael Chekhov when the author first met him at Reseda, California, in 1946.

Giving an acting lesson to Jack and Virginia Palance, numbered among the vast list of stars and directors who were Michael Chekhov's private students. At his home in Beverly Hills, 1954. Their inscriptions at the left of the photograph read: "With all our love and admiration— Virginia Palance. We both feel like Cordelia—Volodenka" (Chekhov's pet name for Palance).

REVISOR

Adaptation by Charles Appleton *

SCENES: Acts One, Three, Four and Five—The parlor in the home of the Mayor of a small Russian town.

Act Two—A cheap room at the inn.

TIME: A day in the year 1830

Characters:

ANTON
The Mayor, really the supervisor of the town district. Coarse-featured, crafty, grafty, pompous; up from the ranks, so he is capable of being as servile as he is arrogant; measures his words; crew-cut gray hair; gold-braided uniform with spurred high boots.

ANNA
His wife. A middle-aged, vain, nosy, bossy, clothes-conscious, small-town flirt; full of airs and pretended culture.

MARYA
Their daughter. Her mother's younger image and jealous of her.

MISHKA
Their manservant. A peasant, young in years and in service.

LUKA
The School Supervisor. Timid, but typical of the scholastically unaccredited who can lord it over the scholastically unaccomplished.

* Copyright © Charles Appleton, 1962.

KHLOPOVA	His wife. Much less timid but far more uneducated than her husband.
AMMOS	The town Judge. He pontificates with a frog in his throat, carefully clearing it before he lets himself leap to a conclusion.
ARTEMY	Manager of Charities which are supposed to begin at his institutions but end at his home; an obese, lumbering, brassy and conniving rascal.
CHRISTIAN	The town Doctor. He's German and doesn't speak much Russian, so his dialogue consists mostly of laryngeal noises.
SHPYOKIN	The Postmaster. As conspiratorial as he is a tippler.
BOBCHINSKY DOBCHINSKY	Local landowners. Both short, potbellied, wildly gesticulative; B. is the shorter and livelier of the two; a grotesque pair.
KHLESTAKOV	The suspected "Revisor" or Inspector General from St. Petersburg. In reality, an underpaid, underweight government clerk of 23; a scatterbrained, overdressed butterfly who flits from place to place and thought to thought.
OSIP	His manservant. Elderly, seedy, rude, clever; speaks in a monotone.
ILYITCH	The Police Chief.
TUNOV	A police sergeant.
WAITER	At the inn.
ABDULIN	A shopkeeper.
FYOVRONYA	A housewife.
EUDOXIA	A widow.

IVAN ⎫
STEPAN ⎬ Important town personages.

ANASTASIA   Stepan's wife.

SERGEANT-⎫
AT-ARMS ⎬ A military attendant from St. Petersburg.

OTHERS   Assorted merchants and townspeople.

[ACT ONE]

The parlor in the Mayor's home. Morning.

Discovered are ANTON, AMMOS, ARTEMY, LUKA *and the* DOCTOR. *The Mayor, in dressing gown and slippers, is pacing the floor agitatedly while the others sit expectantly, curious. The Mayor finally stops and turns on them. (See Alternate Opening Scene in directorial notes.)*

ANTON: Gentlemen, in case you're wondering why you're here —we're in trouble! I got the bad news yesterday and I've been worried ever since, what to do about it.

AMMOS: What news?

ANTON: At any moment, we can expect a little visit—from an inspector!

LUKA: An—an—an inspector?

ARTEMY: What kind of inspector?

ANTON: From St. Petersburg. Maybe even an inspector general!

AMMOS: Why—what for?

ANTON: Please, gentlemen, let's not pretend. To make it worse, he's coming incognito this time—and with secret orders!

LUKA: Secret orders? Oh, my God!

ARTEMY: Just when everything was going so profitab—so peacefully.

Start by creating the atmosphere for the very first little section. It is an atmosphere compounded of despondency, premonition, a danger behind the wall, conspiracy. The players don't have to feel it as yet, only imagine that the air is filled with these elements. They should write the tentative words for this atmosphere at this place in their scripts, and on all pages where other atmospheres start and stop.

Later, when this atmosphere is finally created, and perhaps more succinctly defined, it must be maintained by sheer will power *throughout the scene,* remaining unbroken even when the director has to interrupt with orders and suggestions.

Let them intensify the atmosphere, and under its guidance change places with one another—not yet as characters, but as they personally would be affected by it. And while they are in motion, their bodies should be in harmony with the atmosphere, listening to it and responding as to a piece of music.

They may induce this particular atmosphere still further by rising and finding a place to peek out, as if looking for that danger which lurks behind the wall.

Then let each player choose one sentence—any sentence from the beginning of his part—and speak it in harmony with the atmosphere as the director calls out the name of his character.

Listen for tone levels* now. How does it sound, for example, when the actor playing Anton says, "Gentlemen, in case you're wondering why you're here—we're in trouble!"? Is it consistent with the atmosphere? Would it be compatible with the character? No need to make corrections yet; merely make a mental note of the shortcomings and go to the next step. Often these early imperfections, if any, erase by themselves as the characters begin to take form.

* Also see page 125.

The next step is the same sentence spoken in keeping with the proper *movement* as well as the tone level of the atmosphere. Is the atmosphere maintained as each actor combines tone level with movement? Is each character beginning to peep through both in sight and sound?

Test it by contrast. Still maintaining the atmosphere, let all the players simultaneously speak a series of sentences from their respective parts and move toward one another as if having a conversation. The gabble may make no sense, but no matter. Watch and listen only for the differences: Is each character beginning to *contrast* with the others? If not, then the atmosphere is not yet being properly felt by all.

Therefore, try the start-and-stop method of acquainting the players with the sensation of being in and out of the atmosphere—donning and doffing it instantly, as it were. At the signal "Curtain!" let them start reading their lines in proper sequence and within the atmosphere; at the call of "Stop!" let them read the same lines without the atmosphere. None should strain or fake to make the difference apparent; it will automatically become so if the atmosphere is truly felt and applied.

ALTERNATE OPENING SCENE

For my own productions of the play, I found that the effect of the opening was greatly enhanced by not having Anton, the Mayor, on stage when the curtain goes up. Instead, the other four characters sit or stand around, waiting for him with curiosity and impatience, a couple of them taking turns at consulting their pocket watches. After an establishing pause, Anton comes down the stairs in dressing gown and slippers. At the bottom of the stairs, he stops to count heads. No "Good mornings" are exchanged, but those who sit rise respectfully, and all follow Anton's movements while he mysteriously closes the door, carefully peers out the window, and paces in deep thought, hands locked behind his back and now and then flashing a piercing look at one or the other of the group.

ANTON: Maybe that's why I was warned.

ARTEMY: Warned? By whom? You didn't tell us.

ANTON: It was a dream. Two nights ago, I had a recurring dream about two rats. Big, black monsters. They scurried in, sniffed everywhere, then—vanished. They did it over and over again. Then came this letter from Alexei to bear it out.

LUKA: About the—the—rats?

ANTON: No, no. They were only the symbol of what Alexei writes about in his letter. Listen.

(*He extracts the letter from his pocket and starts reading.*)
"Dearest godfather, friend and benefactor . . ."

(*Mumbles along until he reaches what he is looking for.*)
Ah, here it is. . . . "Duty and devotion compel me to advise you that a big official is now here, getting orders to inspect all governmental operations, especially in your district."

(*He waggles a significant finger.*)
"I can't reveal my highly placed source of information, but I can warn you to be on the lookout for a private citizen who pretends to be touring the country. While I'm sure you will claim that you have nothing to hide, my advice would be to hide it a little better."

(*Looks around uncomfortably.*)
Heh-heh. Alexei always likes his little joke. But I wish he wouldn't put it in writing!

When this active pause has been sufficiently "milked," he suddenly stops and faces them. Ammos and the Doctor sit down; Artemy and Luka remain standing. Holding them in his gaze, Anton begins.

———————•◦•———————

BIZ (business): Before the word "inspector" on the first page of the play, Anton takes a step toward them, turns and looks around behind him.

After "secret orders," also on page 114, Ammos rises with a "Whew!," as if he has an impulse to depart. Artemy draws a chair near and leans on it.

On "Maybe that's why I was warned," Anton sinks into a chair. All but the Doctor venture a little closer. Before Anton speaks about the rats, he should motion them to draw even closer, which they do. And before the word "vanished," he scrutinizes their faces to see what impression he created. The others nod, mumble "Yes," and otherwise indicate that it is indeed an ominous sign.

Before Anton starts reading the letter, he takes his chair with him to the table and looks to see if the door is closed. Ammos, behind him now, follows his gaze.

The atmosphere of suspicion should be increased as Anton reads the letter.

While Anton is reading the letter, all but the Doctor try to look over his shoulder or sidle up for a glimpse of it. Anton changes positions on his chair several times in order to prevent this, and once or twice drives them back with a hard look.

Anton should stress such phrases in the letter as "especially in your district," "private citizen," "in your midst right now," "get the goods on you." A beat after each and a look up at one or more of the others will further heighten the effect.

(Continues reading.)

"For all I know, this inspector may be in your midst right now, innocently snooping around to get the goods on you. Sister Anna Krillovna—" The rest is all personal, about the family.

(Returns the letter to his pocket.) †

So you see, gentlemen, the rats *are* scurrying around and the trap *is* about to be sprung—but on us!

ARTEMY: Why on us? It's only you, the Mayor, he's investigating.

ANTON: And what about the Mayor's appointed public servants. . . .

(Paces and stops in front of each.)

The manager of our charities, Artemy? The supervisor of our schools, Luka? The head of our judiciary, Ammos? And the guardian of our health, Dr. Christian? What if they have been guilty of their depredations and inefficiencies without my knowledge or consent, as I shall most certainly claim?

AMMOS: No need to be hasty, Anton. I'm not convinced that our imperfections are so glaring that they shine all the way to St. Petersburg. There are districts with worse—ah—conditions.

LUKA: Yes, yes. This sudden investigation seems to have some kind of political overtones.

ARTEMY: Such as what?

LUKA: Yes, what—and why us?

AMMOS: I'm thinking that our government may be preparing for war, so they're sending undercover officials around to see if there are any subversives in hiding.

† For extra business, Anton may leave the letter on the table instead of returning it to his pocket. Artemy picks it up after his first
speech on this page. Toward the end of the next speech, Anton sees
Artemy and snaps the letter out of his hands without interrupting
himself, replaces it on the table.

Build the Mayor's characterization. Beginning with the others'
secretive interest in the letter and to the end of the act, Anton
suspects everyone present. Each is a partner in his crimes, each
knows about the depredations that can send him to Siberia. In the
succeeding pages, this suspicion develops in him the tendencies to
prevent, throttle and stop them. He is on guard against these potential enemies.

Thus, these tendencies become his characteristics, stemming as
they do from his main objective, which is to annihilate this larger,
menacing thing which has suddenly appeared in his life. Annihilating it permeates and dominates all his other or minor objectives
in the play, which include finding out if the menace is real or a
phantom, and if real, how to draw it into his claws, how to grapple
with it, how to subdue it and crush it. The main objective drives
him until the end of Act Four, when he thinks the threat has been
nullified by becoming his son-in-law and he dances in triumph.

When Ammos speaks, he has a tendency to draw himself up and
stretch his neck like a rooster before crowing.

Also establish here that the slowest characters in speech and
movement are Luka and Osip. The quickest are Khlestakov and
the Mayor.

(Notes should be taken by each member of the cast of suggested

ANTON:

(*Derisively.*)

Now, there's a political pundit for you! Of all the really vulnerable border cities and towns, they pick out this remote, Godforsaken district. Why, your behind would be saddle sore for three years before you could gallop to the nearest frontier.

AMMOS: You don't understand. Governments are always more devious than the people they govern. There must be a reason why—

ANTON: Certainly. Somebody has tattled or complained. But whatever the reasons, you can't say I haven't been loyal and not warned you all. He shall find my administration without blemish, and my advice to all of you is to be similarly prepared for examination. Especially you, Artemy. The first things they pry into are the charity hospitals and homes, because that's where government tax funds usually develop their most mysterious diseases and infirmities. So make sure that everything is neat and clean, and that the patients and inmates don't look like they've just come up out of a coal mine.

ARTEMY: I'll budget a little more for laundry and a scrub woman this week.

ANTON: And you, Christian: on every hospital bed there should be a chart with the patient's case history, written in Latin or your native German, or something else that nobody can understand. And don't let them smoke so much; their cheap tobacco makes the wards and halls smell like opium dens. Also, get rid of a lot of them before the inspector pops in. It's no compliment to your medical skill, Christian, or to your management, Artemy, that the places are always so crowded.

ARTEMY: It would be a debit to us if they were empty. Each head has a little profit on it, you know.

ANTON: As for you, Ammos, tell your bailiffs the waiting room of a courthouse is no place to keep and trade their geese. The place stinks like a poultry yard. All we need is for the inspector to slip on some goose droppings!

characterizations and other pointers concerning his performance.)

When Anton starts instructing his officials, these moods should be evidenced:

He is locked in combat with Artemy—two dogs growling and ready to leap at each other, but never doing so.

With Ammos he adopts a chiding tone, as though criticizing a playmate.

To Luka he is all ridicule in tone and gesture.

The Doctor he ignores as ineffectual and hopeless.

Artemy resents everything Anton tells him.

While Anton is lecturing the Doctor, Artemy and Ammos make another attempt to read the letter on the table. A stony look from Anton in the middle of his speech drives them back. Artemy's lips move as he reads, and continue moving after his eyes leave the letter.

When his name is called, the Doctor looks up as if from a snooze, stares blankly at Anton. Remembering that the Doctor doesn't speak Russian, Anton thinks shouting will help him understand. When it doesn't, Anton buttresses shouting with sign-making.

AMMOS: We'll keep them hidden in the kitchen until he leaves. By the way, wouldn't you like a goose for dinner today?

ANTON: Your own chamber doesn't look and smell any better. It would be more seemly to have some lawbooks around instead of those motheaten old hunting trophies. And tell your court clerk to chew some garlic or onion; with a vodka breath like his, it's dangerous to light a match.

AMMOS: He doesn't smoke.

ANTON: I'm not criticizing him, or anybody. God gave us all our special little sins. It's only that inspectors take an atheistic view about them.

AMMOS: Well, some sins have to be hidden more than others. I've never made a secret of the fact that I take bribes. But my bribes happen to be white greyhound puppy dogs and I'm not ashamed of it.

ANTON: Puppies or pussies or servant girls, a bribe is a bribe.

AMMOS: A puppy isn't worth as much as your five-hundred-ruble fur overcoat, or that expensive shawl your wife has been wearing lately.

ANTON: By God, you think like an atheist, too! At least I go to church, but you stay in bed with a different servant girl every Sunday.

Ammos waits for an answer to his offer. Anton's ferocious scowl tells him this is not the time for gallows humor.

MULTIPLE LEVELS

A performance of any consequence should have a minimum of two levels. In fact, any line spoken by a player should have at least these two levels: 1) the intellectual meaning, or *what* the actor has to say; 2) supported by the psychology behind the meaning, or *how* the actor says it.

Shakespeare stated it originally in King Claudius' apron speech: "My words fly up, my thoughts remain below; / Words without thoughts never to heaven go." Neither do an actor's.

When the *how* or thought behind the words is missing and the actor speaks only what the author has written—no matter how properly, logically or clearly the words may convey the meaning— it is not yet a performance. It is reading aloud, it is conversation, it is lecturing, but it is not theatre. Not until the *what* is coupled with the psychology behind it do the words come alive, take on true body and soul and feelings. Every sentence has its appropriate psychological overtone. The function of the actor is to find it, and that of the director is to help him do so.

There are also dual levels in tempos, qualities, moods, etc., as we shall see in the subsequent pages, and these in combination make a beautiful kaleidoscope of human emotions—and a delightful performance to watch.

———————————◆·◆———————————

Anton and Ammos lean toward each other like two bantam cocks when comparing bribes. Artemy is arrayed with the Judge against the Mayor in this skirmish.

AMMOS: I like my view of the Creation much better. Besides, I consider myself blessed enough that God made my bed more comfortable than our church pews. Any philosopher would agree with me.

ANTON: You know what the old peasant proverb is: Turn to higher education, turn away from God.

(*Turns to* LUKA.)

And speaking of education, Luka, couldn't you recruit a more personable set of teachers, whose habits are not as ludicrous as their looks? Right now your faculty resembles a bunch of escaped convicts from the Siberian salt mines.

LUKA: If they were any better, would they stay here on the salaries we pay them? Some of them have had to grow long beards to hide the fact that they cannot afford neckties.

ANTON: That has nothing to do with those crazy faces that fat literature teacher makes when he's reciting. And the one who teaches history—does he have to dramatize every battle and smash the chairs? They come out of our budget, you know.

LUKA: Don't think I haven't spoken to them about it. But pedagogues are all so peculiar, and so set in their methods.

ANTON: It will be even more peculiar when the inspector walks in on them incognito and catches them at their antics. In fact, it will be most peculiar for all of us, to put it mildly, if that somebody we least suspect should drop in unexpectedly.

(SHPYOKIN, *the Postmaster, enters.*)

SHPYOKIN: Good morning, gentlemen. What's this I hear about some official coming?

ANTON: How did *you* find out?

ARTEMY: How wouldn't he find out? He's the Postmaster, so he reads all the mail.

Ammos' retort on his atheism is more angry and sarcastic than clever.

———— •—• ————

The atmosphere that pervaded from the beginning undergoes a change on this page with the quick entrance of Shpyokin, the Postmaster. The cast should so note it on their scripts, as they should all other atmospheres at their places of transition.

The second atmosphere is actually a retention of the first plus this difference: it is now intensified with an "on the alert" element. For the Postmaster not only is associated with the menacing letter (the reason is at the bottom of this page), but his sudden entrance, at what is for him an abnormal hour, and in the midst of the tense atmosphere that already prevailed, precipitates its new phase.

The Postmaster's entrance may have to be repeated several times, without dialogue, in order to ascertain whether this new element in the atmosphere is being evoked and making itself felt. Again, straining or faking must be avoided; it will not be necessary if the first atmosphere was genuinely present.

———— •—• ————

Anton's attack on Luka and his school is loaded with digust and ridicule. When Luka moves closer to Anton, the better to hear him, Anton pushes him aside.

Artemy and Ammos make another try at reading the letter on the table. Without stopping his speech, Anton frustrates them by plucking the letter from under their eyes and pocketing it. The letter-peepers turn their backs on him and retreat into a whispered conversation, which Anton also notices.

BIZ: After his sudden appearance, the Postmaster completes the entrance like his Russian prototype of the period. He spits on his hands and slicks down his hair, then goes to shake hands with everybody, speaking his lines while doing so, making it a kind of cheap sociability. But he should do it truthfully, without exaggeration, and respond to the atmosphere of the others in his own way. For his individual atmosphere is that of a provincial Khlestakov.

SHPYOKIN: That's a libel. Bobchinsky was at the post office and it was he who told me.

ARTEMY: Then Bobchinsky must be reading the mail for you.

ANTON: That's enough. . . . Well, Ivan Shpyokin, what do you make of it?

SHPYOKIN: It's quite obvious. We'll soon be at war with the Turks.

ANTON: Ah! Another political pundit. You may join the learned Judge over here.

SHPYOKIN: It must be war with the Turks, stirred up by the French. If not the Turks, then who else?

ANTON: With us. It's we in this town who are going to get it from our military, not the Turks. The letter you delivered from Alexei yesterday warns us.

SHPYOKIN: Oh? Have they some information, something we should all be afraid of?

ANTON: It's not for myself I fear, but for the stalwarts in this room. True, my present unpopularity with the merchants and townspeople is annoying, but it will pass. It always does. I may have taken a little too much from some, but they know that I will take a little less the next time.

(*He leads the* POSTMASTER *aside.*)

What I suspect is that some hotheads may be complaining to St. Petersburg about me.

SHPYOKIN: I wouldn't be surprised. They don't appreciate that good government is expensive, and that public servants can't live on their monthly stipends alone.

ANTON: Exactly. You're a very analytical man, Ivan Shpyokin.

SHPYOKIN: Thank you. I, too, serve the government, so I know.

ANTON: Well, then, couldn't you—that is, every suspicious-looking letter, or every other letter coming or going—couldn't you kind of open it for official inspection—or maybe even unofficially— you know, for everybody's benefit. . . .

Shpyokin habitually puts a finger to his pursed lips to indicate that he's thinking.

Anton takes the letter out of his pocket, taps it against his left fingertips. Shpyokin reaches for it; Anton withdraws it, pockets it again.

Shpyokin's self-importance increases during this friendly isolation with Anton; he is pleased to be made privy to something special. Some of the others edge near, to hear better as well as share in this intimacy.

Shpyokin's psychology behind this speech is not so much a protest against government salaries as it is resentment against those who have complained about him, too, in the past.

A rocking motion of Anton's hand follows his "couldn't you," and a gentle elbow nudge precedes "you know."

SHPYOKIN: If I have your permission, the instruction is quite unnecessary. You'd be shocked at what some of those letters contain. People think a sealed envelope is like a locked bedroom door. I wouldn't say such things to a common prostitute.

ANTON: There you are. Has there been any hint about an official coming from St. Petersburg?

SHPYOKIN: No, nothing to or from St. Petersburg. But there may have been something in one or two of the letters I missed.

ANTON: Suppose, then, for all our sakes, we don't miss any again. And if somebody complains or denounces me, you just bring the letter here, and you and I can make some private—and advantageous—disposition of it.

SHPYOKIN: How advantageous?

ANTON: Trust me.

SHPYOKIN: It will be a pleasure.

AMMOS: Just be a little extra careful. Tampering with the mail is a criminal offense. Tampering by a government official against the government is both criminal and treasonable.

ANTON: If you want to save your own skin, too, save your legal interpretations.

SHPYOKIN: There are always mitigating circumstances, my dear Judge. If I do it—and I don't say that I shall—it will be at government request, with government consent and for government benefit.

ARTEMY: What government—Turkey?

SHPYOKIN: No, *us.* Are we not, all of us, the government's representatives?

ANTON: Quite correct. And don't use the word "tampering" so loosely, Ammos. It will merely be a little censorship, which every government is entitled to. Because when that inspector walks in, incognito, and makes charges and accusations, we would be derelict in our duties not to know whose letter brought him here, and not to be prepared with a counteroffensive against that treacherous citizen.

BOBCHINSKY *and* DOBCHINSKY *enter breathlessly.*)

After "letters contain," Shpyokin takes several letters out of his inside coat pocket and flashes them like a seller of filthy post cards. He quickly stuffs them back as Ammos and Artemy start to come closer.

Here Anton virtually gives him his blessing to the crime.

Shpyokin does not necessarily mean material things by the question, but favor with Anton's daughter, Marya (see middle of page 154).

—————————•—•—•—————————

With the entrance of Bobchinsky and Dobchinsky, the second atmosphere also undergoes a change. What will be the third atmosphere starts on Bobchinsky's line: "You'll never guess what happened!" This new atmosphere conveys the addition of impending catastrophe. Thus, the alertness of the second atmosphere is vastly increased here and, musically speaking, becomes its crescendo. Of course, the temptation to force the new atmosphere with outward acting also becomes greater and must be resisted even harder. Sensing it in the air, feeling it inside, will automatically lead to more natural and more characteristic responses. Trust the atmosphere to do the major work of bringing them out.

This third atmosphere prevails until Ammos' speech "going to the inn as a delegation?" (page 140).

—————————•—•—•—————————

The entrance of Bob. and Dob. also startles them. They rise or stiffen in alarm on "A tremendous piece of news!" move toward them in a semicircular wave, slowly framing them.

BOB.: You'll never guess what happened!

DOB.: A tremendous piece of news!

(*Reactions and ad-lib inquiries from* ALL.)

BOB.: Totally unexpected. Just as we were going into the inn—

DOB.: Yes, both of us were going into the inn and—

BOB.: For heaven's sake, Peter Ivanovich, who's telling the story?

DOB.: Let me tell it. Please.

BOB.: No you don't. You'll garble it.

DOB.: And you won't remember everything. You seldom do.

BOB.: I will, I will.

(*Appealing to the others.*)

Please, gentlemen—let me tell it. And tell him not to interrupt.

ANTON:

(*Exasperated.*)

Bobchinsky! Dobchinsky! Find seats and be quiet! No, I mean only one of you talk.

DOB.: Which one?

ANTON: It doesn't matter, so long as it's only one at a time. Now sit down.

(BOB. *and* DOB. *find seats, the others draw theirs around them.*)

We sit on pins and needles, while you two fence with each other and our emotions! Now start again, from the beginning, Peter.

BOB.: Well, it was—

DOB.: Just a minute. He didn't say which Peter. I'm Peter, too, you know. Which of us did you mean, Mr. Mayor?

ANTON:

(*Bursting.*)

It doesn't matter! Only *somebody* get on with it!

BOB.: Well, since I came in first, I should tell it first.

Note: While the characters of Bob. and Dob. were originally written and performed as wild gesticulators, I have had more success with making their movements less exaggerated—provided I could get from them the qualities of timidity, amazement and astonishment. Except when otherwise necessary, they constantly use their hands in a kind of knitting or embroidering motion, like two little old women observing and storing up gossip.

Though breathless, Bob. and Dob. are expert gossipers who have learned not to race their narrative, and to make their words count. Also, they accent their consonants for extra emphasis. Anton and Artemy maneuver the pair onto the sofa during their introductory speeches here, and stand facing them. The others follow, grouping themselves near the table, behind Bob. and Dob.

PSYCHOLOGICAL DIVISIONS AND SUBDIVISIONS

There are three main parts or sections in the psychological construction of every play, whether it is a one-act play, or five-act play like this, as I have illustrated in *To the Actor*. Once we have found these three sections, the next step is to find the subdivisions within each.

While the major sections are fixed at three by all the laws and practices of good playwriting, there is no restriction on the number of subdivisions which may be found in each. Some yield more, some less, depending on the director's judgment and determination as to what is logically and psychologically a subdivision, as with the climaxes (page 137, *et seq.*).

This is a most important factor in directing and developing the play, and if you do not grasp it entirely now, it will further clarify itself later on. For the time being, let us consider what the subdivisions of Act One are, before we have gone too far into it. In

DOB.: And I'll tell everything you leave out.

BOB.: Nothing will be left out, and I'll start from the beginning, as you requested, Mr. Mayor.

(*Clears his throat.*)

When I heard about the letter you received—

ANTON: What letter?

DOB.: The one from your godson, Alexei—

BOB.: He didn't ask you. . . . The one from your godson, Alexei.

ANTON: And how did you know about it?

DOB.: Me? I heard it from Peter Bobchinsky.

ANTON: Who heard it first? Now you've got me doing it, too. From whom did *you* hear it, Peter Bobchinsky?

BOB.: From your housekeeper, Avdotya, when you sent her to Filipp Antonovich's for a small keg of brandy.

DOB.: French brandy.

BOB.: Immediately, I ran to confirm it from our good Postmaster here, and on the way I found Dobchinsky—

DOB.: At the bublichki bakery.

BOB.: But when we reached the post office, Ivan Shpyokin had already heard about it, too.

ANTON: From whom?

BOB.–DOB.: From Avdotya.

ANTON:

(*To* SHPYOKIN.)

Then why did you tell us that you learned it from Bobchinsky?

SHPYOKIN: From him, too. It is more gallant to protect a woman than a man.

this first act alone, which constitutes only half of the First Section, I have found as many as five subdivisions. For example:

In the beginning of the act, the psychological effect is one of conspiracy, and that is the content which must be radiated. First seen as a closed bud, the conspiracy opens in five steps. The first step begins with the Postmaster's entrance (page 126), the second with the entrance of Bob. and Dob. (page 130), the third with their ensuing expository scene (pages 132 through 140); the fourth will be Anton's preparations for meeting the incognito inspector general (page 142), and the fifth will inject a new psychological quality when Anna and Marya romanticize the panic (page 152).

On Bob.'s "the letter you received," Anton stops, eyes Bob. obliquely, his suspicions intensifying.

When asking Bob. how he knew about the letter, Anton looks around, first at Artemy, then Luka, then Ammos. They give him, in turn, a "Why ask me?" gesture, a shake of the head and a shrug.

Anton returns his gaze to Bob., who is already shaking his head in denial.

On "bublichki bakery," Bob. gets up and Dob. follows. Anton pushes Bob. back and sits beside him, while Ammos pulls Dob. back from behind and comes around to take a chair next to him. Artemy also takes a chair near them, and Luka moves up to stand behind it. Shpyokin moves into the place vacated by Artemy. With all leaning their heads toward Bob. and Dob., the effect is that of a tightly packed bomb awaiting detonation.

REHEARSAL TASKS

Aside from those separate rehearsals devoted exclusively to develop-

ANTON: I can see our Avdotya has been quite busy. She must have eavesdropped when I mentioned it to my Anna and Marya last night. Now the whole town must know it. . . . Continue, Peter.

(DOB. *makes a start*; ANTON *stops him.*)

Bobchinsky. You, Dobchinsky, may only interrupt. You were at the post office, Bobchinsky.

DOB.: We both were.

BOB.: When we left, I said to Dobchinsky, "You've gorged on bublichki, but I'm starved. Let's go to the inn. I heard they've just got some fresh sturgeon." Well, just as we entered, we caught sight

of this young man—

DOB.: Quite attractive, he was, and dressed in civilian clothes of fairly good quality.

ANTON: Yes, yes, go on.

BOB.: He was not just a stranger, but there was also something strange about him.

DOB.: Because he was pacing the lobby, deep in thought.

BOB.: His face and manner were so unusual that I immediately became curious.

DOB.: So I called Vlas, the innkeeper, aside and quietly asked him who the young man was—

ing the business (page 155), each of the early rehearsals should include a specific task or concentration along with the routine steps. That task should be to pay particular attention to, even to stress, what at the moment appears to be the weakest ingredient of the performance.

True, the cast is thoroughly saturated with the atmospheres before starting rehearsals of each act, but if the atmospheres are forgotten and fall away, they should be made a special task, too, for one or more of the rehearsals. Another rehearsal might be given over to watching the inner and outer tempos of the characters, or their individual qualities in the difficult scenes. The objectives of the characters and the objectives of the scenes are frequently lost sight of, so also deserve special attention during a rehearsal or two.

Pointing out in order to point up the main and auxiliary climaxes,† as well as the psychological sections and their subdivisions, can be tasks included in the normal rehearsal pattern. However, because these are such vital tiers in building the play, I have found it more expedient to devote entire rehearsals to going over only the scenes in which these climaxes and divisions occur: one rehearsal for the main and auxiliary climaxes, and another for merely the beginning and end of each subdivision. That is usually sufficient to implant them a little more deeply in the players' consciousness.

On "young man," they are all on the *qui vive* again, heads turning from Bob. to Dob. and back again as first one, then the other, supplies the next scrap of information.

† THE CLIMAXES

Graphing the main and auxiliary climaxes within the three sections as so many peaks to be climbed and linked, the play's chart would look like this:

BOB.: And what do you think Vlas said?

DOB.: Now who's interrupting whom? Wasn't it I who called Vlas aside?

BOB.:

(*Ignoring him.*)

He said, "He's an official of some sort, I'm sure, though when I asked him, he pretended to be only a government clerk on his way from St. Petersburg to Saratov. But he doesn't seem to be in any hurry. He's been here two weeks. Mighty queer behavior, especially since he orders everything put on his bill and has yet to pay me a cent."

DOB.: You forgot his name. Vlas told me it is Ivan Alexandrovich Khlestakov.

BOB.: The moment I heard it, it seemed to ring a bell and I said, "Aha!"

DOB.: It was I who said "Aha!"

BOB.: Did you? Then it was I who wondered why, if he's going to Saratov, does he stay here so long?

DOB.: "To find out something," I said. "To listen to gossip at the inn, without being seen around town."

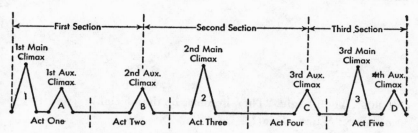

1. FIRST MAIN CLIMAX starts with the first line of the play, Anton's "Gentlemen . . ." page 110. Ends on Luka's "Yes, what— and why us?" page 120.

A. *First Auxiliary Climax* starts with Bob.'s "Then he must be the official," page 140. Ends on Anton's "Oh, Lord . . ." same page.

B. *Second Auxiliary Climax* starts with Anton's "Your highness is pulling my leg," Act Two, page 180. Ends on Anton's "more like four hundred," same page.

2. SECOND MAIN CLIMAX starts with Khlestakov's "there is only one St. Petersburg," Act Three, page 210, last speech. Ends on Khlestakov's "Ridiculous! A government official . . ." Act Three, page 218, last speech.

C. *Third Auxiliary Climax* starts with Anton's "bless you and forgive my sins and stupidity," Act Four, page 288. Ends on Anton's "what a turn events have taken!" same speech.

3. THIRD MAIN CLIMAX starts with Anton's "My throat is slit . . ." Act Five, page 324. Ends on Anton's "He didn't even resemble . . ." page 326.

D. *Fourth Auxiliary Climax* starts on the Sergeant's entrance, Act Five, page 328. Ends with his announcement of the real inspector general, same page.

Note: It will be more convenient to mark these climaxes in your script so that you will not have to keep referring to this page for their starting and ending points.

N.B.: While a play may have any number of auxiliary climaxes as links connecting the main climaxes—depending, like the subdivi-

BOB.: Then I said, "Then he must be the official."

ANTON: What official?

DOB.: The one you were notified was coming incognito—the inspector.

ANTON: Oh, my God! Then it's true. And he's here already!

BOB.: He must be, from the way he looked us over, and from the way he studied our plates when we were eating our sturgeon.

DOB.: As if he expected us to slip some sort of bribe under them.

ANTON: A bribe? For whom?

(BOB. *and* DOB. *shrug. A thought reflects in the Mayor's eyes.*) Did you happen to learn his room number?

BOB.: Yes. Five, over the parlor.

DOB.: Where people usually gather to gossip and scandalize.

ANTON: And in two weeks, he could have heard a lot! That I beat Corporal Ivanoff's widow for a strumpet, that the prisoners missed three meals, that the streets look like a city dump . . .

(*Holds his head in despair.*)

O Lord, there's a whole universe of sins to punish. Couldn't you have overlooked a few of ours?

AMMOS: Instead of trying to soften God's wrath, wouldn't it be better to do something as atheistic as going to the inn as a delegation?

ARTEMY: That would be too obvious. First we should send the warden, a couple of the clergy and a few leading businessmen to smooth the way for us.

ANTON: Oh, no. I have a better idea. This isn't the first time I've had to cope with such things and come out smelling like a rose.

sions, on the director's taste and judgment—no play should be divided into more than three main climaxes, like the main sections. For it is a characteristic of bad plays that they suffer from too many main climaxes and not enough auxiliary climaxes.

———— •• ————

After Bob.'s "Then he must be the official," there is a breathless stop. Anton looks around to see if the others are thinking what he is before he asks, "What official?"

On Dob.'s "the inspector," the bomb explodes under Anton. He leaps up before delivering his "Oh, my God!" speech.

"He's here! He's here!" Anton can repeat to the officials, as if recalling all their sins like a nightmare, to them as well as himself, making them cringe. Then he throws up his hands and clutches his head. His fear is infectious. . . . It is a moment of great importance to the development of the act, and to the whole composition of the play. Because if it is not perfectly registered, its counterpart, the entrance of the Sergeant-at-Arms (page 328), will not have the powerful impact intended for it.

Dob. tries to rise on his "some sort of bribe under them" line, Bob. after him. But Anton pushes them back; he wants more information from them.

Only Bob. and Dob. are listening to Anton's recital of what the inspector could have found in two weeks. The others are concentrating on their own derelictions. It is only after his appeal to God that they approach him with suggestions—first Ammos, then Artemy.

———— •• ————

Ammos' suggestion of going to the inn as a delegation drops the fourth tense atmosphere into their midst. Its name is Panic, and it continues until Anton and his retinue depart (page 150).

———— •• ————

Artemy's speech, following Ammos' suggestion, restores some of Anton's aggressiveness. He pushes both aside as a referee might a

Perhaps the good Lord will overlook the atheist in our midst and help me again this time.

(*To* BOBCHINSKY.)

He's a very young man, you say?

BOB.: Twenty-three. Not more than twenty-four.

DOB.: Although that may be one of his incognito disguises, too.

ANTON: Not very likely. It's easier to conceal an elephant than one's true age. A young man, especially, is all on the surface.

(*He crosses to the window, opens it and calls to someone outside.*)

Hey, Officer Tunov! Go fetch your Chief and bring him back with you. On the double!

(*Returns to the gathering.*)

My advice to you gentlemen is to go at once and put your houses in order and wait—and pray for my success while waiting. Meanwhile, I shall take my usual police entourage and go for an unofficial little drive, perhaps as far as the inn, just to check on whether all visitors to our town are being properly received. On your way, gentlemen.

(*The visitors prepare to leave, lingering to banter among themselves. Those without speeches ad lib sotto voce.*)

ARTEMY: Well, Judge, it looks like there will be some cases which you will not be trying.

AMMOS: Even a judge is innocent until found guilty. But who ever burrows into a court's verbiage if he can possibly avoid it, and who would ever understand the verdicts I write, anyway? I'm afraid I have nothing to fear.

ARTEMY: And I'm afraid I have.

AMMOS: No doubt, but no use getting jittery. Put clean hospital gowns on all the patients and they'll cover a multitude of your sins.

ARTEMY: But you'll still be able to smell a lot of others. Instead of hospital diets, the stench of cabbage borsch in the corridors

couple of clinched fighters, and walks through the gap as he starts his "Oh, no" speech, pacing and plotting while he delivers it. The others follow him with their eyes, listening, trying to penetrate and anticipate his strategy.

When Anton stops to ask Bob. if K. is a young man, Bob. and Dob. jointly get off the sofa and come to him with their answers. Then, when Anton turns away from them and resumes pacing, the pair trail him with small steps (not grotesquely).

Here, with the beginning of Anton's order-giving, he starts building up a series of crescendos. The actor playing Anton should mark these orders in his dialogue and bear in mind that each must be a little more emphatic than the last—so that by the time he rushes out (page 150 L), it is as if a cyclone had just departed.

Bob. and Dob. start to join this departing group near the door, but Anton pulls them back and walks them upstage for more questioning, which is conducted in whispers while the next five speeches are going on.

Artemy's fear and despair about the conditions in his hospital raise his voice in pitch and volume, drawing Anton's attention back

would suffocate you. And by nose alone you couldn't tell the wards from the lavatories. If only that inspector hadn't swooped down upon us so suddenly!

ANTON:

(*Loudly.*)

Gentlemen, gentlemen! We're wasting time!

(AMMOS, ARTEMY, LUKA, SHPYOKIN *and* CHRISTIAN *file out as they exit.* BOB. *and* DOB. *are about to follow but remain when* OFFICER TUNOV *appears in the doorway.*)

TUNOV: The Chief is coming, sir.

ANTON: Good. Is the phaeton ready?

TUNOV: Yes, sir.

ANTON: Where are Officers Vitzyn and Morda? I didn't see them outside with you. Didn't I give orders that all three of you are to guard my house and accompany me everywhere?

TUNOV: Officer Vitzyn will have to be excused for today.

ANTON: Excused? Who excuses me from my duties?

TUNOV: You are not as drunk as he is, sir. He's dead to the world at the widow Eudoxia's. Two buckets of water couldn't revive him.

ANTON: Good God, what a police force! Go sober him up and get him out of there before the inspector hears of that, too.

(TUNOV *starts to go.*)

No, wait. First things first. Run up to my room and get me my sword and new hat, and my best uniform.

(TUNOV *exits. He confronts* BOB. *and* DOB.)

Which of you wants to go along with me?

BOB.: I do.

DOB.: So do I. Please.

ANTON: All right, Dobchinsky, it'll be you. The phaeton can only hold one more.

to the group still at the door. Interrupting his whispered interrogation of Bob. and Dob., he turns to them in anger.

Tunov executes a military heel-click and a salute before addressing Anton.

Tunov should start to reply "The Chief—" but catch himself before incriminating his superior, then deliver his "Officer Vitzyn . . ." line as a diversionary tactic.

Anton's "No, wait" interrupts Tunov in the middle of a heel-click and a salute. Leg and arm remain poised in the air for a beat or two. He brings them back slowly and silently.

BOB.: I'll tag along on foot if you drive slowly. And I'll keep to the background, or just look through a crack in the door. But I wouldn't miss your meeting with him for the world.

(TUNOV *re-enters with the apparel.* ANTON *takes the sword and hat box, removes a plumed hat from the box, then examines the scabbard.*)

ANTON: Look how scratched this scabbard is. A disgrace to my office. And I blame it all on that miserly shopkeeper, Abdulin. He knows I need a new one, but does he provide it? Oh, those two-faced traders! It wouldn't surprise me in the least if each of them already had a petition against me in his coat pocket.

(*To* TUNOV)

Now, here's what I want you to do. Round up all the sober policemen you can. Give each a broom and let them sweep up the street around the inn. Clean. None of your usual tricks that I've heard about, like dropping by for tea at the inn and stuffing silver spoons into your boots. Or what you did to the merchant Chernayev: cadged two yards of cloth for your uniform and walked off with half a bolt. One thing you must learn in government service, Tunov: never graft more than your rank entitles you to. Now get going!

(TUNOV *exits.* ANTON *starts pacing again, thinking; then he tries on the sword, next the plumed hat, takes it off, walks to the window and looks out, muttering.* BOB. *and* DOB. *urge him into clothes, help him dress.*)

ANTON: Where is that confounded Police Chief?

(*As he returns to stage center,* ILYITCH *enters.*)

Here you are at last, Ilyitch. What the devil kept you so long? Where were you?

ILYITCH: I merely stopped at the gate to hear a report from Tunov.

Bob. virtually pleads. How can he be excluded when his inseparable rival is not?

The Police Chief's rank spares him from saluting or heel-clicking. He does that only at important functions. Instead, to announce himself and make Anton turn around, he can ad-lib, "You sent for me, sir?"

ANTON: Well, hear this: an official from St. Petersburg has been here incognito for two weeks. Why didn't you know about it? What do you propose to do about it now that you know?

ILYITCH: I approved your orders to Tunov to round up all policemen and clean the streets.

ANTON: And where is Morda? I want him to drive the phaeton.

ILYITCH: I've sent him to get the fire engine and hose down the sidewalks.

ANTON: And at a time like this Vitzyn has to be drunk. Couldn't you have put a stop to it?

ILYITCH: Not so long as God makes lonely widows to tempt virile men.

ANTON: Then this is what you'd better do. That very tall waiter at the inn—Pugovich; dress him in a uniform and station him at the bridge to make a good appearance. Then remove that broken-down fence near the shoemaker's and drive surveyor's stakes into the ground, so that it will look as though we are in the process of paving the street. And have the storm drain at the end of that street dredged out. At least thirty carloads of trash must be deposited there. People! Make a hole anywhere and they'll fill it with their rubbish every time. Or put up a statue, and immediately it's surrounded with debris.

(*Groans in despair.*)

Another thing: if that inspector asks any of our officials if they are satisfied, they are to reply politely that they are perfectly satisfied. Those who say they are not will have plenty to be dissatisfied about later.

(*He reaches for his hat and picks up the hatbox instead.*)

The good Lord forgive me for having to be such a sinner. But when this danger has passed, I'll offer the biggest candle the church has ever seen. I'll make every one of those conniving shopkeepers contribute a hundred pounds of wax for it. Are you ready, Dobchinsky?

(*Claps the hatbox over his head. It covers his face and he quickly makes the proper exchange.*)

While the Police Chief is getting a dressing down, he joins Bob. and Dob. at helping dress up the Mayor. Throughout the speeches on this page and Anton's long speeches on the next page, the three voluntary valets must synchronize the difficult business of getting Anton into the various items of his official uniform. The step-by-step process is too long to detail here and too difficult to graph, but must be carefully worked out during rehearsals so that each movement required for each piece of apparel serves to punctuate Anton's dialogue rather than detract from it. The dressing part of the scene must not be played broadly, but as a sublevel with a contrasting tempo, and at no time must it becloud Anton's instructions to Ilyitch; in fact, Bob. and Dob. are trembling at Anton's mounting wrath, so it is hardly a time for clowning. But if properly synchronized, the scene will pay off in a big way. The laugh to top it will come when Anton, fully dressed in every other detail, thinks he is reaching for his hat and, instead, puts on the hatbox. It will be the audience's momentary release from the tempo and the tension. To repeat, the scene is basically very funny, but the fun must be delayed so that the content of the dialogue, so vital to the character and plot structure, is not destroyed.

POSTPONE THE COMPLETE RUN-THROUGH

As you will remember from the chapter on better rehearsals, I do not believe in going through a play in sequence, or through the entire play in early rehearsals. The exception is the first reading of the play, when the cast sits around the room or at a table. But once the cast is on its feet, a full run-through is not recommended until the penultimate and final rehearsals. In the Hollywood production of this play, and my own productions of it in New York and Europe, a complete run-through was not attempted until the thirty-third or thirty-fourth rehearsal. In commercial productions, where the rehearsal period is limited to four weeks, run-throughs may have to come earlier, but they should be postponed as long as possible.

In other words, if the rehearsals have been conducted according to my suggestions, two run-throughs will be enough; more will make

The devil take it! Nobody has his wits about him since that monstrous inspector entered our lives.

(*To* ILYITCH *again.*)

One more thing: if he asks what happened to the money that was appropriated to build a chapel at the hospital five years ago, everybody is to say that it burned down just as we got it completed—which is what I said in the report I sent in. But some idiot is liable to forget and tell him that construction never began. And if I were you, I'd get Vitzyn out of the widow Eudoxia's and padlock both of them, separately, until the inspector has left. When both of them are drunk and go roistering around the town, nobody needs the St. Petersburg Gazette. Are you ready, Dobchinsky?

(*He starts to go, the others to follow, but turns back and brings them up short.*)

And get word to the barracks that every soldier must wear pants and underwear instead of just high boots and a long overcoat. When they get drunk and start to fight, they peel off their overcoats and—underneath they look like sin incarnate!

(*He turns and exits, followed by the others. After a pause,*

ANNA *and* MARYA *enter hurriedly. They survey the bare stage.*)

for confusion and neglect of important details. For it is easier to memorize a play a little at a time than to ingest the whole of it at once; it is easier to see and correct a few imperfections at a time —in close-up, as it were—than to view it en masse and try to detect its hidden blemishes.

In the early rehearsals, it is not even necessary to run through a whole act or acts in sequence. Rehearse only the opening atmospheres of the acts scheduled for the day, and those segments of the acts wherein the atmosphere changes. For setting the atmosphere is first and foremost in getting the proper moods, qualities, tempos, etc., out of the cast.

Later on, the director can hop all over the play in rehearsing those acts and scenes where the main climaxes occur and where the auxiliary climaxes link them. The same with those portions of the play where the beginnings and ends of the psychological divisions are to be found, and the scenes where the subdivisions must be designated as so many steps, each of which leads to the next stair landing.

Forgive the paraphrase, but a scene at a time saves nine.

———— •◦• ————

With the entrance of Anna and Marya, the atmosphere of Panic is supplanted by that of Alarm, which is the last atmosphere of the first act.

A run-through of all the first-act atmospheres is advisable. The cast should start by imagining no atmosphere at all. Then, under the influence of the first atmosphere, they start rehearsing their lines until stopped. Maintaining the first atmosphere, they start reading again with the addition of the Alert of the second atmosphere, until stopped. Still maintaining the first two atmospheres, they resume with the third, Impending Catastrophe. Stopped again, they maintain all the previous atmospheres, and when started again, they build them still further with the addition of Panic. The four atmospheres, all related in content and comprising the main at-

ANNA: Where is everybody? Don't tell me they've gone.

(*Opens a door and calls out.*)

Anton! Antosha! Where are you?

(*Calls upstairs.*)

Antosha, my husband! Are you there?

(*Returns stage center.*)

We get all dressed up for them and they leave without a word. The least they could have done is waited for us. It's all your fault, you and your everlasting dawdling. "I want a scarf, Mama. Have you got a pin to go with it?"

(*Goes to the window and looks out, hurriedly opens it and calls.*)

Anton! Where are you all going in the phaeton? . . . What?

ANTON:

(*Off, shouting.*)

To see an official.

ANNA:

(*Shouting back.*)

Is it the inspector? Has he arrived?

ANTON:

(*Off.*)

Yes, we think so.

ANNA: Has he got a mustache?

ANTON:

(*Off.*)

We don't know. He's incognito.

mosphere of the act thus far, prevail until the men exit. With the entrance of the women, the fifth and last atmosphere, Alarm, supplants the other four.

Anna's Characterization: She fancies herself a woman of high society and strives to create this impression with cultured voice and precise speech, but her aggressive, businesslike manner comes through regardless.

Anna should enter first, stop, look around. Marya swirls in dancingly after her, also stops.

After Anna asks, "Where is everybody?" Marya resumes her dancing movements, continues them while Anna searches, gets in Anna's way as she recklessly propels herself.

Marya's Characterization: Bated breath, innocence, but otherwise her mother's mimic and inept rival.

While Anna is talking at the window, Marya is behind her, hopping on one foot or standing tiptoe to glance over her mother's shoulder.

Note the two levels on which Anna probes: the queenly exterior and the fishwifely thoughts; how she struggles to maintain that cultured voice even when compelled to shout her uncouth inquiries.

ANNA: Oh, I hope he has a mustache, and that he's at least a colonel.

ANTON:

(*Off.*)

I'll give you a full report later.

ANNA: No, I've got to know at once. Wait! I'll go with you.

ANTON:

(*Off.*)

There's no room in the phaeton.

ANNA: Anton! Wait for me! Wait, Anton!

(*She closes the window, turns back to the room angrily.*)

He's gone! I'll fix him for this. And you, too. Because you're the one to blame, with all your primping and whining. "Oh, Mama, dear, help me pin my scarf. How do I look? I wish you'd let me borrow your new dress. I won't be another moment"—and another moment, and another moment, and another moment—until we've missed all the important events. You and your ridiculous coquetry! And for what? An oily Postmaster who's attentive to you only because you're the Mayor's daughter, I'm sure.

MARYA: No use taking it out on me, Mama. The things you want to find out will be just as good a couple of hours from now.

ANNA: How consoling we are. Thank you very much. Why not wait a couple of weeks, or a couple of months? By then, perhaps, the tale will have a new twist in it.

(*Goes back to the window and looks out ruefully; then, seeing someone outside, she opens the window and calls.*)

You there, Avdotya! . . . Did the Mayor tell you where they were all going? . . . I can't hear you. Make signs to me. . . . He didn't, huh. Just waved at you and drove off. . . . Why didn't you ask him, or was your head too full of foul thoughts about men, as always? . . . No, she says, the stupid peasant. . . . Well, run after the carriage and find out where it went and whom they are seeing, you hear? I want you to bring back a full description of what he looks like—whether he has a mustache and what kind, and whether

On the lines that mimic Marya, Anna speaks faster and makes faces.

Anna moves about on this long speech. After "coquetry," she petulantly throws herself down on the sofa, her arms spread across the top of it, expansively the queen venting her spleen.

BIZ REHEARSALS ONLY

It being the end of the act, and no further directorial suggestions being necessary that could not be invented by the director himself, permit me to use the space to obviate a problem which often plagues actors as well as directors and playwrights—stage business.

I would recommend that at least one rehearsal a week be set aside for nothing but this troublesome task, the business of developing and establishing the business—setting the action and the precise movements of the cast during it. It can be a vital part of a scene, an act, and sometimes of the whole play itself. Cases in point are the scene in which Bob., Dob. and Ilyitch dress the Mayor, and the biz of the concluding scene of Act Five, which sums up all the gestures that preceded it.

he has blue eyes or black, how tall he is and what color hair—everything about him. You hear? . . . All right, now hurry! And hurry back immediately!

FIRST ACT CURTAIN

No dialogue should be used during these business rehearsals other than that which serves as the cues. In fact, it is better if the director marks the lines that cue the important business and reads only those aloud (or the stage manager can prompt them), then watches the players' response to each.

Cues alone are preferred because in the process of remembering lines, it is natural to forget the execution of business, and vice versa. The strictly business rehearsal is designed to overcome that, since concentration on the cues can be a better help in forging reciprocal mnemonic links between "what and how to say it" and "what and when to do it."

[ACT TWO]

A sparse room at the inn. Its cheap furnishings are a bed, a table and two chairs, dresser and washstand. Two huge suitcases, oddments of male apparel, some toilet articles and a couple of empty flasks complete the décor.

OSIP, *the manservant, is discovered lying on the bed, holding his stomach while gently rolling and keening. A knock on the door brings him leaping to his feet. He opens the door cautiously.*

OSIP: Ah, it's you. Come in.
(*The* WAITER *from the inn, a middle-aged man, enters.*)
You've come to take my master's order for dinner, I hope.

WAITER: No. I saw him go out a while ago and took the first opportunity I could to come up. I've been trying to catch you alone —to ask you about him, and yourself.

OSIP: If it has nothing to do with my master's food, I'm not interested.

WAITER: It has. . . . He's not getting any more until his bill is paid. That's what I came to warn you about.

OSIP: Such a generous heart must beat for something. What?

WAITER: Friendship, that's all.

OSIP:
(*Suspiciously.*)
Friendship, hmm? Is there an etiquette book in which it is written that family retainers should fraternize with waiters, and vice versa?

For the beginning of Act Two, the elements composing the atmosphere are Emptiness, Dejection and Hopelessness.

Khlestakov and Osip might try reading a few lines in this atmosphere for proper orientation, wandering aimlessly around the stage, moving things, murmuring to themselves.

This atmosphere prevails until Osip bursts back into the room (page 174). There it ends abruptly.

—●—

Osip's Characterization: He suffers immensely, hence he should be played soberly and without striving for comedy. His humor derives mainly from the situations which surround him. His attitude toward Khlestakov is that of an old, sulking, chiding nurse.

The importance attaching to this expository opening scene between Osip and the Waiter is that it implants in the audience's mind the background of two main characters—Khlestakov's and Osip's—and at the same time reveals a bit of the subsidiary character of the Waiter himself.

Since the nature of the scene is predominantly expository, it cannot be hurried too much. But neither should it be permitted to drag, which it will if the lines are merely tossed back and forth, especially by two characters whose inner tempos are naturally slow and servile.

A two-level trick with the tempos can avert that dangerous drop in audience interest which frequently attends all expository dialogue occurring *after* the first act, as this does.

The remedy, simply, is to have Osip start playing the scene with a slow outer tempo and the Waiter with a faster one. Then, when the two old serfs become sympatico, these outer tempos reverse.

WAITER: Yes. In the book that says "family retainer" is just another name for serf.

OSIP: True, true. But only a man who was once a serf himself can have the compassion to appreciate the hardships.

WAITER: I was and I do—and I never forget to remember it. So I help them whenever I can.

OSIP: It's good to have nothing else on one's mind. Me? These days I even have trouble remembering to whom my young government snotnose owes money, and when to avoid running into them.

WAITER: You see? I guessed he must be in trouble, and you with him.

OSIP: Sooner or later everybody does. Oh, you don't know the miserable life I lead with this young fop of mine! Right now my stomach is carrying on as though an army of buglers were inside blowing "Charge!" Since we left St. Petersburg two months ago I have never been sure when the next meal is coming or if we'll ever get home again—alive, that is.

WAITER: Has he really no money—from his position or his family?

OSIP: Yes, but he gambles away most of it and spends the rest on folderol and fancy living.

(*Snaps his fingers, impersonating his master.*)

"Osip, the best room! Osip, the best dinner! If it isn't the best, it offends me!". . . In every town he shows off like a celebrity, but he's only a low-grade little government clerk. He fancies himself a card shark, too, so he cultivates other travelers—and gets cheated every time.

WAITER: On his salary, how can he manage to live that way, especially in St. Petersburg?

OSIP: Oh, he manages, all right. As soon as his father sends him some fresh money, he squanders it on sprees. Rides all over town in hansom cabs, buys theatre tickets every night—and in a few days I'm back at the old clothes shop to sell his best coats and trousers. There have been times when I've sold everything but the things on his back in order to raise some quick money.

Osip's outer tempo is stepped up; he comes alive because his new friend may help him get some food. The Waiter's outer tempo is slowed down.

The same for their inner tempos, identical with the outer tempos save that Osip's inner tempo is a little more pronounced because of the prospect of something to eat. The Waiter's inner tempo, like his outer, has no prospect but commiseration.

ACT TWO SUBDIVISIONS

It is not my purpose to impose arbitrary psychological subdivisions for this play, only to illustrate to the director how I arrived at them for myself in the hope that he will agree with them. If he does not, he is free to find his own, as he most certainly will have to when he directs another play. I merely point out the necessity of establishing such subdivisions in his mind to facilitate directorial approaches, to show him how they can result in more inspired directing.

Hence, after this act, I shall try to avoid what to some of the more experienced practitioners of our craft may seem like elementary finger-pointing and let them exercise their own imaginations in finding the psychological subdivisions for the other three acts. If they should be stumped, and for those who do not feel like exercising, the directorial notes will contain enough clues.

The following, then, are the psychological subdivisions I submit for Act Two:

1. Sadness, a bundle of misery. Osip and Khlestakov are both unhappy creatures at the beginning.
2. Hysteria. K. and Anton are like two hysterical women in the market place, each trying to top the other, both wanting to speak at once, only waiting for the other to finish so that his own words will be heard.
3. Happiness. It starts with the climactic scene when Anton gives him the money (page 180). K., Anton and Osip are all happy, each in his own way, each for his own reasons.

WAITER: Why doesn't he stick to his job and work for a career instead of gadding and gambling about?

OSIP: Ach! If I only knew. And if his father knew, he'd take his little government official and beat his fanny black and blue! Instead—I have to suffer the humiliation of being told by an inn-keeper's waiter that there will be no more meals until the bill is paid.

WAITER: Shhh! I was not supposed to tell it to anybody but him, and only when the time came.

OSIP: The time will come, you may be sure.

WAITER: The boss still thinks he's a somebody and doesn't want to risk offending him until he's sure he's a nobody.

OSIP: To hell with offending *him*. I'm the one who's suffering the most. He gets a good meal once in a while; I get only the dregs. Please, for old times' sake, couldn't you arrange to—not exactly steal, but sort of put something aside for me? How about a little remembrance and compassion like some cabbage soup and a piece of stale bread?

WAITER: Shhh! That's what I came to tell you. If he can't pay his bill, I'll manage somehow to sneak something in to you, the first chance I get.

(OSIP *embraces him. The* WAITER *goes to the door, peeks out and exits hastily.* OSIP *locks the door and is about to fall into bed again when a rapping, as with a cane, brings him back to reopen it.* KHLESTAKOV *enters, hands* OSIP *his cane and hat. While* OSIP *is helping him doff his gloves and coat,* KHLESTAKOV *glances toward the bed.*)

KHLESTAKOV: I see you've been making free with the bed again.

OSIP: Free? It is free only to those who can pay for it, and I know that *I* can't.

KHLESTAKOV: Then don't muss it up.

(*Paces the room.*)

See if there's any tobacco left in my pouch.

Khlestakov has to knock several times with his cane. Osip must indicate that he heard him, all right, but will take his time about going to open the door.

K. enters like a Beau Brummell, wearing one glove on the hand which holds the other. He gives Osip his cane and gray top hat. Then Osip helps him doff his overcoat and hangs it near the door; hat and cane he puts on the dresser. Not until K. is removing his other glove does he notice that Osip has been on his bed.

osip: Unless the elves filled it again, there isn't. You smoked the last of it four days ago.

(khlestakov *continues pacing, contorting his face, coming to a resolve which he voices loudly.*)

khlestakov: Now, look, Osip—I want you to go downstairs and—
osip: Where and what?
khlestakov:
(*Almost entreating.*)
To the restaurant—and tell them—tell them I must have my dinner.
osip: Oh, no. Not me.
khlestakov: You stupid old man! How dare you refuse me?
osip: It's easy; because it would spare you embarrassment.
khlestakov: What embarrassment?
osip: Well, I've heard it whispered that you are not to get any more meals until—
khlestakov: This is ridiculous! They wouldn't dare!
osip: Is it? Wouldn't they?
(*Building it.*)
It has also been rumored that the hotelkeeper intends to complain to the Mayor about us. He's telling everybody that you haven't paid him since we arrived two weeks ago. He also suspects that you and I are a couple of card cheats besides. He knows swindlers when he sees them, he says, and you look like a very clever one to him. So— your credit is discredited.
khlestakov: You seem to be deriving great pleasure in repeating all this to me. Go on, have your fun. Anything else?
osip: I am only telling you what I heard. The innkeeper says he has been victimized by his last deadbeat and intends to make an example of you. This time, he'll go straight to the Mayor and prosecute you to the fullest extent.

Khlestakov's entreaty for food is delivered slowly and in a low voice. . . .

But it bounds back up when Osip refuses to go for his dinner.

There is no anger between K. and Osip at any time. Impatience and criticism, yes, but never any bitter, fighting-mad anger. The relationship, to repeat, is that of a crafty but exhausted old nanny and her incorrigible charge.

KHLESTAKOV: It won't help you, Osip. You are still going down there and tell him to send up my dinner.

OSIP: And suppose he refuses?

KHLESTAKOV: I'll have to risk it.

(*His arrogance deflating.*)

I'm so terribly hungry I could risk anything. I tried to forget my appetite by going for a walk, but it clung to me. How can nothing cling to you so? Ah! If I hadn't squandered so much in Penza, we'd be home by now. But who would ever suspect that an infantry captain could cut cards like that? Cleaned me out in no time. If only I could have another go at him sometime! But what's the use? My luck's lousy these days, and this is a lousy town. You can't even hang up the grocer for anything. These provincial merchants don't trust anybody.

(*With a slight appeal in his voice.*)

So be a good fellow and see what you can do about some dinner.

(OSIP *sighs, shrugs and goes to the door. But as he opens it, the* WAITER *stands revealed, holding a bowl of cabbage soup covered with a piece of black bread.* OSIP *covers his embarrassment with silence.* KHLESTAKOV *becomes his lordly self again.*)

WAITER: Excuse me. I must have the wrong room.

KHLESTAKOV: Come in, my good man, come in.

(*The* WAITER *steps in.* OSIP *quickly closes the door.*)

Surely that is not my dinner you are bringing me.

WAITER: No, it is for a poor peasant down the hall somewhere. I couldn't remember the room.

KHLESTAKOV: Well, then, so long as you are already here, suppose you take my order for dinner. And rush it up, will you? I have some important business to attend to and I'm in an awful hurry, my good fellow.

(*The* WAITER *casts a baleful glance at* OSIP, *then steels himself.*)

WAITER: I'm sorry, sir, but my boss said he cannot let you have

After "My luck's lousy these days," K. whirls away from the table and is directly in front of the window, right, when he adds that it is a lousy town. He remains there until the Waiter enters.

On seeing food in the Waiter's hand, K.'s nostrils flare and he comes stage center with regal affability—until he gets a better look at the meager menu.

The Waiter always averts his eyes from K. when replying or addressing him, most likely a subconscious effort not to betray that he knows the truth about him. Instead, the Waiter looks at Osip or down at the floor.

On the Waiter's fabrication about the peasant, K. becomes the affable master again. He gives the Waiter the instructions about the dinner, then turns away as though to decide what might tempt his palate before placing the order.

The Waiter's rebuff stops K. midway. And on the mention of the

anything more on tick. He's even thinking of going to the Mayor and lodging a complaint against you.

OSIP: So you see, it wasn't entirely my imagination.

KHLESTAKOV: Quiet, you fool!

(*Reasonably to* WAITER.)

Why should he complain? You can see that I have to eat. Everybody has to eat. Would you want me to turn into a cadaver? Being hungry is no joke.

WAITER: I'm sorry, sir, but that's what the boss said: "No more food till his bill is paid up in full."

KHLESTAKOV: Couldn't you convince him otherwise?

WAITER: How?

KHLESTAKOV: Persuade him that eating is a very serious matter. Does he want his guests to die on him? Would it look good for his inn if people saw corpses being removed every day?

WAITER: I'll try, but I don't think it will do much good.

KHLESTAKOV: My friend, I have the utmost faith in your ability to make him see the light.

WAITER: Thank you. But in case I fail, couldn't I leave this cabbage soup and bread for your manservant here? I'll get another order for the poor peasant.

KHLESTAKOV: Absolutely not! Osip eats from my table or not at all!

WAITER: Yes, sir.

(*The* WAITER *casts a frustrated look at* OSIP, *who almost faints, his eyes glued on the food. The* WAITER *exits.* KHLESTAKOV *resumes pacing and talking.*)

KHLESTAKOV: And what will I do if he refuses me? In all my life I've never known such starvation!

OSIP: Maybe I ought to sneak out with some of your clothes and try to raise a little cash on them? On the way back, I could stop at the grocer's and—

Mayor, K. strides back and stands imperiously before the Waiter,
as if to make him cringe for his audacity. The Waiter tries to stand
his ground, but the menial's inbred respect for swank still comes
through.

Osip's line brings K. back to reality, so he attempts another
approach.

K.'s "Being hungry . . ." line is very sincere, and plaintive.

A reasoning, instructing quality serves K. best on this speech.

Osip's head and eyes go heavenward in despair.

KHLESTAKOV: Absolutely not! I'd rather die in this miserable place than return to St. Petersburg without my best clothes. Oh, what wouldn't I give if Joachim would rent me one of his best carriages again, and I could drive up to one of our neighbor's fancy homes, with the lamps aglow and you in best livery! I can just hear the commotion. "Who is this princely guest honoring us with a visit?" Then you would run up and announce, "Ivan Alexandrovich Khlestakov of St. Petersburg!" "Show him in without delay," they would say. "My house is always open to him." And soon the pretty daughters would materialize and goggle and giggle, and I would press their slender, scented fingers to my lips and sigh, "Enchanted, mademoiselle!" Ah! Meanwhile, I starve to death among these muzhiks here!

(*A knock on the door freezes them.* OSIP *almost tiptoes as he goes to open it a crack and peer out. Then he flings the door wide open to reveal the* WAITER *with a loaded trayful.*)

OSIP:
(*Like a footman.*)
Your dinner is ready to be served, sir.

(KHLESTAKOV *claps his hands and dances in glee as the* WAITER *enters and sets the tray down.*)

KHLESTAKOV:
(*Singing and dancing.*)
Dinner is ready to be served. Then serve it, my good fellow. Dinner is ready to be served. I'll eat it whether it's red or yellow!
　　OSIP: How did you ever manage it, my good friend?
　　WAITER: It wasn't easy, believe me.
　　(*To* KHLESTAKOV.)
My boss says this is positively the last time on credit.
　　KHLESTAKOV: Tell your boss I spit on him—twice! What did you bring us? That's more important.
　　WAITER: Some soup and a roast of beef.

Not death but the gay life—that is what his butterfly mind flits to on his mention of St. Petersburg. He sits on the table and lets his thoughts run riot.

K. reads the imagined parts loudly and with great pomp.

At the pretty daughters goggling and giggling, K. twinkles and twirls his toes in the air.

And on "starve to death," he brushes an angry palm across the empty table.

On seeing the loaded tray in the doorway, K. leaps off the table hopefully, but pauses momentarily like a pointer. After all, it might only be another guest's dinner and the Waiter merely came back to say "No."

K.'s dancing is done with a chair, and when finished, he sets the chair down before the table, which Osip moves into place. Then Osip helps the Waiter transfer the things from the tray. K., arms folded across his chest, stands watching like an overlord.

K. sits down before the table, rubbing his palms in great anticipation while Osip comes behind him and ties a napkin around his neck, European style.

KHLESTAKOV: Is that all? Hasn't he any more imagination than just two courses?

WAITER: Just two courses. That's all.

KHLESTAKOV: Ridiculous! What is he trying to do, humiliate me? Leave this here and go tell him it's not enough.

WAITER: He'll say it's too much and he'll make me bring it back.

KHLESTAKOV: The kitchen is loaded with food. I saw them preparing all sorts of delicacies as I passed through this morning. I even saw two chubby little men eating sturgeon in the dining room.

(*Lifts up some dish covers.*)

Where is the gravy?

WAITER: There isn't any.

KHLESTAKOV: No gravy, no fish, no chops? Why do you lie to me?

WAITER: We have them, but for other guests.

KHLESTAKOV: And am I not a guest? Am I not as good as they?

WAITER: Well, they *pay*.

KHLESTAKOV: Argue with a fool and you get a foolish answer.

(*Ladles out some soup and tastes it.*)

Is this what you call soup? It's Volga River water, heated up and laced with pepper. Take it away and bring me another kind.

WAITER: If I take it away, you'll never see it again. I know the boss.

(KHLESTAKOV *covers the tray with his hands.*)

KHLESTAKOV: All right, leave it. But I want you to know I'm not accustomed to such treatment.

(*Continues eating.*)

Great God in heaven, I've never tasted such horrible liquid! I hope the pigs here get better slop than this.

(*Finds something on his spoon.*)

What's this lump supposed to be—chicken?

(*Bites into it, makes a face.*)

When K. asks the Waiter what he brought, he is already looking under the lids.

The Waiter steps back before he replies.

The Waiter's replies are terse, but not sassy or bold. On the contrary, he gets frightened the more K. complains.

Here, especially, the Waiter avoids looking at K. when he answers him. His appeals are mostly to Osip, who would understand and sympathize.

Here the Waiter gives Osip the sympathy he wants himself, looking at Osip and nodding his head as if to say, "And this is what you have to put up with!" K. interprets the nods to mean that the Waiter is agreeing with *him*.

This entire eating scene affords us a wonderful opportunity to reveal the two contrasting and amusing levels on which the Khlestakov characterization should be played at all times: the *beggar on horseback*, the *starving* copy clerk aping what he imagines is the way of an aristocratic *gourmet*. Only a fool would dare to try it, and that is another of K.'s characteristics—foolish daring.

It's as hard as your boss's heart. Give me the roast beef, Osip. I've left you a little soup.

(*He digs into the meat while* OSIP *empties into his quivering lips what's left in the soup tureen.*)

What sort of meat is this, anyway? Are you sure it's roast beef?

WAITER: What does it taste like?

KHLESTAKOV: Like some uncured leather for boot soles.

(*But he continues eating ravenously.*)

That dog of an innkeeper, to feed his guests this garbage! One could get lockjaw from chewing it.

(*Uses his finger for a toothpick.*)

And once it gets into your teeth, it takes gunpowder to blast it out. A thief and a scoundrel, that's what your boss is!

(*Looks among the emptied dishes.*)

What else is there to eat?

WAITER: Nothing. You've had it all.

KHLESTAKOV: The dirty swindler! He might have included a taste of dessert, at least. Take it away and tell him I shall not pay for the meal—or anything!

(OSIP *helps the* WAITER *pile the dishes together. They exit while* KHLESTAKOV *continues his diatribe.*)

Did I say meal? Forgive the word. It wasn't even an appetizer. I might just as well not have eaten any of it. And what I did barely manage to get down will give me a bellyache during the night, I'm sure. Oh, the cheat, the rogue, the villain, the blackguard, the—

(OSIP *bursts back into the room, slams the door shut and leans against it breathlessly.*)

OSIP: The Mayor is here! Downstairs! I heard him asking for you!

KHLESTAKOV:

(*Apprehensive.*)

Oh, that foul, treacherous innkeeper! Then he did lodge a complaint against me, that Judas! How am I going to save a face if they throw me into jail? What will the townspeople think when they see the man who set the fashion for them these past two weeks, who had the merchants' daughters flirting with him and waiting for

Osip should turn away to gulp the soup, else K. will incur genuine audience hatred for treating another human being like that, even though it was the accepted master-servant attitude in the Russia of Czar Nikolai I.

———————————◆◆———————————

On Osip's line, "The Mayor is here!" (bottom of page), the atmosphere of Horror suddenly replaces that which opened this act. It takes command instantly, without transition, with no remaining vestiges from the preceding atmosphere.

Anton enters in the same atmosphere of horror. Both he and Khlestakov are virtually ready to jump out of their skins but fight hard to restrain themselves, turning the urge into a will impulse and subatmosphere. Later, when the Mayor offers K. money, it is still in this atmosphere. Its high tension begins to relax only when Anton says, "Helping visitors in this town is one of my duties" (page 180).

———————————◆◆———————————

The first half of K.'s second speech, until "any of it," is shouted out the door after Osip and the Waiter. Then he bangs the door shut and delivers the rest of the speech around the room, with attenuated beats between each word of the invective in the last sentence—as though he were searching for the appropriate names and making a sort of game of it.

Osip should repeat "The Mayor is here!" immediately after he says it the first time. And when he completes the announcement, K.'s bravado plummets.

him to pass every day—what will they say when they see me being led off in chains? Oh, the humiliation! To be treated like a common tradesman! I won't stand for it! I'll defy them, defy them all! I'll—

(KHLESTAKOV *advances to the door but pales and withdraws as he sees the knob slowly turn and the door slowly open.* ANTON *timidly enters,* DOB. *following and seeking refuge in his shadow. The two principals stand transfixed with fear of each other.* ANTON *finally manages a trembling salute.*)

ANTON: My greetings and compliments to you, sir.

KHLESTAKOV: And my respects and welcome to you, too, sir.
ANTON: I do hope you won't regard this as an intrusion.
KHLESTAKOV: I'm sure no harm has been done—
(*Under his breath.*)
As yet.

ANTON: As the Mayor of this progressive town, I make it my duty to see that the nobility and visitors of rank should be made comfortable and subjected to no inconveniences or indignities.

KHLESTAKOV:
(*Tentatively.*)
I—I don't know—what they told you about me. But—but—you understand—it wasn't my fault if—and I have every intention of— yes, discharging my obligations here. Yes—momentarily I expect a communication from home and—and—I shall settle everything, I assure you.
(*He gets braver as he sees* BOB. *peep in the door and withdraw in fright as their eyes meet.*)
But it's the innkeeper himself who's most responsible for my sternness and obstinacy. He has virtually starved me ever since I've been here. His soups could give one dropsy, and his meats are like the

And with Anton's salute, a heel-click, at the same time taking furtive little glances around the room to see where somebody else could be hiding and eavesdropping.

K. stands stiffly when replying to the greeting, observing the verbal formalities but not the physical. Anton accepts that as the prerogative of what he imagines is K.'s rank.

So Anton is further intimidated. He removes his hat and holds it before venturing his next speech.

The movements of the two antagonists are in slow tempo here. Everything is tentative, each is feeling for a way to reach the other. K.'s destination is the Mayor's heart; Anton's is the inspector's throat.

K. inches back during this explanation, as if he would like to hide or escape if it did not betray his fear.

Here K. decides to try blame and criticism, carefully noting the Mayor's reactions to this approach. He has now inched back as far as the bed.

leather seat under a sweaty coachman. Do you wonder why I am determined not to be hoodwinked?

ANTON:

(*Intimidated.*)

No, no. I was not aware of it and I am not to blame, believe me. I have always insisted that the meats in our markets be of the best quality. It is I who have been hoodwinked, I see, and I promise to remedy the situation at this inn. In the meantime, if you will allow me, I shall be happy to escort you to other accommodations.

KHLESTAKOV: How nicely you put it—"other accommodations." Such as what—your jail? But you don't fool me. You want to discredit me! And why? Because I found some things wrong here. But you'll regret it if you do. I'm still in the service of the government at St. Petersburg and I know all your tricks!

(*Pounds the table.*)

By what right do you confront me like this? The Minister himself will hear of it!

ANTON:

(*Quaking.*)

Please, sir. Have mercy! Don't believe everything those disreputable shopkeepers have told you. I am a good husband with a wife and little children. It would ruin me!

KHLESTAKOV: And to save your wife and children, you propose to take me elsewhere—to another jail. This inn is jail enough, thank you, and I refuse to leave no matter how badly it may turn out for you.

(BOB.'s *head pops in the door, soon disappears again.*)

ANTON:

(*Beside himself.*)

Please, sir. No man is infallible. Everyone is born into temptation, especially the poor. Not all of us can hold important government posts, and you know that the salary of a small-town mayor barely pays for his tea and sugar. If I have been accused of accepting

On "other accommodations," K. suspiciously moves further along the bed until he is stopped by the wall. There he mops his brow. Having retreated as far as he can, K. can do nothing now but advance, which he does during this speech. . . .

On "all your tricks!" he is back at the table, more militant for his bravery, so he pounds on it.

Now their respective fears and feelings of guilt impel them to hysterics. They are as near to involuntary tears as two men can come, as though each were contemplating his death sentence. Also, while Anton may quake, he does not shout; his "Have mercy!" speech has emphasis rather than volume. Before the man he believes to be the inspector, he is anything but the tyrant he was at the end of Act One.

bribes, I assure you they were only trifling things for the table or some inexpensive garments. And no matter what the scoundrels have told you, I don't beat widows just for nothing; it was to help her make something of herself instead of leading our soldiers astray —and some of our best citizens, too!

KHLESTAKOV: Your scoundrels are no concern of mine. As for flogging widows, I wouldn't advise you to try it on me. I'll pay that worthless innkeeper his money—under protest, but I'll pay it. At present, I happen to be out of cash. My money from St. Petersburg has been delayed—that's the only reason I put up with this place.

Right now I haven't a single penny to my name.

ANTON:

(*Trying humor.*)

Your highness is pulling my leg. But if you wish me to take it as a hint, I stand ready to oblige. Helping visitors in this town is one of my duties; and if it is money you need, I am at your service.

KHLESTAKOV: Yes, I do. Could you really lend me some? Then I could get that miserable innkeeper off my neck. Two hundred rubles, perhaps? Even less would be appreciated.

(ANTON *takes a packet of bills from his pocket and hands them to* KHLESTAKOV *with a bow.*)

ANTON: At least two hundred rubles, sir. But don't be surprised if the count is more like four hundred.

K. is confused by Anton's recitation. Why is the Mayor telling him all this before arresting him? Is he hinting that he can be bribed, or is it his indirect way of telling him what punishment is in store?

Having no money to bribe him with, and fearing the punishment, K. starts backing up again. Reaching the wall once more, he presses against it as he attempts to explain his situation.

———————

The third atmosphere of the second act lap-dissolves in, as it were, when Khlestakov takes the money (bottom of page). It may be described as a courtly, aesthetic, high-life kind of atmosphere: calmness in the highest degree, fine manners except when dealing with underlings, a quality of Mozartian music. It continues thus until the end of the second act.

———————

Before delivering the last sentence of the first speech, "Right now . . .", K. takes his wallet out of his inside breast pocket, opens it and inverts it to show Anton that it is empty.

Anton is just as confused by K.'s retreat. Ah, that clever one, he thinks, pretending he's timid and trying to trap me into offering a bribe. Though still fearful, he has no choice but to risk a gentle probe: "Helping visitors . . ." etc.

The sight of the money draws K. forward like a magnet, his eyes glued to the pretty paper as though it were hypnotizing him.

K. starts to count the money, but stops when Anton assures him that it is more than he bargained for. Anton chuckles self-consciously, disarmingly, more to hide his inner feeling of success.

KHLESTAKOV: I'm greatly indebted to you, Mr. Mayor. I'll return it immediately I get home. You *are* a gentleman, and I am

happy to see that relations between us are so vastly improved. Osip! Fetch that insolent waiter at once!

(OSIP *exits.*)

Why is everybody standing? Please be seated, gentlemen. We need not be ceremonious with each other now.

ANTON: Nevertheless, I feel that we should observe the amenities. When a distinguished visitor wishes to enjoy our town—shall we say incognito?—far be it from us to discomfit him.

KHLESTAKOV: No trouble at all. I'm delighted you've come, gentlemen. Do sit down, please.

(ANTON *sits in the chair.* DOB. *negotiates the edge of the bed.* BOB. *peers in again and is pleased with the progress.*)

ANTON: Peter Dobchinsky here is one of our more prosperous landowners.

(KHLESTAKOV *bows to him.*)

We frequently go on these little strolls together. Other mayors may not concern themselves so much with the problems and welfare of their communities, but we like to go around and look in on our various citizens. Pure Christian good fellowship goes beyond official duty, you see. And I must say that occasionally we are rewarded for our efforts, such as coming into the inn quite by accident and making the acquaintance of a personage like yourself.

KHLESTAKOV: Your graciousness is reciprocated. I must confess that without your help, I might have been stuck here for longer than I planned. An innkeeper who insists on having money will brook no explanations, not even if you bared your whole life and soul.

ANTON: May I ask, sir, what place you plan to—ah—*visit* next?

KHLESTAKOV: A village I come from, in the Government of Saratov.

K. shakes hands with him to express his gratitude. Each man now adds a quality of joy and relief to his character, but each is still dominated by his own main objective.

When K. orders Osip to bring the Waiter, he surreptitiously gives him a riffling glance at the bills, then stuffs them into his wallet like a lump of clay.

After K.'s "be seated" speech, Dob. gets a chair for Anton and places it near him. Anton pretends to ignore it, waves Dob. back.

Anton sits on K.'s second request. But when he sees K. still standing, he rises politely and pushes the chair back to K. Dob. solves the amenities by bringing the second chair for K., then goes to sit on the bed himself.

K. forces a little laugh after Anton's "a personage like yourself." Anton echoes the laugh.

Anton's "May I ask . . ." is his second gentle probe, the first having worked so well. What he means to say is: "Now that you've got your money, when are you getting out of here?"

ANTON: The *Government* of Saratov, no less. Hm-hm! That's quite a trip. But I suppose one doesn't mind distances when one travels for—shall we say pleasure?

KHLESTAKOV: No, my father has summoned me. He's disappointed because I haven't moved up as fast in the service as he would like me to. Thinks you can win promotions every day. I'd like to see how far *he'd* get in a government office.

ANTON: Then you won't be staying there too long.

KHLESTAKOV: Not any longer than I can help. Living among the peasantry suffocates me. Whatever my fate in the service, being in St. Petersburg is reward enough.

ANTON: Quite true, quite true. Even in a place like this, no matter how hard you work in it to serve your country, no matter how many sleepless nights you spend, no matter how much you give of yourself—the reward always remains an unknown quantity.

(*Looks around.*)

At least in St. Petersburg the rooms are better than this, and less damp.

KHLESTAKOV: And less dirty, and less bug-ridden, and less gloomy. Why, this inn doesn't even provide a candle to read or write by at night.

ANTON: It's outrageous! . . . If you wouldn't think it presumptuous of me, I'd like to suggest—

KHLESTAKOV: What?

ANTON: Of course, it is nothing worthy of you, and I'm sure it doesn't begin to compare with what you have in St. Petersburg, but—

KHLESTAKOV: But what?

ANTON: There is a beautiful room at my home. Nothing pretentious, you understand, but clean and sunny and most comfortable. If my suggestion doesn't offend you—

KHLESTAKOV: Offend me? Nothing would give me greater pleasure at this moment than to be out of this cesspool. I accept your most generous invitation!

ANTON: My wife and I will both be delighted beyond measure

Again an example of the minimal two-level performance. Anton is not merely making polite conversation. He is probing for chinks in K.'s armor, feeling for soft spots in his back at which to make the annihilating stabs if he has to.

The afterthought "the rooms are better," etc., is really the forethought of this speech. That's what Anton intended when he started it; that is his way of launching the minor objective of bringing K. to his home.

After K.'s "But what?" Anton rises for his next speech, standing behind his chair with his hands resting on it. This is an accent of the main objective of luring and snaring the menace.

On "I accept . . ." rises and offers his hand. They shake each other's hands in a kind of double handclasp.

to have such a distinguished personage as our guest. I say this not out of flattery; that is not one of our indulgences. We are simply very hospitable people by nature.

KHLESTAKOV: Your candor and kindheartedness touch me deeply. I dislike two-faced people intensely. All I ask of life is sincere friendship and respect.

(OSIP *enters, followed by the* WAITER. BOB. *is seen outside when the door is open.*)

WAITER: You sent for me, sir?
KHLESTAKOV: Yes. I want my bill.

WAITER: I brought you several bills already.
KHLESTAKOV: Who can remember your illiterate scribblings. How much do I owe?
WAITER: Let me see. Dinner the first day. Then only salmon the second. Then—then everything else was on credit.
KHLESTAKOV: I am not supposed to keep track of everything; you are. What does it all come to?
WAITER: I'll go to my boss and find out.
ANTON: You shouldn't have to bother yourself with such paltry details, sir. Please let me attend to it.
(*To* WAITER)
Tell your boss I said the money will be sent to him. Now vanish!
KHLESTAKOV: How simple. Thank you, sir.

(KHLESTAKOV *pockets the money. The* WAITER *exits. Again* BOB. *takes advantage of the open door to stick his head in and out.*)

ANTON: And now, sir, may I suggest a tour of inspection of our town and our leading institutions?
KHLESTAKOV: Is there something special going on just now?
ANTON: Oh, I thought you'd like to see what models of management everything here is. Especially our charity institutions.

With his request for the bill, K. takes out his lumpy wallet and places it on the table.

The puzzled Waiter looks from K. to Anton, back to K., then delivers the line more to Anton.

K.'s "I am not supposed to . . ." speech is flung at the Waiter loudly and haughtily.

Anton stamps his foot at the Waiter on "Now vanish!" as if at a barking dog.

Anton approaches K. at the table and stands there with grand-society geniality while suggesting a tour of the town. This is an-other accent of the main objective, enticing and nullifying the menace.

KHLESTAKOV: Well, if you think so, of course.

ANTON: Our district school and its unique pedagogical methods might also be of special interest to you.

KHLESTAKOV: They might, mightn't they?

ANTON: On the way, we could drop by our police headquarters and town jail.

KHLESTAKOV:

(*Swallowing hard.*)

We could? You're sure it's not another trick to get me into your jail?

ANTON:

(*Laughing.*)

Your highness is having his little joke. . . . It's always fascinating to strangers to see how the prisoners are disciplined.

KHLESTAKOV: I have a good imagination. So if it's all the same to you, we'll pass that one up.

ANTON: As you wish. Will you ride in your own carriage, or will you do me the honor to come with me in my phaeton?

KHLESTAKOV: Your phaeton will do nicely, thank you.

ANTON:

(*To* DOB.)

You'll make room for his highness, Peter, won't you?

DOB.:

(*Bowing.*)

He is most welcome to my place. I need the walk back, anyway.

ANTON: Ah, yes, you are a fast walker, aren't you? Well, let's see how fast you can deliver a couple of notes for me.

(*To* KHLESTAKOV.)

May I write a line to my wife and prepare her for our honored guest?

KHLESTAKOV: Please don't let her go to any unnecessary trouble for me. The ink is there, but I'm sorry that I used up all

my paper. Ah, here is an old bill.

ANTON: That will do, thank you.

K. would rather go gambling or wenching, but . . .

At the mention of jail, K. takes a backward step and a glance at Osip. The old suspicion returns. He tries to make light of it.

Before answering Anton's question, K. glances at Osip for his opinion. Osip's lips form a silent "Phaeton" behind Anton's back.

After K.'s acceptance of the phaeton, Osip pours water into the washbasin near the bed and to the left of the door, and gets a towel ready. K. goes to wash.

Briefing Dob. on delivering the notes for him is a continuation of the Act One conspiracy, so is conveyed in an intimate tone.

During this speech about not going to any unnecessary trouble, K. is drying his hands and going about finding pen and ink, placing them on the table for Anton.

After K. gives Anton the old bill, he returns to the basin to resume his ablutions.

(*Continues talking as he writes.*)

I'll also write to the manager of our charities and tell him to have a nice lunch ready for us and a bottle of imported wine. The local vintages can floor a mastodon. However, you may try our local Madeira if you wish; you're not a true tourist until you do.

(*Finished writing,* ANTON *hands the notes to* DOB.)

Now your fast walking will not be in vain. Hurry away, my friend.

(DOB. *bows to* KHLESTAKOV *and turns to go, but before he can reach the door, it suddenly swings open and* BOB. *falls in on his face. There are surprised reactions.* KHLESTAKOV *helps him up and* BOB. *grins sheepishly.* ANTON *scowls at him.*)

KHLESTAKOV: Are you hurt? What were you doing out there, anyway?

BOB.: Just a bump on my nose. I was waiting for my friend here, Peter Dobchinsky. I'm Peter Bobchinsky.

(DOB. *exits hurriedly, as though to disown him.*)

ANTON: Oh, it's nothing, nothing, I'm sure. Let's go, sir. Your servant can bring the luggage over later.

(*To* OSIP.)

Gather up your master's things, my good man, and take them to my house. Everybody knows where the Mayor's house is. . . . After you, sir.

(*Steps aside for* KHLESTAKOV *to exit, and before he does so himself, he turns on* BOB.)

You dunderhead! A fine time you picked to make a spectacle of yourself. You looked like a sprawling octopus!

(*He exits,* BOB. *following.*)

SECOND ACT CURTAIN

K. finishes washing while Anton is writing. Osip then brushes
K.'s clothes, drapes the overcoat over his master's shoulder (the
dandy's style of the time), gets his hat and cane. K. takes the gloves
from inside the hat, places them in his left hand; with his right
hand, he next puts on his hat and takes the cane. Osip then goes to
a place near the door, standing ready to open it for their exit.

Handing the notes to Dob. one at a time, Anton signals with one
finger on the first one, with two on the second. Dob nods, steals a
glance at K. to see if they were observed.

For added emphasis, Anton should also shake his head at Bob.
in controlled anger but with more apparent disgust.

Having put his hat down before writing the note, Anton is about
to walk out without it. Bob. taps him on the shoulder and stops
him at the door, long enough to run and bring the hat to him.
Anton snatches the hat and claps it on his head before he bawls
the "You dunderhead!" line at him.

[ACT THREE]

The parlor of the Mayor's home.

Discovered are ANNA *and* MARYA, *in virtually the same positions near the window as when the curtain went down on Act One.*

ANNA: It's over an hour now and we're still waiting! Waiting because of your stupid little vanities. It was not enough to get all dressed up so early in the morning, but you had to fuss and delay with everything you put on.
(*Looks out the window again.*)
It's maddening! Nobody on the street, as though the world had come to an end just to spite us.

MARYA: Oh, Mama, why do you torture yourself? Somebody will be along in a minute, I'm sure.

ANNA: Avdotya should have been back long ago. Where *is* that sow?

(ANNA *comes downstage;* MARYA *replaces her at the window.*)

MARYA: She probably couldn't find them.

ANNA: More than likely she's in the back room with the wine-shop keeper.

MARYA:
(*Looking out.*)
Wait! I think I see someone.

(ANNA *quickly joins her at the window.*)

ANNA: Where, where? . . . You're imagining things again.

MARYA: There on the other side. He's crossing over.

ANNA: Yes, it *is* somebody. It looks like a short man in a frock coat, but with my eyes I don't recognize him.

The atmosphere at the beginning of the third act is one of Despair; the game is lost. Anna and Marya may test their opening lines in harmony with it, adjusting tone level and movements as necessary.

Now add the quality of a staccato tempo and the atmosphere of this opening scene is set until the entrance of Peter Dobchinsky (page 194).

———————◆◆————————

Leaving the window, Anna may sit at the table, disgusted, her fingers tapping her aggravation. Marya contrasts her mother's little snarls with a sighing, soothing quality.

Anna's excitement and inner tempo are only radiated. Outwardly, her words and movements are still deliberate. She is still maintaining her dignity, still holding herself erect.

MARYA:

(*Let down.*)

Oh, Mama, it's only Dobchinsky.

ANNA: It can't be Dobchinsky. He went off in the phaeton with your father.

MARYA: But it is, I tell you, it is.

ANNA:

(*Peering hard.*)

For once I think you're right. It's Dobchinsky's trot.

(*Opens the window and calls out.*)

Hey, there! Dobchinsky! Can't you walk any faster? Where are they all? What happened? . . . He's very severe? . . . Who, the inspector or my husband? . . . What? I can't hear you! . . . Don't wave a piece of paper at me! Say something!

MARYA: He's says he's coming in.

ANNA: I know he's coming in. But why can't he tell me from out there, after I've been waiting so long, the stupid little frog!

MARYA: Maybe it's something confidential.

ANNA: Nothing is confidential in this town. Everybody knows even how you waste your time primping and prinking for the Postmaster.

(DOB. *enters.* ANNA *is upon him at once.*)

You should be ashamed of yourself. All of you fled as though from the cholera and nobody had the decency to tell me where you were going and why. I should think the godmother of both your children deserved more consideration.

DOB.: Believe me, my dear godmother, that I am out of breath from running to pay my respects to you. Good afternoon, Marya.

MARYA: How are you, Peter?

ANNA: Don't waste time with salutations. What happened at the inn; where are they now?

DOB.: This note from your husband will explain everything.

ANNA: Never mind my husband and his notes. Who is the man you all went to see? Is he a general?

DOB.: No, I don't think he's a general—we haven't found out

Anna is almost in tears with impatience.

———◆◆———

With the entrance of Peter Dobchinsky, the atmosphere of staccato despair, still maintained, merges with that of Curiosity. It obtains until Anna calls "Mishka! Come at once!" (page 198) and vanishes there.

———◆◆———

everything yet—but he looks and acts every inch a general: cultured, dignified, important!

ANNA: Then you're sure it's the one described in the letter.

DOB.: No doubt about it. The same one Peter Bobchinsky and I first discovered.

ANNA: Why must you torture me with details? Just tell me what happened.

DOB.: Thank the good Lord everything is all right now—I think. But he treated us rather sternly at first. He was angry because the inn was so mismanaged and the food so bad, and he thought Anton was in league with the innkeeper and wanted to put him in jail for complaining about the service and demanding credit, which was his due as a government official from St. Petersburg, you understand.

ANNA: Anton should have thrown the innkeeper into jail instead.

DOB.: Not a bad idea, if only for those prices he charges for his sturgeon. Anyway, when Anton convinced him of his innocence, and offered to make amends on behalf of the town, he became much friendlier and everything went smoothly. Now they're off on a tour of the charity institutions.

ANNA: I don't care about all that. What I want to know is what he looks like. Is he young, old, handsome, ugly; is he tall, short? Those are the things that matter in an official.

DOB.: Oh, he's young, all right—about twenty-three or four. But he talks with the authority of a veteran, and moves with such distinction.

ANNA: Yes, yes, but what about his looks—is he blond or brunet, is he—

DOB.: More on the chestnut side, I would say; and his eyes are so quick and penetrating they give you the shivers.

ANNA: That tells me exactly nothing. Maybe my husband has more to say.

(*Grabs the note out of* DOB.'s *hand, reads.*)

Anna is absolutely without interest in Dob. or what happened to her husband, so listens rather impatiently to *h*is speech. Her sole objective in the scene is to find out how *socially* prominent the St. Petersburg visitor is and how *attractive* he is.

On Dob.'s "twenty-three or four," Marya gives a trilling little laugh. Anna shushes her; it's so undignified.

Marya complies with a little shiver.

"My Dearest: A hasty note to advise you that we are not in the clear yet, but trusting in God's mercy, two dill pickles, one-half portion of caviar, one ruble twenty—"

(*Looks up, bewildered.*)

Has he gone crazy?

DOB.: There wasn't any other paper. It's an old bill from the inn.

ANNA: Oh.

(*Turns the bill over and continues reading.*)

"Everything will come off smoothly. We will have a distinguished guest, so fix up the room with the ocher wallpaper. Nothing extra for dinner because we'll have a big lunch with Artemy at the hospital. Only make sure Abdulin supplies some Rostov. Arrange for guest's manservant. I kiss your hand, my dearest, and pray." . . . Good grief, he doesn't give us much time, does he?

(*Hurries to the door and calls.*)

Mishka! Come at once!

(*Returns to* DOB.)

Look at all the time wasted. Couldn't you have delivered this sooner?

DOB.: First I had to bring a note to Artemy, to alert him about the lunch and the Madeira, and getting the hospital shipshape. Now I'd better get back over there and—

(*Smacks his lips.*)

and see how the inspection is getting on.

ANNA: Of course. God forbid you should miss free food and drink.

DOB.: Good-bye, Anna Andreyevna. Good-bye, Marya Antonovna.

MARYA: Good-bye, Peter, and thank you.

After Anna calls for Mishka, the succeeding atmosphere might best be described as a kind of charade, a preparation for the festivities, a children's game. It disappears when the women exit to dress up (page 202).

———◆◆———

All heads are close together when Anna reads the letter. She holds herself erect while reading it, intones it impersonally.

It is only when Anna has finished reading the letter that she responds to it as though it is meant for her. Her outward tempo increases against her will.

Anna sits on the sofa as she sarcastically dismisses Dob. Marya remains standing.

(DOB. *exits as* MISHKA, *stepping aside to let him pass, enters.*)

ANNA: Mishka, as soon as Avdotya returns, send her down to Abdulin to bring back a case of his oldest Rostov claret. Then I want you to prepare the ocher room for a distinguished guest.

MISHKA: I know who it is. Avdotya told me.

ANNA: That harlot! Why didn't she tell *us?* We've been waiting on pins and needles. I'll give it to her! Where is she?

MISHKA: She got waylaid somewhere, so now she's having a nap.

ANNA: Just as I guessed! Well, she'd better be up in time to fetch the wine and help me with dinner or out she goes on her big red nose, bag and baggage! . . . And speaking of baggage . . . after you've made the room ready, be on the lookout for our guest's manservant and give him a hand, and find a place for him to sleep.

(MISHKA *nods and exits.*)

Now, Marya, my dear, if we don't want this big-city swell making fun of us, we'd better dress to receive him. Your little blue gown with the ruffles would be most becoming for the occasion.

MARYA: Oh, Mama! You know I abhor that blue dress. The flowered print is much more becoming to me.

ANNA: Not that horrible thing! Really! If I had said the flowered print, you'd have said the blue gown. But just because I want to wear my strawberry, you want to clash with your print.

MARYA: But Mama, dear, your strawberry doesn't suit you at all, but you insist on wearing it whenever I select my flowered print.

ANNA: And why, may I ask, doesn't the strawberry suit me?

MARYA: Because it's a better color for people with dark eyes.

---•◦•---

After Mishka's exit, Anna breaks the atmosphere as soon as she begins her discussion of dresses. This is no longer a charade or a children's game. It is developing into a Contest for a man, a Quarrel over who is to attract him. Now there is some urgency in Anna's voice, but outwardly she is mostly calm and dignified. It is more accent than atmosphere.

---•◦•---

On "little blue gown with the ruffles," Marya nestles up to Anna like a cat, her feet under her on the sofa, a feline precaution before disagreeing with her.

Anna stresses the word "because" in criticism, to point up Marya's contrariness.

ANNA: And what are mine, pink? When I have my fortune told, isn't it the queen of clubs that always represents me?

MARYA: I should think it would be the queen of hearts.

ANNA: What are you saying? The queen of hearts is for flirts and cocottes! Queen of hearts indeed!

(ANNA *exits with a flounce,* MARYA *following. After a brief stage wait, the door to the guest room opens and* MISHKA *sweeps out some dirt, looks around, then sweeps it under the parlor carpet.* OSIP, *struggling with two heavy suitcases, enters in time to catch him.*)

OSIP: I know, I know. It's good for the moths. Well, it is. They breed much better. . . . Now, where do I put these?

MISHKA: I've just swept out a place for them.

OSIP: Good.

(*Sets suitcases down.*)

I'll rest a minute first. The emptier the stomach, the heavier the load.

MISHKA: When is the general coming?

OSIP: General? Which one?

MISHKA: The one you take orders from.

OSIP: Who said he was a general?

MISHKA: Isn't he?

OSIP: Oh, sure—in reverse.

MISHKA: That means he outranks a regular general.

OSIP: You won't think differently when you see him.

MISHKA: No wonder they're making such a fuss about him.

OSIP: Are they? Then how about paying a little attention to me, too—like getting me something to eat?

MISHKA: Dinner for you and your master isn't ready yet.

Marya challenges the "queen of clubs" statement by getting to her knees on the sofa and looking into Anna's eyes as she delivers her "queen of hearts" line. At this, Anna pushes her away and gets up indignantly, pacing through her next speech until she exits majestically. Marya bounces off the sofa and dance-swirls after her.

———◆———

The third full atmosphere begins with Osip's entrance. It is a mixture of suspicion, spying and caution. Its tempo inclines to legato. It prevails until Osip exits after Mishka (page 204).

———◆———

Osip sits down after "rest a minute," really tired. Mishka crouches down beside him to continue the conversation.

Osip puts a friendly arm around Mishka's shoulder before asking for something to eat.

osip: Between you and me, I don't eat much of what he eats. Isn't there something simple in the kitchen?

mishka: If you wouldn't mind some cabbage borsch, kasha and bublichki . . .

osip: Well—I'll tell you what: you help me put the luggage into the room while I think about it.

(mishka *hefts the suitcases and carries them into the guest room.*)

mishka: When you decide, there's a door in this room that leads to the kitchen.

(osip *puffs out his chest and, one arm akimbo, struts after him.*)

osip: I'll follow you, never fear.

(osip *exits, shutting the door behind him. . . .* tunov *and* ilyitch *fling open the doors to the street, enter and stand to each side as* khlestakov *struts in, much like* osip *strutted out, followed by* anton, artemy, luka, dobchinsky *and* bobchinsky, *whose nose now sports a patch of adhesive.* anton *detects a piece of paper that Mishka failed to sweep under and stabs a finger toward it.* tunov *and* ilyitch *collide in their haste to scoop it up.*)

khlestakov: Model institutions, all of them. And a most enjoyable tour, I must say, most enjoyable. Other towns showed me nothing.

anton: Perhaps it's because in other towns, the public servants are more concerned with serving themselves than the public. Here, I demand that our sole thought shall be to merit the government's faith in us to preserve the ideals of law, order and progress.

Osip gets confidential when explaining his diet, drawing Mishka toward him, establishing the camaraderie of the servant classes.

———•◦•———

The fourth atmosphere suffusing the third act begins with Khlestakov's entrance. It is definitely on the staccato side and has the tension of a gambling house in which a huge fortune is being wagered. Which will it be for gambler and house—win or lose?

In this atmosphere, K. predominates. He is the big, reckless operator in the spotlight, the gambler gone mad. The others are not only subservient to him but have no independence and no individualities of their own; they only try to acquiesce and blend with him. When K. asks a question, they reply in the same tone; when he changes his tone, so do they, trying to merge their personalities with his. They also react to his every movement in the same way.

Inwardly, the Mayor resents all the others; he seethes when they try to say something to K. or answer his questions; he feels that only he should be their spokesman and in the vanguard.

Artemy, Anton's chief rival for the great man's attention, always tries for proximity to K., but the Mayor constantly maneuvers him back.

This fourth atmosphere lasts until K.'s exit (page 218).

———•◦•———

On Anton's "other towns" speech, K. has wandered over to the mirror. Discovering himself in it, he starts to preen. Also during it, Artemy comes out of the group and tries to get a word in, but Anton pushes him away.

KHLESTAKOV: And so you do. That was a most delicious lunch. I'm afraid I overindulged. Does the staff lunch like that every day?

ANTON: Only on special occasions, to honor a special guest.

KHLESTAKOV: You have. I eat to live, but I live to eat well.

ANTON: Well put, your highness.

KHLESTAKOV: That divine fish—what did you call it?

ARTEMY:

(*Taking the bows.*)

Labardan.

KHLESTAKOV: Heavenly! Fancy finding something so rare in a hospital. It was the hospital we dined at, wasn't it?

ARTEMY: Yes, your highness, at one of the charities under my supervision.

KHLESTAKOV: Of course. Beds all over the place. I don't remember seeing many patients, but I suppose they were there.

ARTEMY: Only about a dozen. We don't pamper them. Cure them fast and discharge them fast, that's been our policy since I took over the management. We tolerate no malingerers.

(ANTON *motions dismissal to* ILYITCH *and* TUNOV. *They exit.*)

When K. mentions the lunch, Artemy wants to press forward again, but a threatening look from Anton restrains him.

———— •═• ————

QUALITIES to watch for in this major scene are:

Khlestakov gets progressively crazier in his descriptions, love-making overtures to Anna and Marya and other actions, until he is helped off to his room.

Anton is concerned that the others in the room may say the wrong thing; therefore, each is a menace and he prevents their speeches.

Artemy is subservient, fearful, crushed, overwhelmed along with Anton. Whenever Anton speaks, he has the same urge.

Luka is pale, bewildered, almost lifeless. Psychologically, he tries to vanish.

Anna blooms when K.'s hands touch hers, radiates her passion, is ready to give herself to him.

Marya observes and absorbs everything. Absorbing K. becomes her objective.

Bob. and Dob. are agape with interest, exchange awed glances a few times, make themselves insignificant in the background.

———— •═• ————

Artemy won't be restrained any longer. He rushes up to K. to say his "Labardan."

K. rewards Artemy with a couple of pats on the shoulder. Anton's eyes flash daggers at Artemy.

Artemy starts moving back on his second speech, drawing K. after him and away from Anton. Not giving up, Anton follows behind K., waiting for his turn to brag about himself.

ANTON: And the hospital is only one of a Mayor's responsibilities. It's enough to make your brain weary just thinking about them. There's sanitation, alteration, reparation—God only knows what else, but I thank Him for His help in keeping things going smoothly. May the day never come when I stop my devotion to duty, nor the night when I do not ask myself, "Is the government satisfied with my sacrifices?" I am not motivated so much by whether the government will reward me or not, but by my desire to do better than the average Mayor and know that my conscience is clear. Honors are vain and shallow compared to the peace and contentment that comes from having served your country well.

KHLESTAKOV: Quite true, quite true. I like a bit of philosophy now and then. It's so much more refreshing than ordinary prose or poetry. But tell me, what do you do for entertainment here? Are there any card clubs about?

ANTON:

(*Suspicious, guarded.*)

Well, I suppose some card-playing does go on, privately, in some lower-class homes. But there are no card clubs as such. In fact, there aren't any clubs of any kind here. I myself wouldn't know a queen of clubs from a queen of hearts, and I am not in sympathy with those who waste their time on them.

KHLESTAKOV: It's not such a waste of time when you win— ahem—I'm told.

(ANNA *and* MARYA, *dressed in their finest, enter.*)

ANTON: With your permission, sir, allow me to present my family—my wife and daughter.

KHLESTAKOV:

(*With a bow.*)

A distinct pleasure, ladies, to meet you.

ANNA: Our pleasure is even greater in meeting such a distinguished guest.

At the sound of Anton's voice behind him, K. turns so suddenly that Anton now has to start backing up.

K. sits on the arm of the first chair he comes to, swinging a leg while forcing himself to listen to Anton's tedious recital.

K.'s "Quite true" response is sudden and loud, as if to prove that he has been listening. Luka, Bob. and Dob. are startled by it and move a little nearer to K., as though it were his command to them.

All but K. instantly become aware of the ladies' entrance and clear a path for them to K.

When Anton announces Anna and Marya, K. looks up at him stupidly. Anton has to repeat it, gesturing toward the women. K. gets to his feet to acknowledge them. Anna and Marya move center as if they were already favorite ladies at court. K. sidles over to them, waits for them to present hands to be kissed, Russian society style (the man bows with one foot behind the other, holding the position while taking the lady's hand and kissing it). The women present their hands.

KHLESTAKOV:
(*Grandly.*)
You flatter me. Mine is the greater pleasure, I'm sure.

ANNA: It's most kind of you to be so condescending and com-
plimentary. Please do sit down.

KHLESTAKOV: Why sit when just standing near you is joy
enough? After you, please.

(*He gestures her to the sofa, is instantly seated beside her.*)
But since you insist, I am most happy to join you.

ANNA: Forgive me for reveling in your compliments, but the
truth is I enjoy them.

(*With a glance at* ANTON.)
They are so rare in a town like ours. After the courtesy and culture
of your capital, traveling in the hinterlands must be a great hardship.

KHLESTAKOV: Hardship is an understatement. When one is
accustomed to the—*je ne sais quoi*—of society's upper strata, and
then is subjected to ill-kept inns, indignities and abysmal stupidity
. . . But no matter . . .

(*Regarding her suavely, unctuously.*)
Sitting beside you now is compensation enough for all I've endured.

ANNA: How terrible to have suffered so.

KHLESTAKOV: This moment has made me forget everything.

ANNA: You mustn't say such things. I don't deserve them.

KHLESTAKOV: Ah, but you do, you do.

ANNA: I am only the wife of a small-town Mayor.

KHLESTAKOV: Oh, don't misunderstand me. Small towns have
their charm, too. Hills and dales and brooks, and the like. No com-
parison, of course, to St. Petersburg; but, then, there is only one St.
Petersburg. Ah, such life, such gaiety, such splendor! Don't think

I am only a copy clerk because I'm dazzled by it all and rave so
about it. On the contrary. The head of the branch of our service
and I are on most intimate terms. Always has me to dinner and
consults me on matters that need looking into. He even offered me

Anna starts moving, fanning herself, Marya with her and K. mincing alongside them until the sofa is reached.

When K. gestures Anna to the sofa, she draws Marya to the far side of her, sits down and leaves room for K. to join her. Marya has to look around her mother's expansive bosom to see K. when he finally sits down.

Anton takes a standing position near the sofa, half turned so that he can be in K.'s view and still keep an eye on the others.

The entrance of Anna and Marya has intensified K.'s irrationality. Now he speaks part of a sentence to Anna, the rest to Anton; then begins a sentence to her again, finishes it to nobody in particular, goes blank, stares at Luka, who only draws away in fear.

K. tries in various stages to reach Anna's hand, and when he does, he only timidly plays his fingertips on it.

Anna's responses are an invitation to K. to move closer. Anton, seeing that K. is afraid, gives him a smiling nod to indicate that it's quite all right. Inwardly, Anton would even give *all* of Anna to K. if that would win the latter's favor.

On K.'s first "St. Petersburg," there is a pause. It is the beginning of a climax and everybody reacts and prepares to listen. The pitch starts going up, and up.

K.'s "copy clerk" line is delivered to Anton—*he* would understand.

a promotion as a college inspector, but I've had enough of colleges, thank you, I told him. . . .

(*Looks around.*)

Why is everybody standing? Please sit down, gentlemen.

ANTON—ARTEMY—LUKA: We respect our differences in rank. It is an honor to a distinguished guest.

We are quite comfortable, thank you.

KHLESTAKOV: Rank or no rank, do be seated.

(*The three,* BOB. *and* DOB. *find seats.*)

Ceremony does not appeal to me. I prefer going and coming unobtrusively, but no such luck, it seems. The moment I appear anywhere, they discomfit me with attention. It's embarrassing, always to be pointed out as somebody important and be deferred to. Not long ago, I was even mistaken for a commander-in-chief, and the soldiers rushed up and presented arms.

ANNA: How exciting it must be, nevertheless!

KHLESTAKOV: Oh, sometimes it is, when your adorers are lovely actresses. I write vaudeville sketches for them occasionally, more for my own amusement than for money. But I prefer the company of literary men such as Pushkin, who is also a devoted friend. He's quite a character, that Pushkin. Most imaginative and creative. It probably stems from his Negro ancestry, you know.

ANNA: How thrilling it must be to be able to write! Do you contribute to the magazines and newspapers, too?

KHLESTAKOV: Oh, yes, many of them. I also have several major works to my credit—*The Marriage of Figaro, Robert the Devil, Norma*—the rest of the titles escape me. It all came about through a chance meeting with the *régisseur* of the St. Petersburg Art Theatre, and he asked me to try my hand at it. Next morning, he had his first operatic story, much to everybody's amazement. I am fortunate in having a nimble wit. Everything you've read under the name of Count Artzybasheff is mine, too.

ANNA: Then *you* are Count Artzybasheff!

KHLESTAKOV: One of my *noms de plume,* if you'll pardon the confession.

ANNA: I shall never forget your *The Belated Executioner*.

KHLESTAKOV: Yes. Fetched me fifty thousand, that one.

MARYA: Forgive me, Mama, but isn't that book by Yuri Pavlevsky?

ANNA: There you go contradicting me again, and offending our honored guest.

KHLESTAKOV: No offense.

(*To* MARYA)

The one you read was probably Pavlevsky's. But there is another *The Belated Executioner* which preceded his, and that is the one I wrote.

ANNA: You see? Yours is the one *I* read. Utterly devastating!

KHLESTAKOV: Confidentially, literature is my main source of income. One cannot prosper in government service and maintain such a home as mine, one of the finest in all St. Petersburg. You must all call on me next time you visit, and attend one of my grand balls.

ANNA: Ah, yes, I've heard about those fabulous St. Petersburg balls.

KHLESTAKOV: St. Petersburg is a round robin of balls every night of the week. Mine especially do me proud. The bill for watermelons alone is nearly a thousand rubles. The soups are imported directly from Paris, tureens and all, and you never smelled such heavenly aromas. It's like walking down Montmartre itself. Then there's my whist club, composed of nothing but the leading foreign ambassadors and myself. We play till all hours of the morning and sometimes into the next night. I get so exhausted, I dash home—I mean up to the fourth floor and tell my cook, Marushka, to take my coat—she sleeps up there—my apartment is on the first floor and costs— Anyway, long before I arise each morning, my foyer looks like a battlefield of counts and princes contesting for my attention and sounding like an angry beehive. Occasionally, the Minister of State . . .

K. is taken aback and is momentarily lost when Marya corrects him on Pavlevsky. For an instant, he fears exposure, even considers flight; he could kill Marya—until Anna comes to his rescue and gives him time to cover up. It's a crucial moment for Anton, too. But it is an inner satisfaction for Artemy to see the Mayor and his family incurring K.'s displeasure. The others are just terribly shocked by this *faux pas.*

On "You must all call on me . . ." K. abstractedly takes the fan from Anna and fans himself, his head practically reclining on her shoulder.

At the end of this speech, Anna elbows K. so knowingly and familiarly that she dislodges him from the couch and, in his semi-drunken condition, he slips to one knee. Anton starts to help him but K. waves him back. When K. rises, simultaneously beginning his "St. Petersburg" speech, the others rise after him; but he waves them to sit down while he continues standing, talking and wandering among them.

Marya reacts to K.'s "high life" descriptions like a teen-ager with suppressed little squeals, shudders of joy, self-conscious giggles. Intermittently, Anna has to shush, shake and pinch her. These responses should be carefully synchronized and kept unobtrusive.

Marya giggles loudly on K.'s "fourth floor," gets a gentle slap from Anna.

(The men rise in wonder and respect.)
Perhaps it's because my letters sometimes address me as "Your Excellency." They still remember the time I was drafted to be in charge of the whole department. The head of it vanished, mysteriously, and there was a lot of talk, especially about who could replace him. Generals by the dozen were hungry for the position, and many of them tried and failed. Everybody thinks it's easy to run a complex governmental operation—until they've tried it. Finally, in desperation, they appealed to me. Messengers flowed in and out of my home like the tides, each with a communiqué prevailing upon me to come to their rescue. Government clerks and officials congregated outdoors, begging me to save their jobs, to come to their rescue before utter chaos ensued. It was most embarrassing, but finally I stepped out on the balcony in my dressing gown one morning and capitulated. Much as I wanted to decline, I was afraid the Czar would be offended. So I accepted, but on condition that I was to have a free hand in righting all the existing wrongs. And, believe me, anybody who didn't heed my warning suffered for it. When I went through every nook and cranny of that department, it was as if a hurricane had struck! Heads fell all around!

(The men shudder with fear as he works up to a grand fury.)
No, gentlemen, I do not joke, as they all soon discovered. I spared no one, not even the Grand Council, in instilling a respect for duty and a fear of my authority! I let no lapse or misdemeanor escape me. I come and go to the palace as I please, and they know that I have earned my reputation as a stern but just man. I shouldn't be surprised if upon my return home, I am promoted to the exalted rank of a field marsh— Oops!

(He trips and staggers, but everybody rushes to bring him erect again.)

ANTON:
(Quaking, stuttering.)
Your—your—your Ex-ex-ex-excellency—

When the men rise again, K. is up too far in the clouds to notice them. They remain standing, following his orbit with their eyes, inching away as he nears each, clicking heels and generally reacting to his dramatization as though they were part of it—his victims!

In the middle of this speech, K. begins to walk as if he had five legs.

Anton gets to K. first. He pushes the others back, helps K. get up and leads him to a chair. Anna and Marya rise as he falls, the better to see him.

KHLESTAKOV: Yes? Speak up, speak up.

(ANTON *only sputters again.*)

Are you speaking in some foreign language?

ANTON: For—for—forgive me, no, your excellency. I—I—was merely trying to suggest that—that—that you might wish to rest up after such an exhausting morning. Your room is right here, and it's all ready.

KHLESTAKOV:

(*Shaking him off.*)

Ridiculous! A government official, I always say, must be indefatigable! However, after such a magnificent lunch, I don't suppose forty winks would hurt me. That labardan, that labardan!

(*Kisses his fingers to the sky and exits into the guest room,* ANTON *following.*)

BOB.:

(*To* DOB.)

There, Peter, is what it's like to be a great man. One almost dies of fright in the presence of such a personage. I wonder what his real rank is.

DOB.: Oh, I would say he's bigger than a general.

BOB.: Of course he is. He probably has generals shining his boots. Wait till Ammos and Stepan Korobkin hear about this. Let's run and tell them. Good-bye, Anna Andreyevna.

DOB.: Yes, it's about time somebody struck envy in that big merchant's small heart. Good afternoon, my dear godmother.

(BOB. *and* DOB. *exit hurriedly.*)

ARTEMY:

(*In sudden panic.*)

Good Lord, we haven't got our uniforms on! If he finds us without

On Anton's suggestion that K. take a rest, Artemy steps forward as if volunteering to help K. to his room. Anton waggles a warning finger at Artemy and stops him.

The "Labardan" line is actually delivered to Artemy, preceded by a silly "Ha-ha-ha," as K. stops before him while staggering toward the guest room. Artemy gives Anton, who is following K., a vindictive, triumphant look.

At the door to the guest room, when K. drunkenly turns and kisses his fingers to the sky again before he exits, Anna and Marya are certain it was meant for them. . . . A long pause on this exit; everybody looks at the closed door, nobody moves.

———◆●◆———

The fifth atmosphere of the third act is a new one but, unlike the others before it, does not begin all at once; nor is it a blend with the atmosphere that just preceded it. Rather, it starts as a repetition of a couple of the other nuances—fear and children's play —when Bob. says to Dob., "There, Peter," etc. Then, slowly, the cathedral-like qualities of awe, reverence and contrition creep in and dominate; then uncertainty. The great man is sleeping. He may wake up angry for having made a spectacle of himself, blame them for all the wine he guzzled and vent his rage on all. How to propitiate the god?

This atmosphere continues until Osip re-enters from the guest room (page 222).

———◆●◆———

them when he awakens, he's sure to send in a bad report about us. Come, Luka, let's prepare ourselves. Good day, ladies.

LUKA: Yes, good day, ladies.

(ARTEMY *and* LUKA *also exit hurriedly.*)

ANNA: Well, Marya, isn't he perfectly charming?

MARYA: Perfectly adorable!

ANNA: What manners, what refinement, what verve! You can see St. Petersburg written all over him, the way he moves and walks with such elegance. And did you notice the way he stared at me? As though he were drinking me in!

MARYA: Oh, Mama, it was me he was doing it to.

ANNA: You? How silly and vain can you be? It doesn't become you.

MARYA: Nor you. It was me he was looking at most of the time and you know it.

ANNA: Oh, you poor, deluded, man-hungry child. Why would a sophisticated man like that waste his time on an immature girl like you?

MARYA: Nevertheless, he did—when he spoke about his writings, and described his whist games with the ambassadors.

ANNA: Perhaps he did glance at you once or twice; but it was only to be polite, I assure you.

(ANTON *enters from the guest room, softly closing the door behind him and tiptoeing in, finger to lips.*)

ANTON: Sh-h-h. Quiet, you two.

ANNA: Tell me, quickly, what else did he say?

ANTON: What else could he say? He's drunk. And I may be sorry I got him that way. Besides, what he said is enough, even if only half of it is true.

(*Thinking it out.*)

But how can it be otherwise? He may have exaggerated a little, but

The women's discussion of K. starts quietly, in adoration of him. By the middle of the page, it has grown progressively louder until it is an angry dispute between two jealous females.

Marya's line and Anna's retort are accents. It is the first time that the rivalry between them has been voiced. And now that it is out in the open, neither of them is inclined to retreat. Thus, these first six speeches must build in pitch and volume, each up a little more than the one before it—until Anton's return from the guest room commands a halt.

After his warning to the women, Anton falls into the nearest chair, opens a handkerchief wide and mops his whole face. Anna and Marya cross to him with excitement and curiosity.

———•••———

Osip's entrance (page 222) begins the sixth and last atmosphere of Act Three. Actually, it is a resumption of the cathedral-

that's the peacock in all of us. Yet, as they say, a drunken man speaks with his heart on his tongue. I don't doubt for a minute that he gambles with ambassadors and has access to the palace. Ah! The more I try to figure it out, the dizzier I get. All I know is, he completely unnerves me.

ANNA: My feelings were just the opposite. A cultured man of the world always puts me at ease and brings out my warmest emotions.

ANTON: Spoken just like a woman. All frills and featherbeds and fancy words. You haven't got enough sense to be afraid. But the mere thought of his anger, and how defenseless I am against him—

ANNA: Frills and featherbeds and fancy words can be wonderful defenses. Can't they, Marya?

MARYA:

(*Slightly atwitter.*)

Oh, Mama!

ANTON: I hope he flogs you both like I flogged the widow Eudoxia!

(*Angrily crosses to the door and calls.*)

Mishka! Go and tell Ilyitch and Tunov I want them here at once. You'll find them at the gate.

(*Returns stage center and goes into his characteristic pacing.*)

Everything is perverse in this world. Women are padded all over and you can see right through them. But a skinny little rat, you can't even guess what's inside him. Put a uniform on a soldier or a policeman, and instantly you know what he stands for and how he thinks; but God only knows what lurks under a fancy façade. It's like a blind man trying to make head or tail out of an elephant. But that young man doesn't fool me. He may talk in circles, but now and then a telltale sentence does straighten itself out.

(OSIP *enters from the guest room as if to pass through to the street doors.* ALL *waylay him.*)

like atmosphere of awe and veneration, but it is that climactic part of it when the blessings are given. There is, however, this attitudinal difference: each is a priest bestowing the blessings, each a penitent receiving them! So it continues until the third-act curtain.

———————

On her first speech here, Anna spins around gracefully until she stands facing the door to the guest room. As she starts walking toward it, Marya moves as if to join her, but really to intercept her. Anna obviates the need for Marya's action by turning back.

Marya steals a glance at the guest-room door.

Anna is the first to see Osip enter and watches him. So does Marya. Neither has seen him before. Anton turns to see what they are looking at.

ANNA: Just a moment, my good man.

ANTON: Is he asleep?

OSIP: He's still talking. He talks even in his sleep.

ANNA: What do they call you?

OSIP: Osip, ma'am.

ANTON:

(To the women.)

Please. You're confusing the man.

(To OSIP.*)*

Did they give you enough to eat?

OSIP: Oh, yes, quite enough, for the time being. I thank you all.

ANNA: Of course, it's nothing compared to eating from the tables of princes and counts, I suppose. You do have a lot of them visiting your master, don't you?

OSIP: It would not be gracious of me to belittle your meals; but because I know you will do better for me if I say it, then I shall: yes, counts and princes are among his visitors.

MARYA: Oh, how thrilling!

ANNA: Then he *is* a man of rank, wouldn't you say?

OSIP: I would say what you would most like to hear: Yes.

ANNA: And what might that rank be?

OSIP: Oh, the usual rank for a man of his birth and intellectual capacity.

ANTON: Oh, stop your idiotic questions, both of you! There are more important things for him to tell us. Such as . . .

(To OSIP.*)*

What is your master like? Is he a severe person? Does he badger and belittle people? Are his punishments harsh or lenient? Well, you know his characteristics much better than we do.

OSIP: Oh, he's very orderly and methodical. Things must be exactly right.

ANTON: I can see that from the intelligent and efficient way in which you attend him. He is fortunate in having a man like you. Now, what—

ANNA: Yes, what kind of uniform does he wear in his city?

Addressed, Osip stops and bows to them. Anton crosses upstage
to him, takes him by the arm and leads him near the chair he just
vacated.

Anna takes Osip's arm and leads him away from Anton.

Anton leads Osip back near the chair, Anna following.

Marya now joins the group, before her line.

On "Oh, stop your . . ." Anton takes each of his women by an
arm and hustles them away from Osip, near the sofa, then returns
to interrogate Osip alone. Anna is hurt and angry, falls onto the
sofa in a pet. Marya works half the way back in little dancing steps
so as not to miss a word about K.

ANTON: Even in matters of life and death you ask nothing but vain and unimportant questions.

(*To* OSIP.)

They think only of themselves, instead of you. Here, buy yourself some vodka on the journey back.

(OSIP *takes the money* ANTON *gives him.*)

OSIP: Bless you, sir. You're a kind man to the poor.

ANTON: Ah, if people only remembered that about me. Now, as I was about to ask before we were interrupted—

ANNA: Have you noticed what kind of eyes your master favors in women?

MARYA: Yes, and what kind of noses is he partial to?

ANTON: For God's sake, shut up and let me get a word in!

(*To* OSIP.)

When you're traveling, what does he like doing the most?

OSIP: Enjoying the best. He likes to live well and be well entertained.

ANTON: I see.

OSIP: When people receive him, he judges their sincerity by the way they treat his servant. But to a simple person like me, it doesn't really matter.

ANTON: Oh, but it does to me. Here, buy yourself another drink or two.

(ANTON *gives him more money and* OSIP *takes it.*)

OSIP: Your excellency has a generous heart. I'll remember to drink to it.

ANNA: And to me, too. I'll give you something later.

MARYA: I'll go and get something for you now.

(*A cough from* KHLESTAKOV *in the guest room freezes them.*)

ANTON:

(*Sotto voce.*)

Marya now swirls over to the guest-room door, stands staring at it, back to audience. Anna sees her and goes quickly to her side, taking her by the hand to lead her away. Marya turns and dreamily rests her head on Anna's shoulder. Anna caresses her, herself looking at the door as though it were K. she is fondling. Then she leads Marya back to Anton and Osip, looking at herself in the mirror en route.

Silenced by Anton, the women flounce away and sit on the sofa.

Marya rises from the sofa and is halfway out when the coughing stops her.

Stop! No, go, both of you. And for heaven's sake, don't make any noise!

ANNA: Come along, Marya. I think I know enough about our guest and how he would like us to entertain him.

(ANNA *and* MARYA *exit.*)

ANTON: Hm! They think there is no other way to a man's heart. Talk, talk, talk—as men of your age and mine well know, Osip. But tell me, now, my friend—

(ILYITCH *and* TUNOV *enter rather noisily.*)

Quiet, you elephants! You sound like a bunch of horses thundering across a wooden bridge! Where have you been since I sent for you?

TUNOV: I ran as soon as Mishka gave me your order.

(ANTON *claps a hand over* TUNOV'S *mouth.*)

ANTON: Quietly, I said! Do you have to roar like a lion in a cave.

(*Mimics him, roaring.*)

I ran as soon as Mishka gave me your order! From where—the wine shop? You're supposed to be at the gate.

(*To* OSIP.)

Forgive them, my friend. But don't let us detain you any longer from whatever you were going to do when we stopped you.

OSIP: I've forgotten what it was now, but I'm sure it will wait . . .

(*Jingles money in his hand.*)

Until I've paid my respects to you, your excellency.

(OSIP *exits.* ANTON *goes into conspiratorial action.*)

ANTON: As for you two, get out there on the front walk and stand guard as you've never stood it before. Not a stranger is to enter this house. More important, not a single shopkeeper. It'll be worth your life if any of them slip by you, you hear? The

Anna rises, goes to Marya, takes her by the hand on "Come along . . ." At the stairs, she stops to deliver the rest of the speech directly at Anton, already unbuttoning her dress.

After his "since I sent for you," Anton beckons Ilyitch and Tunov downstage, away from Osip.

After mimicking Tunov, Anton surreptitiously jerks his head and thumb back at Osip, warning the policemen not to say too much in front of him. Then he rejoins Osip to dismiss him politely.

Anton waits until he is certain Osip is out of earshot, then whirls on the policemen.

moment you see any of them, or anybody else who looks as if he might have a petition against me, grab him by the seat of his pants and kick him into the gutter. Do you understand? Any shopkeeper, stranger or anybody with a piece of paper in his hand or in his pocket—bang!—into the street on his ear! Now go, go!

(He waves them out like barnyard fowl and exits after them.)

THIRD ACT CURTAIN

[ACT FOUR]

The parlor in the Mayor's home. Later that afternoon.

As the curtain rises, SHPYOKIN, AMMOS, LUKA, ARTEMY, BOB-
CHINSKY *and* DOBCHINSKY *enter on tiptoe, cautiously squeezing
into the room. Each is attired in a full-dress uniform or costume of his respective official rank or civilian status. They
stand around awkwardly and in disorder, whispering back and
forth in their discomfort.*

AMMOS:
(*Asserting his seniority.*)
For heaven's sake, gentlemen, look at yourselves! Here you are,
about to face a man accustomed to storming at the nobility in
palaces, and you stand around like ducks at a mud puddle. Let's
get some semblance of rank and order here.
(*He begins positioning them.*)
Bobchinsky should stand there . . . and Dobchinsky over here
. . . and you, Artemy . . .
(*He pushes* ARTEMY *into place.*)
ARTEMY: I wish there was some other way of doing this.

AMMOS: If you don't like this arrangement, what would you
suggest?

ARTEMY: Something that may satisfy him more than a formal
reception.

AMMOS: Such as what?

ARTEMY: The same thing that satisfies us—something in the
palm.

In the Hollywood version of the play, we eliminated this first scene of Act Four because it was repetitious and contributed nothing new to the plot, therefore did not progress it fast enough for today's accelerated methods. Thus, the fourth act began with Osip's return from the street, then Khlestakov's entrance from the guest room.

But the once discarded scene is included in this new version for two reasons: (1) the scene plays much better in this simplified, modern-stage adaptation; (2) it will serve as an exercise for the director and/or players in finding and creating the proper atmosphere, tempos, qualities, etc., on their own. For that reason, the right-hand pages opposite pages 234 and 236 are designed to receive your own directorial notations.

———— •◦• ————

Khlestakov's entrance (page 236) precipitates the longest and most complex atmosphere of the play. It prevails for almost twenty minutes, until changed by the offstage voices of the merchants (page 264). Its complexities derive from the fact that it starts very slowly as an atmosphere of curiosity, and by almost imperceptible degrees becomes laden with pleasure and then overburdened with happiness. To build this progression, the players who come for individual interviews with K. must listen carefully and ascertain the degree of happiness reached before each exit, so that they may sustain the volume and pitch on their own entrances and step it up to the next level from there.

Another facet of this complex atmosphere is that in three of the interviews with the officials, it provides the kind of contrasting levels we spoke of as necessary to illuminate a performance, viz., Khlestakov is happy, but Ammos, Artemy and Luka are inwardly miserable. In other words, an objective atmosphere dissonanced and strengthened by different subjective moods.

———— •◦• ————

AMMOS: I wouldn't take any chances, Artemy. He might react the way a government official is supposed to, get on his high horse and take it out on us for embarrassing him. But we might, perhaps, offer it to him as a contribution to his favorite charity—or to start a fund for a statue of some sort.

SHPYOKIN: I have an idea: tell him there's some unclaimed money in the post office, and would he take it back to St. Petersburg with him for proper disposition.

ARTEMY: You'd better be careful he doesn't take you back to St. Petersburg, in chains. No, things like this have to be done more subtly in a smoothly operating government. In fact, I'm even thinking that we shouldn't all do it together, but meet him one by one, with no witnesses. And you, Ammos should be the first.

AMMOS: No, thank you. Having entertained him at your institution, you are on speaking terms with him, so it would be better if you broke the ice.

ARTEMY: Well, let's see, now . . .

(*Looks around the room.*)

It seems to me he would be more trusting with a scholastic representative like Luka here.

LUKA: Oh, no, please. My scholarly attainments are nothing to brag about, as you well know; at least, nothing to compare with his. The moment anybody with a college degree speaks to me, my knees sag and my tongue stiffens. I would ruin everything.

ARTEMY: There you are, Ammos. There's nobody else with your eloquence.

AMMOS: What eloquence? I can expound on hunting hounds and sound pontifical when quoting the law, but when it comes to crawling out on a limb—

ALL:

(*Surrounding* AMMOS.)

You've got to, Ammos.

Don't let us down.

You're the logical one, Ammos.

You outrank us all.

Act Four—Scene One
Directorial Notes

He'll respect you, Ammos.

(THEY *paw him, crush him with their entreaties.*)

AMMOS: Let go of me! You're stifling me!

(*They are interrupted by the entrance of* OSIP *and back up into their places as the latter surveys the scene just a trifle tipsily.*)

OSIP: Why is everybody dressed up? Did I miss something?

(AMMOS *is about to answer somehow but stops short when the sounds of coughing and mumbling come from* KHLESTAKOV'S *room and panic them. They scurry quickly past* OSIP *and converge on the exit, squeezing themselves through and stepping on each other's toes in their hurry to get out. . . . While the puzzled* OSIP *is still shrugging off the exodus,* KHLESTAKOV *enters from the guest room, yawning and stretching.*)

KHLESTAKOV: I must have slept like a dead man. These provincial mattresses and feather beds are really something. I can see why the women spend so much time in them. I wonder if the Mayor's daughter . . . and I'll bet her mother wouldn't look so bad in one, either. Anyway, it's a nice idea and I like it. Not a bad life, you know, not bad at all.

Act Four—Scene One
Directorial Notes

(AMMOS *enters as though pushed in against his will. He stops at the door, quaking as he turns to face* KHLESTAKOV *dumbly*.)

KHLESTAKOV: Whom have we here? Announce the gentleman, Osip.

OSIP: I don't know him. He was here when I returned and I thought you had been receiving him.

KHLESTAKOV: Here, returned? Returned from where? There was no one here but you when I woke up. Are you drunk?

OSIP: Not yet, sir. After all, it was only a few coins he gave me.

KHLESTAKOV: Who gave you? Who has been bribing you, and for what?

AMMOS:

(*Trembling*.)

It was not I, your highness. Allow me to introduce myself.

(*Draws himself to attention, hand on sword hilt*.)

I have the honor to present Ammos Lyapkin-Tyapkin, Judge of the Court in this district, member of the Board of Assessors.

(*Nervously wipes his sweaty brow*.)

Could I—ah—pay my respects alone, please?

KHLESTAKOV: Of course. Go put my room back in order, Osip.

(OSIP *exits into the guest room, carefully leaving the door slightly ajar*.)

Now. Do sit down.

(AMMOS *sits*. KHLESTAKOV *begins circling the chair as he talks,* AMMOS *respectfully turning to keep up with him*.)

So you are the judge I almost met under different circumstances.

AMMOS: Wh-what circumstances.

KHLESTAKOV: Never mind. How long have you been a judge here?

AMMOS: A—a judge? A judge. Oh, I would say about five terms. I was first elected by the nobility in 1816, and—and—I guess they just forgot about me.

KHLESTAKOV: Being a judge pays pretty well, doesn't it?

AMMOS: Yes, and I have the money right here in my hand!

On facing K. after he enters, Ammos clicks his heels like a Russian in official capacity. So do the other government employees coming for an interview.

On Ammos' "Judge of the Court in this district," K. momentarily reacts as to a danger signal, but quickly recovers when he sees how fearful the man is.

Ammos' sitting position is on the edge of the chair, right hand on his knee, the money wadded up inside his fist.

KHLESTAKOV: What? What did you say?

AMMOS: I—I mean—forgive me—the money doesn't mean anything to me. There are far greater rewards—such as when, after I had served three terms, I was recommended to the government for the Order of Vladimir, fourth class.

KHLESTAKOV: The fourth-class Vladimirs aren't so bad. They don't always pay off, but—

AMMOS:

(*Eagerly, extending his clenched fist.*)

Oh, but they do, they do!

KHLESTAKOV: What are you clenching so tightly in your hand?

AMMOS: Huh? Oh, nothing, nothing. See?

(AMMOS *involuntarily opens his hand and the bills within it fall to the floor.*)

KHLESTAKOV: It's quite a pretty nothing. Money, isn't it?

(*He picks up the bills.*)

AMMOS:

(*Muttering.*)

Dear God, I'm lost! All is lost!

KHLESTAKOV: Who did you say lost it?

AMMOS: I don't know—that is, I don't know what to do with it.

KHLESTAKOV: Could I make a simple suggestion? Why not lend it to me?

AMMOS:

(*More eagerly.*)

Delighted! Oh, thank God! And I'll see to it that the person who lost it never finds it.

KHLESTAKOV: Traveling is terribly expensive these days and one runs out of money so much faster. But I'll return it as soon as I reach the next town.

If Ammos had said "Order of Boris," K. would have voiced the same opinion about that. He never heard of either.

Ammos draws his fist away, but the more he tries to hide it, the more conspicuous it becomes.

Not every actor can make this involuntary hand-opening come off realistically, like an uncontrollable reflex. So, if a substitute for this piece of business is necessary, try this: Ammos attempts to pass the bills into his left hand with a quick palming motion in order to show K. the empty right hand on his "See?" line. But he is so nervous and so clumsy at it that the money scatters and falls at his feet. Whereupon K. comes closer to gape down at the bills.

Ammos' "Delighted!" is delivered louder and can be repeated.

AMMOS: No need to, and no explanation necessary. Use it any way you wish. The honor is mine. I could do no less. In serving you, I serve my government.

(*Rising and standing at attention.*)

If you have no further orders, sir, I shall not disturb you any longer.

KHLESTAKOV: Orders for what?

AMMOS: For the Court of this district—or are you now satisfied that we have everything under control.

KHLESTAKOV: Well, not everything, perhaps. But I can see that Justice here is not blind and I need not concern myself with it. Good afternoon, Judge, and thank you for your kindness.

AMMOS:

(*Bowing.*)

Thank *you*, your highness.

(AMMOS *exits.* OSIP *enters from the guest room, grinning about the new windfall.*)

KHLESTAKOV: A nice fellow, that judge.

(*A knock on the door and* SHPYOKIN *enters, also drawing himself up and hand on sword hilt.*)

SHPYOKIN: With your kind permission, your highness, I would like the honor of presenting Court Councilor Ivan Shpyokin, Postmaster.

(KHLESTAKOV *and* OSIP *exchange "another sucker" looks.* OSIP *is waved back into the guest room.*)

KHLESTAKOV: Good company is always welcome. Make yourself comfortable in this chair.

A heel-click right after Ammos rises. Then he stiffens to attention.

Ammos' exit is accomplished with another heel-click, then he walks backward to the door, there clicking his heels once more before he turns to leave.

Shpyokin's entrance speech is broken into three parts, and he takes two steps forward after each break. Their meeting is like that of two dandies; but since it is on an official rather than social level, he, the underling, is a little more dignified. Still, when replying to K., he tries for smiles and easy laughter.

(SHPYOKIN *sits in the chair vacated by* AMMOS *and* KHLESTA-
KOV *begins his circling tactics.*)
Are you the permanent or only the temporary postmaster?

SHPYOKIN: Permanent, by the grace of my government. I have
lived here for some time.

KHLESTAKOV: It's a nice enough place, I suppose. Not many
people, and not too exciting; but, then, it isn't the capital, is it?

SHPYOKIN: Quite right, sir, it isn't the capital.

KHLESTAKOV: However, we in the capital haven't any simple
rustics and you haven't any fashions and grand manners. Don't you
agree?

SHPYOKIN: Quite right. I agree.

KHLESTAKOV: But I'll have to confess that it's possible to live
quite comfortably in a place like this.

SHPYOKIN: Yes, sir. Exactly.

KHLESTAKOV: Because when one is sincerely loved and respected, one can be happy anywhere. Don't you think so?

SHPYOKIN: Precisely.

KHLESTAKOV: It may only be an odd notion of mine, and you
may think me peculiar, but I'm happy that you share my viewpoint.

(*Fixes* SHPYOKIN *with a glassy stare.*)
And I hope you can share my viewpoint on other matters as well—
such as lending your fellow man a helping hand.

SHPYOKIN: Oh, yes, indeed. Quite.

KHLESTAKOV: Well, then, suppose I told you that an odd misfortune occurred to me on the road and I ran out of money—would
you lend me, say, four hundred rubles?

SHPYOKIN: I most certainly would. I would deem your misfortune my great fortune and consider that God has chosen me to
come to your rescue.

KHLESTAKOV: Well, it's not quite that drastic with me, but—
well, you know how it is. When you're accustomed to the best of
everything when at home, you sort of hate to deprive yourself when

When Shpyokin sits down, he inadvertently holds his fist on his knee the way Ammos did. K. is instantly attracted to it and can't keep his eyes off it.

Shpyokin's staccato replies are either preceded or followed by a light hee-hee or ha-ha, whichever comes more naturally to the actor playing him.

On "helping hand," K. stares intently at Shpyokin's fist.
After agreeing with him, Shpyokin, embarrassed by the stare, wipes his clammy hands with a kerchief. K. is dismayed to see that there is no money in that clenched fist, so becomes more direct with his next speech.

Shpyokin's speech raises K.'s hopes again.

traveling. And, actually, why should you, when there are more kindhearted people in the small towns than in the big cities?

SHPYOKIN: Quite correct, sir.

(*Rising and standing militarily erect, he counts out the money from his wallet and gives it to* KHLESTAKOV *with a bow.*)

It is an unexpected pleasure, your highness. Now, if you would like to make some suggestions concerning the operations of the postal department . . .

KHLESTAKOV: None whatever. You look like a man who knows a good postage stamp when he sees one, so our government is safe.

SHPYOKIN: Thank you, thank you.

(SHPYOKIN *bows and exits.* OSIP *emerges from the guest room again.* KHLESTAKOV *counts the money, pockets it with the other,*

lights a cigar.)

KHLESTAKOV: A most obliging fellow, that postmaster. I like obliging fellows.

(*Another knock on the door, and soon* LUKA *seems to be pushed into the room with goading offstage whispers.* OSIP *retires to the guest room again as the newcomer goes tremblingly through the motions of presenting himself like the others.*)

LUKA: Wi-wi-with my kind permission, y-y-your highness, I have the honor to present yourself—to present *to* yourself—Tit-Tit-Titulary Councilor Luka Khlopov, Sup-Sup-Supervisor of Schools.

With a bow *and* a heel-click.

Shpyokin's exit must be managed a little more characteristically, thus: When he bows and clicks his heels again, K. offers his hand, and when Shpyokin takes it, K. leads him to the door. En route, the Postmaster revels in the intimacy of the handclasp, keeps pumping K.'s hand and laughing all the way out.

When taking a cigar from the box on the table, K. should pocket several more before lighting the one in his mouth.

One glance at Luka tells K. that here is a dolt, a cipher. Even before Luka has finished his speech, K. has picked up a chair and is ready for him when he comes stage center. For as the play develops, Luka's characterization becomes that of a man unable to cope with the intrigues of the conspiracy, so that his body grows lifeless and expresses itself by expressing nothing. Physically, he is not all there, and he is going that way mentally, too, as he will evidence in the last act.

KHLESTAKOV: Nice of you to come. Here, have a seat, have a cigar.

(*Shoves a chair under him and a cigar into his hand, which* LUKA *holds awkwardly, indecisively.*)

Smoke it, smoke it. It's not quite what I'm used to, but it's not bad. In St. Petersburg, you can buy cigars for as much as a ruble apiece. Why don't you light it?

(*Gets him a candle, but* LUKA'S *shaking hand can't touch cigar to flame.*)

No wonder. You've put the wrong end in your mouth.

(LUKA'S *fright pops the cigar out of his mouth and he spits and quakes with embarrassment.*)

LUKA: Forgive, me, forgive me.

KHLESTAKOV: Obviously, you are not a cigar smoker.

LUKA: It's—it's just that I'm not accustomed to—to—such a fine brand.

KHLESTAKOV: As they say in St. Petersburg, good cigars and bad women are my burning passions. And you, which do you like best?

LUKA: Oh, I—I like cigars well enough.

KHLESTAKOV: I thought so. Blondes or brunettes?

(LUKA *is baffled, silent.*)

Come, come, you can confide in me. Which kind do you like best?

LUKA: The—the—the big, fat ones with the green-and-gold band.

KHLESTAKOV: You're being evasive, my good man. I want you to be absolutely honest with me about your tastes. Blondes, brunettes, redheads—or perhaps there are some other kinds here.

LUKA: Your highness, I—I—I don't know what to say, I—I—

KHLESTAKOV: I see. You don't want to commit yourself. The chances are that, like me, you hope to try them all some day.

(LUKA *squirms, in silence.*)

You're blushing, so it must be true. Isn't it?

K. speaks a little louder to Luka, as though to a deaf man, in the belief that it will serve a stupid one as well.

K. pats Luka on the thigh after the "bad women" line, as though to make a greater fool out of this fool.

A REMINDER ON PLAYING COMEDY

At this stage of the rehearsals, particularly in this long scene with the village officials and Bob. and Dob., the performances will show a tendency to get out of hand. All, to a greater or lesser degree, will become terribly conscious of the fact that they are playing "comedy." And "terribly," too, is the word to describe how bad the players can become at these moments and how the play can degenerate as a result.

Most glaring will be the attempts of the players to act almost completely outwardly, pretending rather than feeling, imitating and doing all sorts of uncalled-for business to make their scenes even more humorous, striving extra hard to make the audience laugh. That is absolutely the wrong way to play comedy!

LUKA: Y-y-your high-high-high— It's—it's my tongue, sir. It seems hot and dry, but it's frozen stiff!

KHLESTAKOV: I know. I'm probably frightening you. My stare usually does that; women especially have a difficult time resisting it. Would you believe that?

LUKA: Oh, yes, I would, I would.

KHLESTAKOV: Nevertheless, a strange misfortune occurred to me while traveling—

LUKA: Oh, I know, I know. Women can be very treacherous.

KHLESTAKOV: Especially when you haven't any money—and I ran completely out of funds just before I arrived here. Could you lend me, say, four hundred rubles?

LUKA: Why, yes, I would, I would, if I have it on me . . .

(*Reaching into his pocket and extracting bills, which he counts off.*)

Yes, I have, I have! Here you are. Four hundred.

(*Hands* KHLESTAKOV *the money.*)

KHLESTAKOV: Thank you. As I suspected, you have excellent taste in cigars *and* women.

LUKA: And—and—in education also. I assure you it is not necessary to waste your time inspecting the schools under my supervision.

KHLESTAKOV: I certainly don't intend to. The world and its people are the only schools that interest me. The school of life!

LUKA:

(*Bowing, backing out.*)

Thank you, thank you. Good day, sir.

(LUKA *exits.* OSIP *is about to come out of the guest room again, but quickly withdraws as* ARTEMY *enters and goes through the same salutatory posturing.*)

A serious attitude toward the psychology of each character must be maintained, *especially* when playing comedy. A character may be funny, humorous or amusing to others, but he is never, *never* ridiculous to himself! For his ego demands that he take himself seriously as a person, else he cannot relate himself to life.

In this act, more than anywhere else in the play, we must remember that good comedy, or to make comedy good, requires a complete and believable *feeling of truth*, to use Stanislavsky's phrase for it. But when an actor becomes more conscious of his performance than of the inner, sensitive feelings of his character, when he goes overboard on fun and drowns fidelity, the character becomes false and the play implausible.

In the final analysis, the audience is interested in the character, not the actor. Trying to prove how funny the character is by "hamming" only results in shamming, only draws more attention to the actor's artificiality and less to the character's credibility.

Don't forget that when an actor thus demolishes a character, he also demolishes himself as an actor. And, it isn't people who are funny of themselves; it is the things that happen to them that can be.

———•◦•———

K. doesn't even bother to look at the exiting Luka.

When Artemy enters, he makes doubly sure that he has closed the door behind him. Very cautious, he is also concerned with the other door in the room, the one behind which Osip is listening.

ARTEMY: With your kind permission, your highness, I have the honor to present Court Councilor Artemy Zemlyanika, Manager of Charities.

KHLESTAKOV: Ah, we meet again, my wine-pouring friend. Please be seated.

(*Biz of circling chair again.*)

ARTEMY: It was a privilege to show you through the institutions entrusted to my care and administration.

KHLESTAKOV: Ah, yes, that Labardan, that Labardan! A most excellent lunch, most excellent.

ARTEMY: When I serve my government, none but the best is good enough.

KHLESTAKOV: I well remember. After lunch you looked a little shorter.

ARTEMY: That's the impression one creates when he gives so much of himself to his tasks. I regret that I cannot say as much for some others in our local administration.

(*Speaks in a confidential tone.*)

Take the Postmaster, for example. That post office is utter chaos, as you'll discover for yourself when you get around to investigating it. And the Judge who paid his respects to you. He has little respect for anything but breeding dogs and hunting rabbits. Then there's that landowner, Dobchinsky, whom you saw at the inn. His wife and the Judge—you know—the moment he leaves the house. Dobchinsky out the front door, the Judge in the back. All you have to do is look at the children; not one of them resembles their father; even the little girl is a miniature copy of the Judge, poor thing.

KHLESTAKOV: Where does Dobchinsky live? I mean—how interesting, how very interesting!

ARTEMY: Our Supervisor of Schools is another one. How he has fooled the government for so long is beyond me. A real jack rabbit, too, that one; no woman teacher stays here longer than a month. I can write all this information down for you, if you'd like.

K.'s chief interest here is not Artemy but the fastest way of getting money out of him. Artemy being older and cleverer, K. will have to listen abstractedly and wait for his chance to broach the money.

When K. helps Artemy to a chair, he maneuvers a feel for the wallet in his pocket. And at the beginning of each Khlestakov speech, Artemy's own hand goes anticipatorily toward the wallet, as though thinking, *"Now* he's going to ask for it."

On "a little shorter," K. taps Artemy on the chest, again feeling for his wallet. Artemy's reflex action is to feel for it himself.

Artemy looks around for possible eavesdroppers before he launches into his betrayal of the others. As he starts to assassinate each character, he moves a little with his chair or on it, as if trying to get closer to K. and into his good graces—a worming movement.

K., on the other hand, only gets vaguer and vaguer about all the people Artemy refers to in his gossip; he can't even remember their names. Besides, why is the man telling him all this? K. becomes more cautious, more confused, says aimless things, finds it difficult to come to the point.

KHLESTAKOV: You do that. It may make spicy reading when I get bored. You will have rendered me a real service and I will think of you and your children. Have you any—

(A beat.)

You do have children, haven't you?

ARTEMY: Yes, of course. Nikolai, Ivan, Elizaveta, Marya and Perpetua.

KHLESTAKOV: And do they all look like you?

ARTEMY: No doubt about it—I think. I mean—some of them may resemble their mother a little more, but thank God none looks like the Judge!

KHLESTAKOV: You are a fortunate man. Any man is who can call his children his own these days.

(ARTEMY *rises, bows, prepares to go.*)

ARTEMY: With my apologies, your highness. I have taken up too much of your time.

KHLESTAKOV: Not at all. I like this sort of chitchat. You must come again and tell me more. I enjoy a fortunate man, having had a bit of misfortune myself lately.

ARTEMY: You have a wife—I mean your own children are—? Forgive me, I didn't mean to pry.

KHLESTAKOV: Oh, nothing like that. Other men's children, perhaps. I'm not married. The misfortune I meant was that at this point of my travels, I have run completely out of ready cash. You couldn't lend me, say, five hundred rubles, could you?

ARTEMY: I can and I will!

(*Counts out money and hands it over.*)

A pleasure and a privilege, sir.

KHLESTAKOV: You have my thanks and best wishes. May your wife's and other wives' children always look like you.

(KHLESTAKOV *escorts* ARTEMY *to the door.* OSIP *enters from the guest room once more, coming stage center. But just as* KHLESTAKOV *is about to meet him there,* OSIP *signals and*

Before the last sentence of this speech, K. taps the wallet side of his chest when he starts to say, "Have you any—?" But instead of saying "money," he rephrases it to the positive question.

Artemy's reflex on the insinuation about his children is indignation—but he stops himself in time and resumes his unctuousness with a light touch. Besides, K. might not have meant it as an insult at all (which the idle-brained K. didn't), so Artemy answers to what he *could* have meant.

But on K.'s next speech, Artemy is not so sure that he didn't mean the earlier insult. He had better get out, he thinks, before the barbs become more pointed and incite him to do or say the wrong thing.

K. enjoys his "Other men's children" joke, gives a moronic little laugh, and is nonplused when Artemy remains stone sober.

On "could you?" K. quickly reaches into Artemy's pocket for the wallet and hands it to him.

This time, Artemy does give a sardonic little laugh but his face is cold sober. Some joke!

quickly exits into the guest room again. KHLESTAKOV *turns and finds that* BOB. *and* DOB. *have entered and are standing at formal attention.*)

DOB.: Your honor, I have the highness to introduce here me, Peter Dobchinsky, respected resident of this town.

BOB.:

(*Bowing.*)

And here, landowner Peter Bobchinsky.

KHLESTAKOV: I believe we've met before. I remember that one of you, the one with the patch on his nose, fell on his face. Didn't you?

BOB.: Thank you for inquiring. It's much better now.

KHLESTAKOV: Good. I'm glad you're feeling better.

(BOB. *and* DOB. *come stage center and he begins circling them. Suddenly he stops to face them.*)

How much money have you got on you?

BOB.: M-m-money? What kind?

KHLESTAKOV: Paper, gold, anything.

DOB.: Foreign or rubles?

KHLESTAKOV: Rubles would be best. Can you lend me a thousand, for instance?

BOB.: A-a thous—? I don't really think I've got— Have you got that much, Peter?

DOB.: Me? A thousand? You know you've got to give the bank thirty days' notice before you can draw even half that much.

KHLESTAKOV: All right, if not a thousand, then how about a couple of hundred?

(BOB. *scratches around in his pocket.*)

BOB.: Can you dig up two hundred, Peter? All I seem to have, I think, is about fifty.

Bob. knows very well what kind of money. He was outside the door at the inn, and if he didn't see the financial transaction there, Dob. has probably filled him in on it. So pretending ignorance is his way of stalling.

Dob. joins in the delaying tactic only because there is nothing else to do to stave off the inevitable.

(DOB. *peers into his wallet.*)

DOB.: And all I can come up with is about thirty.

BOB.: Look around some more. Some of it may have slipped into the pocket lining.

(DOB. *feels inside his pocket.*)

DOB.: No, the hole was sewed up last week.

KHLESTAKOV: Very well, eighty will be useful, but not much.

(*He holds out his hand and they put the money into it.*)
Thank you for your visit, gentlemen.

DOB.: Before we go, may I impose on you regarding a matter of great delicacy?

KHLESTAKOV: I like delicacies, so it is no imposition.

DOB.: It concerns my eldest son. Your highness may not wish to discuss things of that nature.

KHLESTAKOV: Daughters are more to my liking, but—continue.

DOB.: Well, sir, he was—how shall I say it?—born before I was married.

KHLESTAKOV: That's saying "bastard" simply enough.

DOB.: Please don't misunderstand. He's truly my son, and I love him just as much as if he had been born after my marriage. But I would be so much happier if there was some way of calling him Dobchinsky legally.

KHLESTAKOV: I have no objections. Call him anything you like.

DOB.: Then you'll help me to legitimatize him? He's such a talented boy. He can recite poetry and whittle with a penknife.

KHLESTAKOV: A genius, I'm sure. Very well, I'll speak to someone about it.

(*To* BOB.)
And what confessions would you like to make, my friend?

BOB.: No confessions. Only a small favor. When you return to St. Petersburg and meet with all the nobility and high officials

For this business, Bob. and Dob. go into a huddle, look through each other's wallets, search each other's pockets, while K. walks around impatiently.

K. stuffs the crumpled old bills into his trouser pocket, and while he is thanking them, he is already pushing them toward the door.

On K.'s promise to speak to someone about the boy, Bob. and Dob. laugh hysterically, embrace and kiss each other. Then Dob. turns to K. with inexpressible gratitude, would kiss him if he dared, but just barely touches him.

again, and if they should mention the name of this town, it would give me great joy if you would say, "Why, Peter Bobchinsky lives there!"

KHLESTAKOV: I'm sure they'll be thrilled with this information, but I'll give it to them.

BOB.: I wonder what could happen if you told it to the Czar one day.

KHLESTAKOV: I can well imagine. I will write you about it—from the St. Petersburg Asylum for the Insane. However, you have my promises gentlemen, whatever they're worth, so good day.

DOB.: Thank you for the audience, your highness. We shall remember it always.

KHLESTAKOV: Oh, I'm sure you will.

(KHLESTAKOV *sees* BOB. *and* DOB. *to the door. As soon as they exit,* OSIP *enters from the guest room.*)

OSIP: I hope that's the last of them.

KHLESTAKOV: So do I. For a small town like this, there certainly are a lot of officials. And all of them seem to think I'm somebody with influence in the government. Wait till I write to Tryapichkin about this! He'll do an article for the papers about them and St. Petersburg will laugh its head off. Find me some paper and ink.

(OSIP *searches and finds them.*)

It's a shame to do this to them after all the money they lent me, but . . .

(*Takes money out of pockets and leafs through the bills.*)

Quite a haul for one afternoon, wouldn't you say?

OSIP: I would say something else.

KHLESTAKOV: If only I had that infantry captain here now, I would really show him how to cut cards.

OSIP: I would still say the same thing.

(KHLESTAKOV *sits and starts writing.*)

On this silly request, K. begins to push Bob. and Dob. toward the door in earnest.

Although writing the letter may seem to be only another manifestation of K.'s butterfly mentality, he must light upon the notion emphatically. The letter is vital to the plot and must be stressed: K. slaps his palms together after "about this!" as though coming to a great resolution. His tempo accelerates. He is full of new glee and is already laughing the way he expects the St. Petersburgers to laugh.

MOB SCENES OR MOB RULE?

Some words about group, crowd and mob scenes before we come to one starting on page 264, and bearing in mind the very big crowd scene at the end of the play:

A common error among actors when finding themselves in group or crowd scenes is that each tries to represent the whole group. Everyone thinks his function is to carry the load for himself and the

KHLESTAKOV: What? Give up this wonderful life, no doubt.

OSIP: Exactly. Get out while the getting is good. The money can go faster than it came if something goes wrong.

KHLESTAKOV: What can go wrong if I stay here another day or two? Some more money may come in. But if things begin to look shaky, we'll leave tomorrow, I promise you.

OSIP: Tomorrow may be too late. What man hastily honors today, he is quicker to defile tomorrow. That's an old peasant proverb.

KHLESTAKOV: I'll think about it, peasant, after you get this letter to the post office.

OSIP: I'll send the letter with the servant and start packing to save time. I could get the luggage out through the kitchen.

KHLESTAKOV: First bring me a candle and some sealing wax.

(OSIP *searches for the sealing wax while* KHLESTAKOV *writes furiously, chuckling to himself.* OSIP *places candle and wax beside him, then exits to the guest room, leaving the door open.*)

OSIP:
(*Calling offstage.*)
Hey, there! Mishka! . . . Get yourself ready to take a letter to the post office. Tell the Postmaster to stamp it government business and send it free. Then tell him my master orders a courier coach and pair sent up right away and to charge it to the government. . . . That's right, he travels at government expense. . . . I'll have the letter ready for you in a few minutes.

(KHLESTAKOV *folds the letter, addresses the envelope, seals it with wax, now laughing loudly.*)

KHLESTAKOV: I can just see his face when he reads it. He won't waste a minute getting it into print!

(OSIP *re-enters. He gives him the letter.*)

rest as well. Everyone has a tendency to shout, as though he were the voice of the entire group. The result in such cases is that the actor often loses his own identity, the very characterization he worked so hard to build up.

Either that or he is prone to go to the opposite extreme, where each player tends to shift the burden of carrying the scene to all the others and do little or nothing himself, thereby not only eliminating the identity of the character but also his complete existence as a person with a function on the stage.

Such mob scenes make for chaos, anarchy and just plain bad theatre. To get a good crowd effect, everybody has to be absolutely individual, have his own definite objective and perform his role with even greater concentration on his character than if he were on the stage in a two-scene. For good mob scenes must contain the ensemble feeling *plus* this factor.

Further, participants in group or crowd scenes require just as careful cuing as individual players. Each should have a clear chart of his movements and the nature of the ad libs and sounds expected of him in each instance, and be particularly aware of the crescendos and diminuendos.

In sum, the players in group scenes must try even harder to maintain their own characterizations and objectives, and those who just participate should each have a separate identity, as clearly defined and indispensable a function as those with name parts.

———•••———

Beginning with the offstage voices of the merchants, the atmosphere of happiness and gaiety subsides and converts into a kind of "rushing storm." Thus, Abdulin, Fyovronya and Eudoxia can be called storm-bringing characters. Rising and ebbing, this atmosphere continues until Osip clears out the last petitioners. Then it changes abruptly with Marya's entrance (page 276).

———•••———

The offstage steps incidental to mailing the letter (getting it into

There you are, you pessimistic fool. Now make sure it gets mailed.

(OSIP *starts to leave but is held back by the roaring voice of* ILYITCH *offstage.*)

ILYITCH:
(*Off.*)
And where do you think *you're* going, my fine-whiskered friend! Didn't you just hear me telling the others that nobody, but nobody, is allowed to go in!

(*A tumult of vocal protest comes from offstage.*)
MERCHANTS:
(*Off.*)
Let us in!
We must appeal to his excellency!
By what right do you keep us out!
We'll tell him about you, too!
We're here on business that's none of your business!
ILYITCH:
(*Off.*)
Get out, all of you! Get out, I tell you! I have my orders! He's asleep and he's not receiving anybody, even when he wakes up. Clear the streets at once!

(*An even louder and more unintelligible roar of protests goes up.*)

KHLESTAKOV: What in the devil is going on there, Osip? Go see what it's all about.

(OSIP *goes to the window, opens it and looks out. The babble is louder.*)

OSIP: They look like merchants. They're trying to come into

the hands of Shpyokin primarily), and K.'s method of departure, are quite important to the plot. The audience must form a clear picture of this offstage action, so we must hear every word of Osip's instructions to Mishka. Osip being out of sight when he calls out his speech, he should face the open guest-room door from an unseen position offstage in order that his voice may come through more distinctly.

In other productions, Mishka was called onstage by Osip and given the instructions. But I prefer to eliminate him here because his entrance tends to break the very intimate, conspiratorial mood of the scene. However, in auditoriums where offstage voice projections are difficult, it may be necessary to bring Mishka on when Osip calls for him. In which case he will need only one line of dialogue: When Osip says, "charge it to the government," Mishka repeats, "Charge it to the government?" as a question. Then, after Osip's "in a few minutes," Mishka nods and exits, indicating that he understands and will be ready.

the house, but the policemen are pushing them back. All of them are waving papers wildly and talking all at once. It sounds as if they've come to see you about something.

KHLESTAKOV: Are you sure it's just papers and not more money?

(*He goes to the window and calls out.*)

What do you want, my good friends? What is troubling you?

(*Another unintelligible roar goes up from outside.*)

I can't understand a word they're saying. Maybe we'd better let them come in. Go tell the policemen it's all right.

(*As* OSIP *exits, several waving petitions materialize outside the window, shoved up by unseen hands during the continued mumble and babble.* KHLESTAKOV *gathers them all, opens one and reads it.*)

"To the most illustrious and honorable Excellency of Finance, from Abdulin, the humble merchant. . . ." Excellency of Finance? Is there such a title?

(*While* KHLESTAKOV *is still scratching his head, the doors burst open and the merchants pour in, bearing a large carton of wine bottles and sugar cones.* OSIP *squeezes back in through them.*)

ABDULIN: Forgive us, forgive us. We humbly beg your honor's pardon and help.

KHLESTAKOV: What is it you wish?

ABDULIN: We are being persecuted. For no reason at all, we are the victims of insult and extortion.

KHLESTAKOV: Whose victims?

ABDULIN: The Mayor's. It's impossible to describe the injuries

The merchants remain near the door, behind Abdulin, moving further into the room only when he does. Most of them, like Abdulin, have beards. In addition to the community carton, some carry individual gift boxes and baskets. At first, these smaller presents are hidden from the audience; gradually they work themselves into view.

Abdulin's tone and demeanor are that of a kind, gentle, forgiving man, a persecuted saint who has come to plead not so much for himself as for his followers. It is not he, only his followers, who have anger and hatred in their hearts for the Mayor.

Abdulin includes Osip in the conversation when pleading his case, as though K. were the judge and Osip the jury. In the meantime, K. is circling the area occupied by the merchants, snooping and trying to guess what gifts they brought. Afraid K. may not be

and indignities he has heaped on us. It is not enough that we obey all his new rules and regulations, and show him every respect, and put all the fancy clothes on the backs of his wife and daughter free of charge. No, not for him. He must enter our shops any time at all and take anything he wants without paying. And to add to the injury, we must deliver it here to his house.

KHLESTAKOV: Oh, that cheating, swindling, hypocritical scoundrel!

ABDULIN: We have never been cursed with anyone like him. We have to hide everything the moment he enters our shops, because he'll help himself to everything that isn't nailed down. Try arguing or even reasoning with him, and he'll punish you by quartering soldiers in your home, and they ransack everything! Or he'll declare a quarantine for some fancy disease and order you to lock your shop doors for a week or two.

KHLESTAKOV: A robber like that should be sent to Siberia, no less.

ABDULIN: The farther the better, and may he never return to this world again. Please do something for us, your honor, and allow us to pay our respects with some wine and sugar.

KHLESTAKOV: No, thank you. I am not one of your bribe-takers. However, if you felt that you could make me a small loan, say about three hundred rubles, for example, that would be an entirely different matter.

(ABDULIN *quickly and eagerly produces a roll of bills.*)

ABDULIN: Only three hundred? Why not take five? It's a rounder figure and a greater expression of our gratitude.

KHLESTAKOV: If you insist. And I shan't even mention that you offered me such a loan.

(*One of the other merchants produces a fine small salver.*

listening, Abdulin grabs him by a sleeve and repeats *"all* his new rules and regulations." Osip pulls Abdulin off and shoves him back.

After "the moment he enters our shops," Abdulin includes Osip again, explaining why. On "Try arguing . . . with him," he returns to the ambulating K.

Abdulin tries to pass the carton to Osip. The other merchants with gifts press forward and also hold them out to Osip, who does not take them but waits for a sign from K.

On K.'s "not one of your bribe-takers," the merchants hide their individual gifts behind their backs.

Abdulin sets the carton down at Osip's feet before taking out his money.

ABDULIN *places the money on it and offers it to* KHLESTAKOV.)

ABDULIN: Please keep the tray, too. It's the finest silver and workmanship, and will be a reminder of your help to us.

KHLESTAKOV: I like fine trays. Thank you very much for what's on it, too.

ABDULIN: Why not take the sugar and wine while you're at it?

KHLESTAKOV: I told you, I never take bribes.

ABDULIN: Then take only the sugar, your highness. One can always use sugar while traveling. Perhaps there is something else you may need for your journey—anything, only see to it that our petitions are acted upon. Our necks are already in a noose; without your help, there will be nothing left but to hang ourselves.

KHLESTAKOV: Trust me. I shall do everything within my power.

(ABDULIN *and the other merchants back up, bowing until they have exited.* KHLESTAKOV *begins counting the money. He is interrupted by the shouting voices of* FYOVRONYA *and* EUDOXIA *offstage.*)

FYOVRONYA:
(*Off.*)
You can't keep me out! His highness himself will hear about this!

EUDOXIA:
(*Off.*)
Who do you think you're pushing? Ouch! You're hurting me, you big baboon!

KHLESTAKOV: *Now* what's going on?
(*Crosses to window and calls.*)
What's all the fussing about? What do you want, madam?

FYOVRONYA:
(*Off.*)
Please, your highness. We beg you, we appeal to you!

EUDOXIA:
(*Off.*)

K. removes the money and gives the salver to Osip for safekeeping.

After "while traveling," Osip picks up the carton and takes it into the guest room. A few of the merchants with gifts hastily follow him. They are pushed back onstage by Osip, all returning empty-handed.

Having delivered the speech definitively, K. turns his back on the merchants to indicate that the interview is over, at the same time signaling Osip to get rid of them.

We must talk to you, your lordship! Please order these hooligans to let us come in!

KHLESTAKOV:

(*Shouting, hand to mouth.*)

Officers! Let them come in!

(*To* OSIP.)

Here comes another loan, my foolish friend.

OSIP: Don't be too sure. With women, you don't get it in cash.

(FYOVRONYA *and* EUDOXIA *enter, kneeling at the door before they advance into the room.*)

FYOVRONYA: Your gracious help, I beg you.

EUDOXIA: Help us, your excellency, help us.

KHLESTAKOV: And who, may I ask, are you?

EUDOXIA–FYOVRONYA: Eudoxia, widow of Corporal Vassily Ivanoff.

Fyovronya, wife of the locksmith Poshlyopkin.

KHLESTAKOV: Don't both talk at once. Just tell me what it is you want, but one at a time.

FYOVRONYA: Protect us from the Mayor, protect us, your excellency! May the good Lord punish him and every member of his family and all his relations. May evil be their only reward for seven generations.

KHLESTAKOV: What has he done to you?

FYOVRONYA: What hasn't he done to me? He has had my husband taken away from me to do military duty, even though he is a married man, and has already served once, and it's against the law on both counts. And why? Because the tailor's son should have gone, that young drunkard, but the tailor bought the Mayor off, and so he conscripted my husband instead. "You're too old for a husband," he says to me, "and he's no use to you any more, any-way." "How do *you* know?" I said to him. "I'm young enough for five husbands," I said, "and I wouldn't trust my husband with any of the wenches in your household," I said. So he beat me and took

Fyovronya is in a vengeful mood; she wants to beat somebody or something. For the first time, Osip shows fear for K.'s physical safety and tries to keep her away. K. himself puts a chair between her and him when she comes anywhere near, so that she has to shake her fist to convey her anger.

Eudoxia is less volatile but more seductive. She knows that there are better ways than shouting to get a man's help, and she is concentrated on trying them.

Fyovronya is so fervent as she advances on K. that he has to back away, frightened. When Osip tries to tussle her back, she flings him aside as though he were a matchstick and drops to her knees before K., hands clasped in supplication.

On "You're too old for a husband," Fyovronya springs up nimbly, as if to disprove it, again frightening K. into backing behind his chair.

my husband away. How can I manage without a husband, your excellency?

EUDOXIA: And he had me flogged, too, your lordship!

KHLESTAKOV: What for—if you can tell it briefly.

EUDOXIA: Some women picked a fight with me in the market place, and instead of arresting them, he sent a policeman to arrest me. But when the officer found out how innocent I was, and went back to the police station without me, the Mayor came with the police chief himself and beat me black and blue. If your lordship would like to see—

KHLESTAKOV: That won't be necessary. What would you like me to do about it?

EUDOXIA: Flog him back, then make him pay me a fine, the swine! I'm a widow, your lordship, and I could use the money.

KHLESTAKOV: Very well, I'll see what I can do.

FYOVRONYA–EUDOXIA:

(*Kneeling, each kissing a hand.*)

Bless you, your excellency, bless you!

Thank you, your lordship. If I could only show you where he beat me . . .

KHLESTAKOV: Some other time. Good-bye, ladies.

(FYOVRONYA *and* EUDOXIA *exit.* OSIP *smirks. Another clamor goes up offscene. More petitions are waved outside the window.*)

OSIP: From now on, I'll let in only the men.

KHLESTAKOV: Oh, no you won't.

(*Goes to window and calls out.*)

No, no more! Nobody else! I'm not seeing anybody any more!

(*The clamor gets louder, the petitions more numerous.* OSIP *replaces his master at the window, shouting out.*)

Eudoxia also sinks to her knees before him, weeping and wailing, but remembering to sweep the hair away from her attractive face while she massages her buttocks.

On Eudoxia's "would like to see—" she is already lifting her skirt.

Osip quickly moves around for a better look . . . and gives K. a bitter one when he rejects the opportunity. Eudoxia rises, disappointed.

Eudoxia lifts her skirt a little higher this time.

On K.'s "Good-bye, ladies," Osip comes behind and between them, grabs each under an arm, spins them around and hastens them out.

K. grabs some of the petitions and throws them back at the crowd below.

OSIP: Can't you understand? He said no more! He hasn't any time! Come back tomorrow!

(*Shuts the window.*)

When we're gone.

(*They hear the door open and turn to see a shabby, unshaved figure standing on the threshold, head bandaged and lip swollen. An assortment of other odd, pathetic characters form a line behind him.* OSIP *crosses quickly to stop them from entering and begins pushing and shoving them out.*)

Out! Out! Move back there, all of you! Move!

(OSIP *finally succeeds in clearing them out of the doorway, himself included, and quickly shuts the door behind him. While* KHLESTAKOV *is regaining his composure,* MARYA *enters from upstairs, halts in surprise on seeing him.*)

MARYA: Oh!

KHLESTAKOV: Did I frighten you?

MARYA: Oh, no, not at all. It was a pleasant surprise, that's all.

KHLESTAKOV:

(*Inflating.*)

Were you—ah—going someplace?

MARYA: No, not really.

KHLESTAKOV: Hm. Not going anywhere. Well, why not?

MARYA: Because I was looking for Mama and suspected she might be here.

KHLESTAKOV: But you weren't going anywhere.

MARYA: No, I merely thought you might be occupied with— important details.

KHLESTAKOV:

(*Elegantly.*)

Your eyes are far more important than details.

MARYA: Are all St. Petersburg men so flattering?

KHLESTAKOV: For one as lovely as a princess, yes. Since I cannot offer you a throne, may I offer you a chair?

———◆•◆———

A hasty prank, a gay pastorale, a deft juggling act, Offenbach music—these elements interplay to characterize the atmosphere from the moment Marya enters. Its tempo is staccato.

———◆•◆———

Marya's quality here is a blend of coquetry with genuine innocence and breathlessness. She has never seen such an impressive man, and when K. pays her the supreme compliment of wooing her earnestly, as she thinks, she becomes as frightened as any old-fashioned girl on the verge of the unknown. She carries an album when she enters; getting K. to write something in it would have been her excuse for disturbing him with Mama, had she been there. Now she is unexpectedly alone with him—and at sea.

K. is so happy to see her after his experience with the two coarse women that he reacts like a show dog espying a pure-bred girl friend: one can almost see his tail and ears shoot up.

K. comes closer to look into her eyes. Marya backs away, half embarrassed, half scared.

K. brings her a chair, places it at her side.

MARYA: I really shouldn't disturb you. I really must go.
(*She sits.*)

KHLESTAKOV: That's a beautiful scarf you're wearing.

MARYA: You must be quite accustomed to poking fun at provincial girls.

KHLESTAKOV: On the contrary, mademoiselle. Would I were that scarf embracing your lily-white neck.

MARYA: Oh, it's just an ordinary thing. Isn't the weather peculiar today?

KHLESTAKOV: What does the weather matter when your lips are rosier than a day in June?

MARYA: You do say pretty things, but I'd rather you wrote some verses in my souvenir album. I'm sure you know so many.

KHLESTAKOV: You have only to command me. What kind of verses do you prefer?

MARYA: Oh, any kind, so long as they're new and pretty.

KHLESTAKOV: That's no hardship, knowing so many.

MARYA: Tell me the one you'll write for me.

KHLESTAKOV: I'm trying to think of one that will suit you best. Perhaps you'd like: "Darling, fear not, fear not my love; there's a destiny in human life that unaccountably guides us all. . . ." I can't remember the rest at the moment, but it doesn't matter. I'd much rather recite my love for you as it overcame me when I first glimpsed you.
(*Moving his chair closer to hers.*)

MARYA: I've never understood love, not knowing what it is.
(*Moving her chair away from his.*)

KHLESTAKOV: I could help you understand if you stayed a little closer.

MARYA:
(*Moving more.*)
Shouldn't love be the same far or near?

KHLESTAKOV:
(*Edging closer.*)
It's easier to grasp when it's closer.

When Marya sits, K. gets another chair and seats himself beside her.

Marya offers K. her album. He takes it, leafing through it senselessly.

K. tosses off the "so many" with a bored wave of the hand.

After "Perhaps you'd like," he drops the album back in her lap, stands behind his chair and declaims the verse like a bad actor, with gestures. Unable to complete the stanza, he quickly returns to his seat and resumes the speech.

The biz of moving the chairs is done by both without standing erect. Each simply plants feet on the floor, places hands under the chair seat, and shifts. It becomes a half-gay, half-coquettish game.

MARYA:

(*Moving again.*)

I don't see why.

KHLESTAKOV:

(*Moving after her.*)

You may not see it, mademoiselle, but you'd feel it better if I held you closer. One cannot embrace from far away.

(MARYA *looks toward the window.*)

MARYA: Did you see that? Something flew by. Do you think it was a magpie, perhaps? Magpies mean good luck.

KHLESTAKOV: Then it was a magpie.

(KHLESTAKOV *kisses her bare shoulder;* MARYA *springs up indignantly.*)

MARYA: You're rude and impudent! You weren't even looking.

KHLESTAKOV: Forgive me. Pure love blinded me.

(*He takes her in his arms. She struggles to get away.*)

MARYA: You treat me as if I were a silly country girl.

KHLESTAKOV: No, it was only a little harmless expression of my love. Please don't be angry with me. I'll get on my knees to beg your forgiveness if you like.

(*Sinks to his knees.*)

See? Now do you forgive me? Please say you do.

The chair-chase is now frightening Marya. Her looking toward the window is more in search of an escape.

━━━━━◆●◆━━━━━

When K. kisses Marya, there is a minimal alteration in the atmosphere: her tempo slows to legato while his continues as before.

And when K. falls on his knees before Anna, too (page 282), another change occurs in the atmosphere. It becomes one of noisy and unbridled joy. As in the third-act scene in which he describes St. Petersburg, K. is on a glorious binge of irrationality and confusion. The atmosphere bubbles with his inanities and insanities—until Anton enters it (page 286).

━━━━━◆●◆━━━━━

K. kisses Marya slowly, gently, quietly. A pause follows: both are stunned, overwhelmed. Then her fear returns, and with it her exasperation. When she rises indignantly on "You're rude and impudent!" K. tries to quiet her with a "Shhh!" looking around for Mama in alarm. Then, finishing her speech with "You weren't even looking," Marya bursts into hysterical tears and K. really gets panicky. His biz of taking her into his arms is more to stifle her sobs than make love to her.

The scene can play even better if K. remains on his knees until Anna comes to help him up, stroking his hair. Trying to rise by himself, K. lists, plunges into her skirts and is momentarily engulfed

(ANNA *enters and is shocked by the scene. She covers her eyes.*)

ANNA: Oh! Oh!

KHLESTAKOV:

(*Getting up.*)

Oh, hell!

ANNA: What's the meaning of this, young woman? Have you been flirting behind my back?

MARYA: Why, Mother, I—

ANNA: You've said enough! I can guess the rest. Leave this room at once and don't you dare come back!

(MARYA *exits in tears.*)

As for you, sir, I must confess that I'm shocked beyond words.

KHLESTAKOV: Of what use are words to a beautiful woman like you, whose very look can inflame the senses?

(*Falls to his knees again.*)

Oh, madam, can't you see how love has set me afire?

ANNA: Please, you mustn't get on your knees, not even before me. You'll soil your trousers.

KHLESTAKOV: Oh, yes, I must. How else can I tell you that I'm in love?

ANNA: With me, too?

KHLESTAKOV: Give me love or give me death!

ANNA: Please make it clearer. Are you proposing to me, or are you proposing to me for my daughter?

KHLESTAKOV: It is you I am in love with, madam. Spurn my love and the world will no longer be worth living in. Only your hand can quench the burning passion in my heart.

ANNA: You forget, sir, that I am more or less married.

KHLESTAKOV: True love knows no such distinctions. As the great Markov said, "What the laws have wrongfully put together, love can rightfully rend asunder." Give me your hand. Let us fly to the shadows and the murmurings of delight!

there, clinging to her to save himself from falling. Anna finally manages to disentangle him and caressingly gets him to his feet. Marya is shocked by this byplay but imagines that it may be Mama's way of protecting her.

Anna's three qualities in this scene are indignation, astonishment and love. The more indignant she is, the better the other qualities will contrast. Also, her berating of Marya must not be hurried; she must scorch her with every word.

When Marya exits, she drops her album. (See album biz on page 285.)

Anna looks toward the stairs and the door on this speech. What she is afraid of is not K.'s trousers but the sudden entrance of Marya or Anton.

Anna is neither confused nor displeased by this switch. She just wants to be sure he really wants her.

It is not really an obstacle. She only voices it to play harder to get.

(MARYA *enters hurriedly and stops midway, shocked by the scene. She covers her eyes.*)

MARYA: Oh! Oh!

KHLESTAKOV: Oh, damn!

MARYA: Mama, how could you!

ANNA: Could what? Didn't I tell you not to come back here? Did you expect to surprise me in a compromising situation? Well, I hope you're satisfied.

MARYA: I didn't know, Mama. I thought—

ANNA: Thought! With what? You have no more brains in your head than the other girls in this town. Why must you always ape them when there are other examples for you to follow? Isn't your mother good enough for you?

(KHLESTAKOV *goes to* MARYA, *grasps her hand and faces* ANNA *with her.*)

KHLESTAKOV: Madam, don't be angry with her. Don't let your displeasure stand in the way of our happiness. Bless our eternal love by forgiving and forgetting.

ANNA:

(*Aghast.*)

What! You mean it's Marya you want to . . . ?

KHLESTAKOV: Only if you decide. Will you give me love or give me death?

ANNA: Well!

(*To* MARYA.)

You see, you little idiot? Our distinguished guest humbles himself to get down on his knees for a nitwit like you, and you almost spoiled everything by running in here with your suspicions! I ought to punish you by refusing to give my consent. You're not worthy of him. But, I am cursed with a mother's heart, and—

After "Oh! Oh!" Marya picks up the album she dropped on her exit. That was the excuse she planted for coming back and interrupting Mama's progress with K.

K., still on his knees, hides behind Anna's skirt, pulling on it as he clings and looks around at Marya.

While talking to Marya, Anna reaches a hand behind her and tries to wave K. off. K. gets to his feet, but still hides behind Anna.

On "Thought!" Anna flounces over to the sofa, frustrated, and exasperatedly flings herself on it, leaving K. stage center to face Marya alone.

Anna is truly horrified on her "What!" line. What happened? What had she done to lose him so quickly?

After "consent," Anna cannot control her tears any longer. By the time she finishes the speech, she is crying softly, hiding her face.

(ANTON *bursts into the room and rushes to* KHLESTAKOV *with hands clasped.*)

ANTON: Don't believe them, your excellency! Don't let them ruin me, don't ruin me!

KHLESTAKOV: Why should I want to ruin you, especially at a time like this?

ANTON: I know you let them come in here to complain about me. But I assure you that less than half of what they say is true. If they were not such thieves and shortchangers themselves, I would not have to punish them the way I did. And every word of what the widow Eudoxia said is a lie. If she's black and blue, as she tells everybody, then she flogged herself!

KHLESTAKOV: Hang the widow Eudoxia.

ANTON: I'd like to! They're all of them adulterers and liars and swindlers and cheats. Don't believe any of them, your excellency!

ANNA: Don't excite yourself so, Antosha. There is no need to now. His excellency has just bestowed a great honor upon us.

ANTON: An hon—? He has?

ANNA: Yes, my dear. Ivan Aleksandrovich has just asked for our daughter's hand.

ANTON: Her—what! Are you out of your giddy mind?

(*Appealing to* KHLESTAKOV.)

Please don't be offended, your highness. She's just like her mother.

(*Taps his head.*)

It runs in the family. Heredity, you know.

KHLESTAKOV: Don't be so surprised. I am in love with your daughter and I'm really asking for her hand.

ANTON: Is there a ringing in my ears or did you say that you are in love with my daughter and asking for her hand?

ANNA: That's exactly what he said.

KHLESTAKOV: I'm quite serious, and if I don't win her, I'll go crazy, too.

K. is still holding on to Marya's hand when Anton bursts in, but Anton is too busy with his own problem to notice it.

———————•••———————

Anton's entrance turns the atmosphere's confusions into utter chaos, a fantasmagoria of noise, joy, misunderstanding, appeal, doubt, reassurance, triumph—pandemonium rising and receding until the end of Act Four. At the curtain, only the elements of doubt and triumph remain, the former only a faint glow as yet, the latter a latent but pervading force.

———————•••———————

On this speech, Anna takes Anton by the shoulder and explains things to him as though he were an idiot.

K. also tries a reasoning approach with Anton, speak-ing ve-ry pre-cise-ly in order to convince him that it is not a joke nor only in Anna's imagination. This only makes the thing more impossible for Anton to believe and heightens his bewilderment; he puts his hand to his ear like a suction pump.

ANTON: It's unbelievable! That such an honor should befall me, and I so unworthy of it.

KHLESTAKOV: Worthy or not, I am desperate for her hand and I ask your consent.

ANTON: Surely, you're joking, your excellency. I don't mind a little innocent fun, but—

ANNA: What kind of dunderhead are you? How many times does he have to say it?

ANTON: Am I not her father? I have only one daughter and I must be sure that he means it.

KHLESTAKOV: What must I do to prove how much I want her and must have her? Shall I shoot myself and leave her a widow even before she's married? Think of the scandal if the government looks into *that!*

ANTON: Oh, my God, no! That's all I need right now. Please forgive me. Let your excellency do as he wishes. My head is in such a spin that I'm only making a bigger fool of myself than ever.

ANNA: Well, then, say it. Give them your blessing and be done with it!

(KHLESTAKOV: *stands anticipatorily beside* MARYA.)

ANTON: Bless you, my children. May God bless you and forgive my sins and stupidity.

(KHLESTAKOV *kisses* MARYA. ANTON *turns to* ANNA *in disbelief.*) It's really so! He really asked for her hand! He kissed her and now they're betrothed! He's actually going to be our son-in-law. Merciful heavens, what a turn events have taken! The world will be ours again, only more of it!

Before his "Bless you" speech, Anton makes the sign of the cross, Russian Orthodox version. As he raises his hand to do so, K. and Marya fall to their knees. Anna starts weeping again.

As graphed on page 139, the third auxiliary climax ends on Anton's "what a turn events have taken!" It is important to note this because not only does it mark the beginning of the third section of the play, but also because the performance begins to gather new strength and momentum for scaling the third and last main climax. Let us keep that peak in view and permit no one to drop back so much as a step.

(ANTON *grabs* ANNA *and whirls her around in glee.* OSIP *enters and waits until the glee has subsided.*)

OSIP: The horses are ready and the luggage is in—all of it.

KHLESTAKOV: Horses? Oh, yes, the horses. I'll be along pretty soon.

ANTON: Horses? Horses for what? You're not leaving, are you?

KHLESTAKOV: Yes, I really must be going.

ANTON: But—but—before the wedding date has even been set?

KHLESTAKOV: Oh, I won't be gone long. Only a minute—I mean a day or two. I—I—promised to visit my uncle. The poor man is rich but old. He tires very easily, so I shall probably return tomorrow.

ANTON: Oh, we wouldn't think of detaining you, particularly from a rich uncle. We wish you Godspeed and a safe return.

KHLESTAKOV: Thank you. I'll be back, as soon as I can.

(*To* MARYA.)

Good-bye, my dear. How can I express my joy and what I feel for you?

(*Kisses her hand.*)

Good-bye, my love.

ANTON: Are you sure you have everything you'll need for the journey—such as, perhaps, a little more cash?

KHLESTAKOV: No, no. I couldn't think of it.

(*Thinking it over anyway.*)

But, on second thought, if you insist . . .

ANTON: I insist. How much do you think you'll need?

KHLESTAKOV: Well, let me see. You already gave me two hundred, which, as you said, turned out to be four hundred—so why not lend me a similar amount to make it an even eight?

The dancing subsides when Anton finally sees Osip standing near the door. K. is still kissing and talking to Marya. Osip has to go and tap him on the shoulder and repeat the horses and luggage line. K. lets go of Marya and turns to Osip as if paralyzed. It is a vital junction in the play. Make it an accent.

On K.'s "I'll be along . . ." Anna is startled, Anton alarmed, Marya bewildered. Anton quickly approaches K., Anna following.

Make the difference clear between this offer of money and that of Act Two. In the earlier act, it was dangerous, therefore concealed and loaded with fear and doubt. Here it is overt and handled gracefully as a delicate but social gesture, and as between one close relative and a prominent member of his family.

K. tries for the same level in social graciousness, but his basic characteristics won't permit him to be anything but a phony even in this situation.

ANTON: Eight it shall be.

(*Taking money out of his wallet.*)

Brand-new bills, too, to celebrate the occasion. New money means new luck.

KHLESTAKOV: They also say it means new surprises.

ANTON: Oh, no, I've had enough for one day. My heart couldn't stand it.

KHLESTAKOV: Good-bye, Father. I can't thank you enough for your hospitality and—and everything. I've never been received so well or been more fortunate. Good-bye, Mother.

(*He kisses her hand.*)

Good-bye my darling, my love, my dearest heart.

(*He kisses* MARYA.)

Let's go, Osip, or I shall never tear myself away.

(KHLESTAKOV *and* OSIP *exit. The remaining three, led by* MARYA, *go to the window and open it, the better to see him drive off and to wave good-bye.*)

MARYA: There he is, getting into the coach. Isn't he handsome?

ANNA: You're a lucky girl, you ninny.

ANTON: And I'm a lucky man. You'll never know how lucky.

MARYA:

(*Waving.*)

He's waving at us. Good-bye, good-bye!

ANTON:

(*Also waving.*)

Good-bye, your excellency, good-bye! Have a good journey!

ANNA:

(*Waving grudgingly.*)

Good-bye, good-bye!

(*The coach bells start to jangle and fade away.* ANNA *turns away sadly.* MARYA *closes the window.* ANTON *looks puzzled.*)

On "Good-bye, Father," K. shakes Anton's hand, and after "more fortunate," they embrace Russian fashion. Anna moves closer for her farewell, and after he has kissed her hand, sensually, she virtually engulfs him with hugs and overwhelms him with kisses.

Osip separates them by pulling on K.'s arm, so that Marya, who has stood waiting for her turn, gets only a peck on the cheek for her farewell kiss. Osip waves his good-byes as he drags K. off.

ANTON: Doesn't it seem strange to you that a personage of his exalted rank condescends to travel in an ordinary mail coach? In his place, I'd have nothing but the best.

ANNA: I wish you *were* in his place—and he in yours!

FOURTH ACT CURTAIN

After Anna's curtain line, Anton waves a playful "Oh, go away!" at her, grabs Marya and begins dancing a spirited polka, swinging her around so hard that she screams in fright and protest. Her screams muffle as the curtain descends, dying out when it is all the way down.

Note: Although a fourth-act intermission is indicated in nearly all versions of the play, I have preferred to do without one, merely lowering and quickly raising the curtain to denote a pause in the plot rather than a passage of time. This makes for a better sustentation of continuity as well as audience interest, and I recommend it for other productions of this work.

[ACT FIVE]

The same scene. A few minutes later.

ANTON: Yes, yes, he's quite a capture. Who would ever have dreamed of such a prize, such a turn of good fortune for all of us! I'm sure it never occurred to you that our daughter would one day marry into such a family.

ANNA: I'm sure it has. It's you who are accustomed only to plain people and plain thoughts.

ANTON: But no longer, my dear Anna. From now on, we're flying high! From now on, we're putting the world in its proper place!

(*Goes to window, opens it and calls out.*)
Hey, Ilyitch! Come in here!
(*Closes window.*)
And we'll start with a few of our so-called loyal friends in this town. They thought they had me by the throat, and from behind my back, too! But the ungrateful curs bit the friendly hand too soon.

(ILYITCH *enters.*)
I want you to round up everybody who came here to complain against me. Make a list of names of all who brought petitions here today, including even those who wrote the documents for the illiterate swine. Then I want you to bring the merchants here to me. I'll teach those conniving bastards to denounce me!

(ILYITCH *starts to go.*)
Not so fast, my friend. . . . And while you're about it, I want you to announce that God has chosen me for an honor that comes to few men: that their Mayor is not marrying his daughter off just to some peasant from this town, but to a man of great position and power in the government! Shout it from the housetops! Have the church bells rung for two hours! Let them know that there's going

Triumph from the preceding atmosphere is the chief element of this one. It burgeons and swells Anton into a conquering hero, even a vengeful one. So strong is this atmosphere that it refuses to yield even when the Postmaster enters with the letter which proves to be the undoing of the Mayor and his family (bottom of page 312).

It is only with the impact of the Postmaster's line "—is not an inspector general at all!" (page 314) that the element of shock stuns the triumphant atmosphere into submission and holds it there, perplexed.

———————

As the curtain rises again, Marya's screams go up in volume with it. Anton is still whirling and twirling her in the polka. Anna is studying herself from every angle in the mirror.

When Marya begins to go limp in Anton's arms, crying "Stop, stop, please let me go!" Anton spins her to the sofa and deposits her there, kissing her forehead and pinching her cheek as he delivers the first half of his opening speech. The second half he addresses to Anna.

Marya, exhausted, goes to join Anna at the mirror. Anna pushes her in front of the mirror and begins fixing her hair and straightening her dress.

to be a celebration such as this miserable hole in the ground has never seen before and never will again! . . . Now you may go.

(ILYITCH *exits.*)

And now, my dear Anna, where do you think we ought to live after they are married—here or in St. Petersburg?

ANNA: What a question. How could we continue to live in a town like this?

ANTON: Then St. Petersburg it is. Even the governorship of this place would not appeal to me now.

ANNA: Attending all the court functions, and rubbing elbows with all the ministers—the least you could hope for would be a generalship.

ANTON: No, I wouldn't mind being a general—covered with all sorts of decorations, traveling in grand style with all sorts of couriers and attendants, and captains and mayors like me and everybody jumping to do your bidding. And I'll make them jump, have no fear!

ANNA: Of course, you'll have to give up a great many of your coarser pleasures and be more choosy about your friendships. Don't forget that you'll be moving in an atmosphere of refinement among the aristocracy. And some of your language would shock the drawers off good society.

ANTON: They might enjoy that. Anyway, words are harmless.

ANNA: However, maybe they'll overlook your faults when they visit our house. It'll be one of the finest in the capital. The *décor* will be so rich, it will blind them the moment they enter. And we'll entertain. How we'll entertain!

(*A knock on the door, which is soon opened by* ILYITCH. *He and* TUNOV *herd the merchants in and exit.* ANTON *confronts them imperiously.*)

ANTON: Welcome, you mangy rats, you stinking barrel of cross-eyed herrings!

After Ilyitch's exit, Anton crosses to Anna, puts an arm around her waist and leads her to the sofa on the "And now, my dear Anna . . ." speech. They sit talking like two lovers, his arm around her shoulder, she nestling her head on his. The affectionate picture draws a tender look from Marya; she goes to the window, leans against the frame and gazes out dreamily.

Anna's tone is: "How dare you think of anything less?"

Notice how Anton's basic characteristics come to the fore on the last line of this speech. So let us accent that line.

And the last sentence of Anna's speech here must be an accent, too, because it reveals where her thoughts really lie and that, despite her haughty demeanor, one of her true characteristics is the mentality of a provincial housewife.

The merchants, following Abdulin's lead, bow on their entrance, their arms hanging limply at their sides.

A triumphant, sardonic smile glows on Anton's face as he opens his attack.

ABDULIN: We wish you nothing but good health, your honor.

ANTON: Tell me how things are going with you now, you scrofulous peddlers. So you thought you could make complaints against me, you disease-carrying vermin?

ANNA: Anton! Watch your language!

ANTON: This is not St. Petersburg and they are not the aristocracy, the snot-smeared cowards!

(*To* ABDULIN *and merchants.*)

So you thought you'd put me in prison, did you? But you were even too stupid to guess that the same official to whom you brought your petitions is going to marry my daughter Marya! Now what do you think of that, you excrement? Now it is my turn to make you squirm, you slimy snakes-in-the-grass! Now I'll teach you what it means to cheat people, to make a contract with the government for a hundred and fifty thousand rubles and supply rotten materials. But when you donate a lousy ten yards to me, who serves you and protects you day in and day out, you expect a double profit. I spit on all of you. No, I wouldn't even waste that on you.

ABDULIN: We're guilty, your honor.

(*He goes to his knees, the other merchants following.*)

The devil led us into temptation.

ANTON: Temptation! Who led you into temptation when you contracted to build the bridge? Who helped you charge twenty-two thousand rubles for lumber when not even a thousand rubles' worth was supplied? It was I who helped you cheat, you grafters! I had only to say one word against you, and all of you would now be in Siberia, serving the second year of a thirty-year sentence.

ABDULIN: Forgive us, your honor. We didn't know what we were doing. We give you our solemn word never to complain again. Do what you wish with us, ask whatever you want of us. We will make amends.

ANTON: Of course you will, now that I have the upper hand and you're groveling at my feet. But if the power were on your side, you thieving skunks, you'd sink me in the mud up to my neck and gallop wild horses over my head. I know you, you vultures!

On Abdulin's "good health" line, the merchants echo their "good healths" like an intimidated background chorus.

As Anton turns back to continue his abuse of the merchants, I would recommend that *Anna get up from the sofa, grab Marya by the hand and drag her off upstairs.* For one thing, Anna would not want Marya to hear such language; for another, without the women's presence as a psychological curb, Anton can really work up his violence as well as his execration.

On his line "Now it is my turn . . ." Anton begins taking off his coat and rolling up his shirt sleeves as if he is going to beat them. The merchants cringe.

When Anton finishes this speech, he angrily moves a chair out of the way and beckons Abdulin to come forward. Abdulin advances slowly, fearfully, in a feet-first-stomach-next-head-last posture, head averted but with a tremulous eye cocked sidelong at Anton.

Anton grabs Abdulin by the beard and pulls him erect, holding his face close to his own as he barks out the accusations.

At the end of the speech, he lets go the beard and pushes Abdulin back to his knees.

On the first sentence of this speech, Anton paces upstage and down before the kneeling pack. On the second sentence, he stops to shake a menacing finger at them. On the third, he jabs the finger at them, as if into their eyes.

(ABDULIN *prostrates himself, the other merchants following suit.*)

ABDULIN: Be merciful, your honor! Don't ruin us altogether! Let a ray of kindness shine into your heart!

ANTON: Now he says "Don't ruin us!" That wasn't the tune you sang before. If only I had a torture chamber in this house . . .

(*Throws up his hands in disgust.*)

Ach! God will have to forgive you, not I. It's not in my nature to bear a grudge, but watch your step from now on. Just remember that my daughter is not just marrying into run-of-the-mill nobility, but to a man of tremendous importance in our government. So let your wedding presents be appropriate to the occasion. Don't think you're going to get off with a bit of smoked sturgeon and a pinch of sugar this time. Now go, all of you, before I change my mind and have you flogged!

(*The merchants rise and scurry out. . . . When the doorway is cleared,* AMMOS *and* ARTEMY *enter.*)

AMMOS: Is it true, Anton, is it, that a great good fortune has blessed your house? Congratulations, congratulations!

ARTEMY: I am honored to join in the congratulations. My heart filled with happiness for all of you when I heard it.

(AMMOS *and* ARTEMY *go to kiss* ANNA'S *hand, then* MARYA'S.

. . . IVAN RASTAKOVSKY, *an important village personage, enters.*)

IVAN: Ah, Anton, my good friend! Congratulations! . . . And congratulations to you, too, Anna. And to the happy young couple. May long life and many great-grandchildren bless this marriage.

On Anton's "God will have to forgive you," the merchants look at one another in surprise, start lifting their heads and murmuring their gratitude. On "bear a grudge," they raise up a little more, their ad-lib thanks growing louder. And as Anton talks about his daughter's marriage, they are back on their knees, unhappily surprised and full of renewed fear.

Anton waves them out in disgust on "Now go . . ." On "flogged," he turns away from them, rolls down his shirt sleeves and puts on his coat, while Abdulin and the merchants keep bowing and bowing as they quickly back out, laughing a little with relief and muttering and mumbling their thanks all the way out.

Ammos and Artemy enter with arms outstretched. Anton clasps Ammos' hand, places an arm around his shoulder. But he shakes Artemy's hand limply and turns away.

While Ammos and Artemy are delivering their congratulatory speeches, *Anna and Marya re-enter from upstairs.* They are wearing their best party gowns. They seat themselves on the sofa like a queen and princess awaiting homage from their subjects. Ammos starts the procession toward them. . . . From here until Anton claps for attention toward the end of page 306, the hubbub of background conversations and ad libs grows apace.

Rastakovsky is partly blind and mostly deaf. He speaks loudly and fumbles for Anton's hand. Anton leads him to the women on the sofa, R. waving his cane at the floor to make sure the way is clear. There he congratulates Marya as Anna and vice versa when kissing their hands. Anna motions to Anton to take him away. R. keeps talking as Anton places him in a chair facing the audience.

(IVAN *kisses* ANNA'S *hand, then* MARYA'S. . . . STEPAN KOROB-
KIN, *another important villager, enters with his wife,* ANAS-
TASIA.)

STEPAN: Permit me the heartfelt pleasure of congratulating
you, Anton. . . . And you, Anna. And the lucky bride-to-be.

(*He kisses the women's hands in turn.*)

ANASTASIA:
(*To* ANNA *and* MARYA.)
Oh, oh! I am so happy for both of you, my heart is bursting!

(ANASTASIA *kisses* ANNA *and* MARYA *on the cheek.* . . . BOB.
and DOB. *enter and squirm their way forward through the
guests.*)

DOB.: It's an honor, Anton, an honor! Congratulations!
BOB.: Yes, congratulations! Truly an honor, an honor!
DOB.: A happy event, Anna!
BOB.: A happy event indeed, Anna!

(*They bump heads as they bend to kiss* ANNA'S *hand.*)

DOB.:
(*To* MARYA.)
And may you live in greatest happiness always and wear golden
dresses and drink the richest soups.
BOB.: And with all your riches may God bring you a tiny son
to sit in the palm of your hand, like the picture of the madonna
in the church.

(BOB. *and* DOB. *bend to kiss* MARYA'S *hand and bump their
heads again.* . . . LUKA *enters with his wife,* KHLOPOVA.)

Each time that Rastakovsky hears the word "congratulations," he repeats, "Yes, yes, congratulations" or "Congratulations, congratulations."

After her congratulations, Anastasia sits on the sofa beside Anna, as though to share in the kudos from all the other arrivals.

When Bob. and Dob. enter, the murmured conversations temporarily die down. Everybody wants to hear what this odd pair is going to say.

On Bob.'s word "son," Marya mockingly claps hands to her ears and gives an embarrassed little laugh. Ammos laughs at her embarrassment, the others joining in.

LUKA: It is an honor, Anton, to give you our—

KHLOPOVA:

(*Dashing forward.*)

Congratulations, Anna!

(*She kisses* ANNA, *then* MARYA.)

Believe me, I was so thrilled and happy for you when they told me! I cried and cried with joy until the tears flowed like a cataract. Oh, I know it's silly for women to weep when a daughter is being married off, but there are so many sad things to cry about that we may as well weep over the happy ones, too. Fancy our little Marya making such a wonderful match! But I'm sure you wouldn't have settled for less, and that you had something to do with lighting the fire under the kettle of fish.

ANTON:

(*Calling out the door.*)

Mishka! Fetch some more chairs!

(ILYITCH *and* TUNOV *enter, both clicking their heels this time.*)

ILYITCH: On behalf of the police force, your honor, our warmest congratulations and many years of prosperity.

ANTON: Thank you, thank you.

(*While* ANTON *is shaking hands with each officer,* MISHKA *starts bringing in the chairs.* ANTON *signals* BOB. *and* DOB. *to help, then waits until they are placed around the room before he goes stage center and claps his hands for attention.*)

Please, ladies and gentlemen! Let's all be seated!

(ALL *find seats who have to. As* MISHKA *exits,* ANTON *stops him and whispers something.* MISHKA *nods and continues his exit.*)

AMMOS: Now, Anton, tell us how it all happened—how everything went between you and his highness.

Luka's greeting to Anton is slower than is usual for him, and his wife drags him away before he can finish it and propels him to the sofa. He stands there nodding while she gushes, until he gets his chance to take Anna's and Marya's hand in each of his own and kiss one after the other. Then he goes to Dob. and congratulates him, too. Dob. gets up and moves away, as though Luka has lost his mind.

On "wonderful match," Khlopova draws Marya up from the sofa with a "Please" and sits in her place beside Anna with a "Thank you," snuggling up to Anna possessively as she completes her speech, then demonstratively kissing Anna again.

Anton sees Marya standing forlornly at the sofa behind her mother, hence looks around the room before calling for Mishka to bring more chairs.

Ilyitch calls his greeting from the door, loudly and with a military staccato, so that the others have to turn and acknowledge his and Tunov's entrance. After handshakes with Anton and bowing before Anna and Marya (no hand-kissing from them; they do not rank socially), they retire to the background.

Bob. and Dob. start passing the chairs and carrying them high in the air to the standees. There is much commotion, chatter and ad-lib instructions on the arrangement of the chairs. Most of them are placed at stage right, forming a group composed of Ammos, Artemy, Bob., Dob. and Stepan—with a seat left in the center in the hope of luring Anton to sit among them. *In toto,* the scene should be composed of three groups at this point. They begin to change and interchange only after Shpyokin enters with the letter (end of page 312).

ANTON: It went extraordinarily! His proposal was made in person—to Marya, of course.

(*General laughter.*)

ANNA: And to me. His speech was so respectful and so refined. "Only your rare qualities move me to this moment," he said. I could not believe my ears, that this handsome and cultured man was really proposing. "I swear to you," he said, with such genteel manners, "my life is worthless. You alone can give me love or death!"

MARYA: Oh, Mama, dear, it was me he said it to!

ANNA: Must you interrupt me? . . . And when I protested that we weren't worthy of such an honor, he fell to his knees—in an aristocratic way, of course—and said, "Madam, if my feelings are not reciprocated, nothing will remain for me but to end my life!"

MARYA: You know he said it to me, Mama. You know he did.

ANNA: Of course, he said it to you, too. Indirectly, he meant you.

ANTON: When we hesitated, he almost frightened us to death. "I'll shoot myself!" he screamed, and in another moment he would have put a bullet through his brain.

(*Gasps of astonishment from the guests.*)

AMMOS: How do you like that!

LUKA: It was fated to happen, just fated, that's all.

ARTEMY: Why give fate the credit? Fate is fickle. It was Anton's years of devotion to duty that brought him this reward. Only pigs expect good fortune for nothing at all.

AMMOS: Speaking of pigs, Anton, I could sell you that hound you were interested in.

A suggestion: after Anton's "extraordinarily!" Dr. Christian might enter to break up the speech. Anton gives him a dour look and holds up. The inarticulate man nods to everyone as he goes about finding a chair, finally landing in the one intended for Anton. The group glowers at him. With the Doctor seated, Anton finishes his speech.

Marya, seated on a chair behind the sofa, leans forward and cocks her head at Anna to correct her. A slight recoil from the guests on this. The girl's audacity!

Anna turns her head toward Marya to criticize her, then turns it back to continue addressing the gathering.

A murmur of ad libs follows the gasps: "Can you imagine?" "How do you like that?" "Isn't it thrilling?" "What do you know?" Artemy's ad lib, only slightly audible, is "I could shoot *my*self."

Ammos repeats his ad lib aloud, like a coda.

Luka's "fated" speech is even louder, startling everyone. Bob. leans over to give Luka a puzzled look, shrugs and sits back.

ANTON: At the price you ask for him, I'd rather have a pig.

(*Laughter from the others.*)

STEPAN: Oh, Anton! May I ask where the distinguished groom-to-be is? They say he left in a hurry soon after.
ANTON: Only for a day, on some urgent business.
ANNA: To visit his rich uncle and get his blessings.
ANTON: Yes, he's the next of kin. But he'll return—
(*He sneezes and evokes a gabble of good wishes all around.*)
Thank you, thank you. He'll return tomorrow and—
(*He again sneezes and precipitates another gabble, such as:*)
ILYITCH–BOB.–DOB.–ARTEMY–KHLOPOVA: The best of health, your honor.
A sack of gold and a hundred years to spend it in.
May God double the years and the gold.
Plagues and pestilence upon you.
May the devil rush you to hell.
ANTON: Many thanks, and many of them to you.

ANNA: Your good wishes will go with us to St. Petersburg. We'll be moving there as soon as our new house is ready. It'll be a relief from this unpleasant, small-town atmosphere. And when my husband receives the rank of general—
KHLOPOVA:
(*With consternation.*)
A general!

ANTON: Yes, why not confess it? I'd very much enjoy being a general.
LUKA: Then God grant your wish.
STEPAN: Yes, only God can make the impossible possible.

In the midst of the laughter, Mishka enters with a huge tray loaded with glasses of wine, candies and sweet pastries. He moves among the guests and they politely help themselves as well as those near them. Bob. and Dob. attend the ladies.

During the ensuing lull, when everybody is occupied with the refreshments and voices are down to a minimum, Stepan suddenly and loudly comes to life and hails Anton! . . . Where, indeed, *is* the groom-to-be? Somebody has dared to voice the question for the first time. The guests come very much alive. There is a pause as they wait for Anton's reply. He is caught in the midst of chewing a pastry. He washes the mouthful down with wine before explaining. The guests seem reassured by the three clarifying speeches, but not any happier.

The last two "blessings" are louder than the others and are intended only to draw reactions from nearby guests. Anton does not distinguish them, and it will be so much largess if the audience does. But they should not be rendered separately as old-fashioned "asides."

Anna's announcement of moving to St. Petersburg lifts the pitch a step higher. Everybody attunes to this new level. . . . And on "general," there is many a doubtful "Oh?" Regardless, she is already radiating majestically.

After Khlopova's "A general!" Artemy whispers loudly to Ammos: "Who knows? If this could happen, anything is possible!" Anton glowers at him for a moment, then puts back his smile for the next speech.

On Anton's "general," a zephyr-like laughter sweeps through the guests. Some of the men crowd around him cordially.

Luka shakes Anton's hand as he delivers his "God grant" line, the police officers following suit.

AMMOS: And His wonders never cease.

ARTEMY: As the peasants say: If God wills it, a saddle can fit a cow.

(*To* ANTON.)

Remember your old friends when you become important, Anton, we who stood by you through thick and thin.

AMMOS: And if we have some difficulty here without you, may we call on you for protection?

STEPAN: My son will be ready for government service next year. Do you think you could—

ANTON: Yes, yes, I'll do whatever I can for all of you.

ANNA: Oh, Anton, don't be so free with your promises. How can you burden yourself when your position will make such demands on your time?

ANTON: Every now and then I may find some time, my dear.

ANNA: Every small potato will want to use you to become a bigger one.

KHLOPOVA: I never thought to hear you speak like that, Anna. You are not yet seated at the table and already you've put your feet on it!

(*General laughter. . . .* SHPYOKIN *bursts in, breathless, waving an opened letter.*)

SHPYOKIN: Ladies and gentlemen! Ladies and gentlemen, may I have your attention, please!

(*The assemblage silences.*)

For the second half of his speech, Artemy pushes forward to Anton.

Then Ammos approaches Anton with his speech.

Then Stepan steps up for his, edging the others out of the way.

On Anna's "don't be so free with your promises," she hypnotizes Anton with her stare. Everyone must react sharply. Now she is showing her true colors! This is the way she rewards old friends! Khlopova and Anastasia move away from her, staring their surprise and hurt, then walk about together, whispering. Bob. and Dob. pass looks of bewilderment. For a short while, the comedy becomes drama.

After Anna's "Every small potato" line, it is the men's turn to display amazement and disappointment by backing up or squirming on their chairs away from her. Ammos turns his back to her completely. It resolves into an embarrassed pause, during which there is much rising and shifting and an obvious arraying into two camps. Dr. Christian doesn't understand what's going on and Rastakovsky can't hear, so they suddenly find themselves on the side of the stage with the Mayor's family. Anton looks unhappy over this cleavage away from him in his moment of glory. Everybody is displeased with him—his family for being such a generous fool, the others for being so ungenerous.

When Shpyokin bursts in, all turn almost as one, looking past Anton at the excited Postmaster.

I regret that I must be a bearer of shocking news.

(*Questioning murmurs from the guests, then silence again.*)
The official whom we honored as an inspector general—is not an
inspector general at all!

ALL:

What!

You're mad!

What did you say?

How do you know?

I don't believe it!

Are you positive?

How did you find out?

SHPYOKIN: No, he's not an inspector general. He's not even an
official. The proof is in this letter.

ANTON: Have you gone insane? What letter, what letter?

SHPYOKIN:

(*Waggling letter.*)

This—his own. Your Mishka brought it for franking when he came
to order a coach and pair for him at government expense. Said he
got it from his own man, with the orders.

ANTON: So he brought the letter. Then what?

SHPYOKIN: A franked letter, to St. Petersburg, I said to myself,
must be about government business—and I became alarmed. Suppose, I said to myself, he's discovered some irregularities in the
post office that I didn't know about, and is reporting them to the
authorities? So—I opened it.

ANTON: You didn't! How dared you?

SHPYOKIN: I was in a fog. Some overwhelming compulsion
took hold of me and shook me and shook me until the seal under
my fingers cracked open. My whole body was on fire. But when
I drew the letter out of the envelope, I was chilled to the marrow.

ANTON:

(*Moaning.*)

On Shpyokin's "not an inspector general at all," there is dead silence and absolutely no movement. A full, frozen pause. Everyone is out of his body. Only when Anton turns a stunned, unbelieving stare at Shpyokin, and starts walking toward him, do the exclamations from the others begin. They quickly die down. Everybody wants to hear the rest of the shocking information.

After "The proof is in this letter," Shpyokin waves it at the guests. The letter crackles in the silence. Then he steps toward Anton and holds it gingerly by a corner, mockingly.

On Shpyokin's "I opened it," there are murmurs, gasps and drawn-out exclamations of "Ohhhhh!"

The assemblage supplies audible reactions to Anton's line, too, while Anton angrily tries to snatch the letter. Shpyokin is too fast for him, holds it out of his reach while he explains how it happened —half to Anton, half to the others.

Oh, how could you do such a thing! A letter from a personage of such authority and power!

SHPYOKIN: That's where we were all wrong. He's not a personage, has no authority and no power.

ANTON:

(*Caustically.*)

Oh? And what do *you* imagine him to be?

SHPYOKIN: The Lord only knows. Thin air, I guess.

ANTON:

(*Irate.*)

You're a traitor making treasonable accusations! I ought to put you under arrest!

SHPYOKIN: Do you think you could?

ANTON: Yes, I could!

SHPYOKIN: Have you got the power?

ANTON: Have I got the power! Haven't you heard that he's engaged to marry my Marya—that we're going to live in St. Petersburg—and that my new rank will give me the power of exile and even life and death?

SHPYOKIN: Tsk-tsk-tsk. Perhaps I'd better read the letter. Have I everybody's permission?

(*Ad libs and murmurs of assent. He unfolds the letter and clears his throat.*)

"My dear friend Tryapichkin: A hasty note to amuse you with the weird things that have been happening to me on my journey. First, a fast-shuffling infantry captain cleaned me out at cards, with the result that I had to hole up here on credit at a dirty little inn until

After Anton's "authority and power," Shpyokin takes the initiative. He walks past Anton and delivers his next speech to the group of Act One intimates—Ammos, Artemy, Luka, Bob. and Dob. —with Anton following him. He turns to face Anton when the latter asks, "And what do *you* imagine," etc.

On "Thin air, I guess," there is a light rustle of laughter from the crowd, as if it were blowing in on the wind. Faces do not move; only the light, breathy sounds of mockery come out of them.

With his "Have you got the power?" Shpyokin impudently sticks his hands in his pockets and his chest out, daring to challenge Anton.

———————◄•►———————

As Shpyokin begins to read the letter, the triumphant atmosphere finally collapses completely, after struggling so hard to survive ever since the Postmaster's entrance in this scene. It gives way to one filled with malice and spite. Anton's individual mood of shame and hatred contrasts with it, fights it until the letter is finished (page 322).

———————◄•►———————

A knot of the most vindictive characters—Artemy, Khlopova, Stepan—joins the others around Shpyokin as he starts reading.

As the letter is read, Anton, Anna and Marya begin to shrink. They look around pathetically, as if they would like to run if they could. Instead, Marya goes to her mother on the sofa, to give and receive protection.

the innkeeper was ready to clap me into jail. Fortunately, my St. Petersburg clothes and *savoir-faire* convinced the whole town that I must be an inspector general or something, including the Mayor himself. The fools called for me in state, showed off their crummy little town and installed me in the Mayor's home, where I now am, having a glorious time flirting furiously with his wife and daughter.

I can't decide which one to tackle first. Maybe the mother, because

she seems more willing for a tête-à-tête. Remember all the meals

we had to cadge to exist? Now everybody lends me money right and left as if I were the Minister of the Treasury. They're quite some characters, these yokels, and you'd split your sides laughing at them. They'd make hilarious material for your articles and you have my permission to use them. The biggest jackass is the Mayor himself, who—"

ANTON: I don't believe it! You're making it up!

SHPYOKIN:
(*Extending letter.*)
Here, read it yourself.

ANTON:
(*Reading.*)
"The biggest jackass is—" I still don't believe it. You scribbled it in yourself!

SHPYOKIN: How could I? It's not in my handwriting.

ARTEMY: Continue with the letter.

LUKA: Yes, yes, by all means go on.

SHPYOKIN:
(*Resuming.*)
"The biggest jackass is the Mayor him—"

On the letter's "jail," a muted exclamation from most of the others, more like a whimper of hounds getting the scent. Marya's reaction, though, is quite audible. The more vindictive ones stare their gloating at Anton: he is *their* victim now.

For "flirting furiously," etc., Shpyokin looks up and reads the line directly at Anna and Marya, giving the latter a bitter "double take."

After the letter's "which one to tackle first," the other women look at Anna and Marya and laugh. Anton moves to tear the letter from Shpyokin's grasp, but he retreats into the group surrounding him as behind a protective wall.

On "more willing for a tête-à-tête," Anna almost swoons, dropping her head on Marya's shoulder.

On "everybody lends me money," Anton turns his back to Anna and Marya; the fool ashamed.

Everybody but Anton, Anna and Marya roars with laughter on "The biggest jackass is the Mayor himself." Anton braves a look at Anna. Her face is screwed up in tears; she bursts into sobs, quickly stifles them as undignified. Marya's head is now buried in the crook of her arm, which is draped over the back of the sofa.

When Shpyokin extends the letter to the doubting Anton, he holds it near enough for him to read but not to grab.

ANTON: That's right, repeat it and repeat it!

SHPYOKIN:

(*Continuing.*)

Now I've lost my place. Hm, let's see . . . "biggest jackass . . ."
(*Mumbles.*)

Oh, yes, "The Postmaster, too, is one for the book. . . ." Well,
here he says some foul things about me.

ANTON: Read them! You read mine.

SHPYOKIN: Why? I told you he doesn't spare me.

ANTON: That's not enough. I want to hear them. Read!

ARTEMY: Here, let me.

(*Takes the letter and puts on his glasses.*)

"The Postmaster could pass for the janitor in our office and is
probably just as big a drunkard. The Manager of Charities is—
is—is . . ."

STEPAN: Is that all he says about you? Read us the rest.

ARTEMY: The handwriting isn't legible. But it's quite clear that
he's an ingrate and a skunk.

ANTON: It's not clear at all. Read it, read it!

STEPAN: Let me have it. There's nothing wrong with my eye-
sight.

(STEPAN *reaches for the letter;* ARTEMY *holds it away from
him.*)

ARTEMY: The rest of it is much plainer, so we'll just skip this
small portion.

STEPAN: No, let me.

ARTEMY: Don't you trust me?

ALL: No!

Give him the letter!

Let him have it!

Don't leave out anything!

Anton's "repeat it" line is read with an annoyed, circular motion of his hand from the wrist—as on, and on, and on.

Anton's double insistence that Shpyokin read about himself is backed up by ad libs from many of the others.

A chorus of scornful chuckles on "janitor in our office" breaks the speech there. It is broken again on "drunkard" by shrieks of laughter exchanged between Anastasia and Khlopova, who make a finger-rubbing "shame-shame" gesture at Shpyokin.

On "skunk," Artemy folds the letter and removes his glasses. Anton's demand starts a riotous clamor of agreement.

(ARTEMY *covers a part of the letter with his hand as he passes it to* STEPAN.)

ARTEMY: All right. Read it from there.

ANTON: No, read that part over.

STEPAN: "The Manager of Charities is a pig in a dunce cap—"

ARTEMY: Very funny! When did he ever see a pig in a dunce cap, I'd like to know.   ·

STEPAN: "The Supervisor of Schools reeks of garlic—"

LUKA:

(*To his wife.*)

Do I ever eat garlic? Tell them, tell them.

KHLOPOVA: No, only onions.

AMMOS: Thank God he's spared me.

STEPAN: "The Judge is—"

AMMOS:

(*Jumping up.*)

That's enough! Ladies and gentlemen, the letter is much too long and boring. Why should we waste our time on such utter nonsense?

LUKA–SHPYOKIN–ARTEMY: Why not?

Don't stop now.

Continue, continue.

STEPAN: "The Judge, one Lyapkin-Tyapkin by name, is vastly

mauvais ton—" I guess that's French for something.

AMMOS: Who cares what it's French for? Why doesn't he say it in Russian, like a man?

STEPAN: "Nevertheless, simpletons though they all are, they must be a kindhearted lot because they're so spendthrift with their money. Good-bye, old friend. I'll soon be off to the village of Podolovka in the Government of Saratov. The girls there have never learned to say no."

A quick, general laugh on "pig in a dunce cap."

Artemy's protest gets a bigger and louder laugh, much to his chagrin. He leaves the group and goes to sulk in the background.

Repeat the general laugh on "garlic."

Repeat the bigger laugh on Khlopova's "only onions."

———————◆◆———————

Anton's declaration, "My throat is slit from ear to ear" (page 324) begins the final atmosphere of the act, and the play. This atmosphere combines shame, infamy, catastrophe and admissions of stupidity. Puny souls have been laid bare. Not only have the iniquitous and hypocritical characters been made fools of, but the whole town and even its innocent inhabitants have been ridiculed.

In this atmosphere, what was once comedy turns to tragedy and calls for a different acting style (see *To the Actor,* page 138). The cast plays it for tragedy until the Sergeant's entrance (page 328) restores the comedic overtones.

———————◆◆———————

When Stepan finally reads "The Judge . . ." everyone turns toward Ammos to watch for his reaction.

No laughter on *"mauvais ton."* Nobody knows what it means. But Anastasia and Khlopova like the sound of it, so in the break of the speech they call it at Ammos, waving at him as though it meant something risqué.

KHLOPOVA: Terrible, terrible!

ANTON: My throat is slit from ear to ear. I'm bleeding to death, like a stuck pig's carcass. Go after him, somebody! Bring him back and I'll skin him alive!

SHPYOKIN: You'll never catch him. I gave him the fastest coach and pair.

AMMOS: You've got to bring him back. He borrowed three hundred rubles from me!

ARTEMY: What's three hundred? He squeezed five out of me!

SHPYOKIN: And four hundred from me!

BOB.: .' ad eighty from Peter and me!

AMMOS: Oh, what fools we are! How could we have been such naïve idiots?

ANTON: How, indeed!

(*Pummeling his head.*)

How could *I* have been such an unmitigated and unadulterated blockhead to fall for such a swindle and such an impostor! Thirty years in government service. Not one contractor has ever put anything over on me. Not one merchant could ever hoodwink me. I have outsmarted gamblers and procurers and counterfeiters. And I've even fooled and double-crossed three inspector generals before him, the puny little peacock of a rat! Then he has to come along and rub my nose where the dogs have relieved themselves!

ANNA: I don't believe it, Antosha. I simply can't believe it. Why, he's betrothed to our Marya!

ANTON: Betrothed! Must you remind me? We're lucky he isn't more to her! And what is her loss compared to mine and the indignities I am suffering?

(*Frenzied and frustrated.*)

Look at me! Let the whole world look at what a hopeless moron this Mayor has been turned into!

(*Shakes his fist before his face.*)

Oh, you pompous imbecile! You lardhead! To mistake a skinny little cockroach, a no-account, for a gentleman of great importance! Your senses must have been pickled in mule brine! Not only has

"Terrible, terrible!" cues in a sober, embarrassed quality. Heads are hung or averted. Everyone seems to draw away from Anton, to leave him the center and sole bearer of the degradation. They want to move out of his orbit; to identify with him is to be included in the ridicule which the letter contains.

Anton's self-castigation inflames his anger here. It can almost be seen rising and spreading step by step.

All the other contributors to the "Khlestakov Fund" shrivel on this speech. Inferentially, it describes them, too.

On Anton's "Betrothed!" the general movement away from him, toward the back wall and around toward the door, becomes a little more perceptible.

he made you a laughingstock, but he'll tell it all over St. Petersburg and soon some ink-slinger will splash your humiliation before the eyes of the world. Everybody will clap his hands and roar with laughter. At whom? At you, you ridiculous nincompoops! And at me, at me!

(*He paces the floor while the others suffer their embarrassment in silence.*)

Oh, if I only had that skinny little noodle here right now! That dancing, prancing dandy who called himself an inspector general! He didn't even resemble an inspector general. He was scarcely out of his diapers. And all of a sudden, everybody is calling him an inspector general and bowing and scraping and quaking before him as if he were also an emissary from God!

(*Pauses, puzzled.*)

Who was the first to call him that? Who first referred to him as the inspector general? . . . Speak up!

ARTEMY: You could kill me and I couldn't remember. We were all so frightened and confused.

AMMOS: I'll tell you who it was.

(*Points to* BOB. *and* DOB.)

It was those two intellectual giants.

BOB.: No. May God strike me dead! It didn't even occur to me.

DOB.: Nor to me. I never said such a thing.

ARTEMY: Oh, yes you did. I remember it all now.

LUKA: Yes, yes. You ran in here from the inn and said you saw him.

AMMOS: You said, "Aha! Then he must be the official!"

BOB.:

(*Pointing to* DOB.)

It was he who said "Aha!"

DOB.: But it was you who said he was an official.

BOB.: "Official," maybe. But I never said he was the inspector general.

After "eyes of the world," rueful head-shaking, snorts of disgust, bitter little laughs from most of the assemblage.

On "nincompoops," the crowd's laughter stops. It is a painful reminder that they, too, have been assessed dolts and dupes.

On "emissary from God," he is near Mishka, grabs the tray from him and dashes it to the floor! A shocked and frightened pause. Anton goes into his accustomed pacing gesture during the silence. Only then does he suddenly stop, facing the audience. As the puzzled look suffuses his face, his head slowly goes up. He delivers the first half of his continued speech—"Who was the first to call him that?"—out front. Then he turns for the rest of the speech to face the conspirators of the first act. They rack their brains, or seem to. The other guests whisper "Who was the first?" to those nearest them. Then dead silence. Anton's thunderous "Speak up!" rings in and shatters the silence.

Anton, Ammos, Artemy and Luka begin advancing toward Bob. and Dob., slowly encircling them. Anna and Marya bring up the rear. Fearing that mayhem is about to be committed, all the other guests except the policemen begin edging away upstage, moving

ANTON: Of course, it was you! Both of you, you damned liars, you malicious chatterboxes! All you do is run around town all day and spread your scandal like a madman scatters manure!

AMMOS: A couple of bungling old women!

ARTEMY: Two potbellied guinea pigs whirling in a cage!

BOB.: I swear I didn't say he was the inspector general!

DOB.: And I swear I wasn't the first to say it!

(*A loud knock on the door brings them all to attention.* ILYITCH *goes to open it. A* SERGEANT-AT-ARMS *enters and salutes.*)

SERGEANT-AT-ARMS: I beg to announce that a government official from St. Petersburg has arrived with imperial orders from His Majesty and commands that all of you appear before him without delay. His headquarters will be at the inn.

(ALL *are struck as if by lightning. Cries of amazement mingle with gasps of astonishment. Then, in unison, the group shifts positions and freezes the scene into a tableau, as follows:*

ANTON *stands stage center, head thrust back and arms outstretched. To his right are* ANNA *and* MARYA, *inclining toward him. Behind them is* SHPYOKIN, *facing the audience in the shape of a question mark. On the fringe are* KHLOPOVA *and* ANASTASIA, *grinning hideously at the Mayor's family. At left is* ARTEMY, *listening head atilt.* AMMOS *is almost crouching on the ground, arms outspread and lips pursed in surprise.* STEPAN *also is facing the audience, his eyes screwed up and his tongue stuck out at* ANTON. *At the outer edge are* BOB. *and* DOB., *mouths wide open, eyes popped, gesturing wildly at each other. The others are merely rigid.* ALL *hold positions long enough for the audience to study the principals.*)

LAST CURTAIN

away from the imminent battle arena and toward the door for a quick departure if necessary.

Thus, before the Sergeant knocks loudly on the door three times with the hilt of his saber, the entire cast will be massed and ready to assume the positions delegated to them in the tableau. Then, when the knocks come, they turn their heads slowly, mysteriously, from the impending attack on Bob. and Dob. to the door. After a pause, Anton signals Ilyitch to go open it.

The Sergeant looks around for the official with the authority to recognize him. Anton moves toward him, returning the salute to identify himself. The Sergeant steps toward Anton, salutes again with a heel-click and delivers his speech like a stentor.

———— •• ————

The Sergeant's announcement throws the electric switch that contorts and galvanizes them all into the tableau which sums up the satirical content of the comedy. While this is not exactly an atmosphere affecting the players, it is, nevertheless, an aura which the audience carries away as a reminder of the lesson which the play sought to teach.

———— •• ————

FINAL NOTE: The curtain could come down right here, following everybody's astonished reactions to the announcement—or it may be held long enough for the cast to go into the traditional tableau as described. Whichever is the director's choice, the idea which must prevail just before the curtain is that the whole play has become a marionette show and the players are no longer human beings, but puppets.